다만 빠른 영어
ただ、英語

DAY

DAY 1

preference 선호, 기호

사람과 쥐 모두 단 음식에 대한 맛의 선호를 진화시켜 왔는데, 이것은 풍부한 열량의 원천을 제공한다.
Both humans and rats have evolved taste preferences for sweet foods, which provide rich sources of calories.

hunter-gatherers 수렵 채집인

탄자니아의 Hadza(하드자 부족) 수렵 채집인 사이의 음식 선호에 관한 연구는 가장 높은 열량 값을 가진 식품인 꿀이 가장 많이 선호되는 식품이었음을 발견했다.
A study of food preferences among the Hadza hunter-gatherers of Tanzania found that honey was the most highly preferred food item, an item that has the highest caloric value.

newborn infant 갓난아기, 신생아

인간 갓난아기 또한 단 음료에 대한 강한 선호를 보인다.
Human newborn infants also show a strong preference for sweet liquids.

toxin 독소

사람과 쥐 모두 쓰고, 신 음식을 싫어하는데, 이것은 독소를 포함하는 경향이 있다.
Both humans and rats dislike bitter and sour foods, which tend to contain toxins.

adaptively 적응하여. 적응적으로
adjust 조절하다
in response to ~에 대응하여
deficit 데피싯 부족

그들은 또한 자신의 섭식 행동을 물, 열량, 소금의 부족에 대응하여 적절히 조정한다.
They also adaptively adjust their eating behavior in response to deficits in water, calories, and salt.

first time 즉시

deficiency 결핍

실험에서는 쥐가 소금 결핍을 처음 경험할 때 소금에 대한 즉각적인 선호를 보이는 것으로 나타난다.
Experiments show that rats display an immediate liking for salt the first time they experience a salt deficiency.

intake 섭취
fluid 체액, 액체, 유동체
*deplete 디플리트 고갈시키다

그것들은 마찬가지로 에너지와 체액이 고갈되면 단것과 물 섭취를 늘린다.
They likewise increase their intake of sweets and water when their energy and fluids become depleted.

specific 특정의
mechanisms 기제, 매커니즘
coordinate 코올디네잇 조정하다, 조율하다
consumption 소비, 섭취

이것들은 특정한 진화된 기제처럼 보인다. 음식 선택의 적응적 문제를 다루고 음식 섭취 방식을 신체적 욕구와 조화시키도록 고안된,
These appear to be specific evolved mechanisms, designed to deal with the adaptive problem of food selection, and coordinate consumption patterns with physical needs.

....

38. 글의 흐름으로 보아, 주어진 문장이 들어가기에 가장 적절한 곳을 고르시오.
Experiments show that rats display an immediate liking for salt the first time they experience a salt deficiency.

 Both humans and rats have evolved taste preferences for sweet foods, which provide rich sources of calories. A study of food preferences among the Hadza hunter-gatherers of Tanzania found that honey was the most highly preferred food item, an item that has the highest caloric value. (①) Human newborn infants also show a strong preference for sweet liquids. (②) Both humans and rats dislike bitter and sour foods, which tend to contain toxins. (③) They also adaptively adjust their eating behavior in response to deficits in water, calories, and salt. (④) They likewise increase their intake of sweets and water when their energy and fluids become depleted. (⑤) These appear to be specific evolved mechanisms, designed to deal with the adaptive problem of food selection, and coordinate consumption patterns with physical needs.

정답 ④

'실험에서는 쥐가 소금 결핍을 처음 경험할 때 소금에 대한 즉각적인 선호를 보이는 것으로 나타난다.'라는 내용의 주어진 문장은 사람과 쥐가 물, 열량, 소금의 부족에 대응하여 섭식 행동을 조절한다는 문장과 쥐들은 또한 에너지와 체액이 고갈되면 단것과 물 섭취를 늘린다는 문장 사이인 ④에 들어가는 것이 적절하다.

perishable 페리시블 **부패하기 쉬운**

곡물과 설탕을 제외하고, 인간이 먹는 대부분의 식품은 부패하기 쉽다.
Except for grains and sugars, most foods humans eat are perishable.

deteriorate 디테리오레잇 **악화되다, 저하되다**
*palatability 팔라테빌리티 **맛의 좋고 나쁨, 기호성**
spoil **상하다, 썩다**

장기간 보관될 때, 그것들은 맛이 나빠지거나, 상하거나, 건강에 좋지 않게 된다.
They deteriorate in palatability, spoil, or become unhealthy when stored for long periods.

surplus **과잉, 잉여**
harvest **수확, 수확물**
appropriate **적절한**
methods **방법**
preservation **보존, 저장**

하지만 적절한 보존 방법을 사용하면 수확한 잉여의 동물 및 농작물을 나중에 사용하기 위해 남겨 둘 수 있다.
Surplus animal and crop harvests, however, can be saved for future use if appropriate methods of preservation are used.

식품을 보존하는 주요 방법은 통조림 가공, 냉동, 건조, 염장, 그리고 훈제이다.
The major ways of preserving foods are canning, freezing, drying, salting, and smoking.

restrict **제한하다, 억제하다**
microbe **미생물, 세균**
toxin **독소**
inactivate **비활성화하다**
*enzyme **효소**
undesirable **바람직하지 않은**

모든 방법에서 목표는 해로운 미생물의 성장이나 그것들의 독소를 없애거나 제한하고 음식의 맛에 바람직하지 않은 변화를 초래하는 효소의 작용을 늦추거나 비활성화하는 것이다.
With all methods the aim is to kill or restrict the growth of harmful microbes or their toxins and to slow or inactivate enzymes that cause undesirable changes in food palatability.

*sterile 스테릴 살균된, 무균의
airtight 공기가 통하지 않는, 밀폐된

장기간 보관하는 동안 추가적인 보호를 위해, 보존되는 음식은 멸균한 금속 캔 또는 유리병에 담거나 밀폐된 종이 또는 플라스틱 용기에 넣어 냉동한다.
For further protection during long periods of storage, preserved food is placed either in sterile metal cans or glass jars or frozen in airtight paper or plastic containers.

---

35. 다음 글에서 전체 흐름과 관계없는 문장은?
 Except for grains and sugars, most foods humans eat are perishable. They deteriorate in palatability, spoil, or become unhealthy when stored for long periods. ① Surplus animal and crop harvests, however, can be saved for future use if appropriate methods of preservation are used. ② The major ways of preserving foods are canning, freezing, drying, salting, and smoking. ③ With all methods the aim is to kill or restrict the growth of harmful microbes or their toxins and to slow or inactivate enzymes that cause undesirable changes in food palatability. ④ Palatability is not static: it is always changing, based on the state of the individual, especially in regard to the time of food consumption. ⑤ For further protection during long periods of storage, preserved food is placed either in sterile metal cans or glass jars or frozen in airtight paper or plastic containers.
* palatability: (좋은) 맛 * enzyme: 효소 * sterile: 멸균한

정답 ④

본문이 음식 보존 방법과 그 목적에 대해 설명하는 반면, ④는 음식의 기호성이 개인의 상태나 섭취 시점에 따라 변한다는 내용을 다루고 있어 주제와 관련이 없다.

static 스테틱 고정된, 정적인

맛은 그대로 있지 않다: 특히 음식 섭취 시간과 관련하여 개인의 상태에 따라 늘 변한다.
④ Palatability is not static: it is always changing, based on the state of the individual, especially in regard to the time of food consumption.

antelope 엔텔롭 영양(동물)
skull 두개골, 해골
socket 눈구멍, 소켓
situate 위치시키다, 배치하다

영양의 두개골에서, 눈구멍은 머리의 측면에 위치한다.
On an antelope's skull, the eye sockets are situated on the side of the head.

이것은 이 동물이 영양가가 낮은 음식인 풀을 먹기 위해 고개를 숙인 채 많은 시간을 보내기 때문이다.
This is because this animal spends a lot of its time with its head bent down to eat a low-nutrient food: grass.

graze 풀을 뜯다
predator 포식자, 약탈자
stalk 몰래 접근하다, 뒤를 밟다
range 범위, 영역
vision 시야, 시력

이 동물이 풀을 뜯느라 바쁜 동안, 외부에는 먹이를 찾아 살그머니 접근하는 포식자들이 있을 것이고, 그래서 영양은 그것의 포식자를 알아차리고 도망갈 수 있는 최대 가능성을 가지도록 가능한 최대 범위의 시야가 필요하다.
While the animal is busy grazing, there will be predators out stalking for their food, so the antelope needs the greatest possible range of vision so that it has the maximum chance of seeing its predator and making an escape.

눈구멍이 머리의 후면부와 측면부에 있어, 그것은 자기 주변을 거의 360도 볼 수 있다.
With the eye sockets at the back of the head and on the side, it can see nearly 360° around itself.

또 한 영양의 눈은 머리 후면부에 있어, 이는 그들에게 긴 코를 준다.
The eye of the antelope is also at the back of its head, giving it a long nose.

obscure 가리다, 흐리게하다
evolutionary 진화의, 발전적인

만약 눈이 두개골의 앞쪽에 있다면, 긴 풀에 시야가 가려질 것이고, 그래서 그것의 긴 코 또한 진화적 이점을 제공한다.
If the eyes were at the front of the skull, vision would be obscured by long grass, so its long nose also gives an evolutionary advantage.

....

24. 다음 글의 제목으로 가장 적절한 것은?

 On an antelope's skull, the eye sockets are situated on the side of the head. This is because this animal spends a lot of its time with its head bent down to eat a low-nutrient food: grass. While the animal is busy grazing, there will be predators out stalking for their food, so the antelope needs the greatest possible range of vision so that it has the maximum chance of seeing its predator and making an escape. With the eye sockets at the back of the head and on the side, it can see nearly 360° around itself. The eye of the antelope is also at the back of its head, giving it a long nose. If the eyes were at the front of the skull, vision would be obscured by long grass, so its long nose also gives an evolutionary advantage.

① Better Predator Detection: Eyes' Location Matters!
② Escaping as a Primary Defense Tactic in a Field
③ Closer Eyes, Less Accurate Distance Perception
④ A Win-Win Survival Strategy for Prey and Predator
⑤ Why Do Animals Have Longer Noses than Humans

정답 ①

Better Predator Detection: Eyes' Location Matters
더 나은 포식자 탐지: 눈의 위치가 중요하다

영양의 눈 위치가 측면과 후방에 있는 이유를 설명하고 있다.
이는 포식자로부터 도망칠 확률을 높이기 위해 최대한 넓은 시야를 확보하기 위함이다.
따라서, "① 포식자 탐지 능력을 높이는 눈의 위치"라는 제목이 가장 적절하다.

Tactic 전술, 전략
Perception 지각, 인지

② 들판에서의 주요 방어 전략으로서의 도망치기
Escaping as a Primary Defense Tactic in a Field

③ 눈이 가까울수록 거리 감각이 덜 정확하다
Closer Eyes, Less Accurate Distance Perception
④ 먹이와 포식자 모두에게 유리한 생존 전략
A Win-Win Survival Strategy for Prey and Predator
⑤ 왜 동물들은 인간보다 코가 더 길까?
Why Do Animals Have Longer Noses than Humans?

처음 한글을 배울 때
구조를 분석하지 않았다.
문법을 배우지 않았다. 단어를 외우지 않았다.

외국어로서 공부하기 때문에 느려지고
느리기 때문에 충분한 양에 노출되지 못하여
계속 잊으며, 쌓이지 않고, 읽히지 않는다.

한글 뜻과 영어 순으로
다만 빠르게, 다양하게, 많은 글을 읽어
수능을. 영어를 한다.

다만 빠른 영어
ただ、英語

versatile 벌스타일 다용도의, 융통성 있는
usefulness 유용성, 쓸모 있음

몇몇 형태의 에너지는 활용도에 있어 다른 에너지보다 더 다용도이다.
Some forms of energy are more versatile in their usefulness than others.

myriad 미리아드 수많은, 무수한
applications 용도, 사용처
whereas 반면에
stationary 고정된, 정지된
generate 생성하다, 생산하다

예를 들어, 우리는 전기를 무수히 많은 용도로 사용할 수 있는 반면, 석탄을 태워 얻은 열은 동력을 생산하는 것과 같은 고정된 용도로 현재 주로 사용된다.
For example, we can use electricity for a myriad of applications, whereas the heat from burning coal is currently used mostly for stationary applications like generating power.

substantial 상당한, 많은
due to ~ 때문에
inefficiency 비효율성

석탄을 태워 나오는 열을 전기로 바꿀 때, 공정의 비효율성으로 인해 상당한 양의 에너지가 손실된다.
When we turn the heat from burning coal into electricity, a substantial amount of energy is lost due to the inefficiency of the process.

relatively 상대적으로
inconvenient 불편한

하지만 우리는 석탄이 상대적으로 저렴하기 때문에 기꺼이 그 손실을 받아들이고, 전등, 컴퓨터, 냉장고를 작동시키는 데 석탄을 태워 '즉시' 사용하는 것은 어렵고 불편할 것이다.
But we are willing to accept that loss because coal is relatively cheap, and it would be difficult and inconvenient to use burning coal directly to power lights, computers, and refrigerators.

differing 서로 다른, 차이가 나는
ladder 단계, 사다리

gaseous 개셔스 기체의

사실상, 우리는 가치 사다리의 맨 위에 전기를, 가운데에 액체와 기체 연료를, 밑바닥에 석탄이나 장작을 놓으며 다양한 형태의 에너지에 다른 가치를 부여하고 있다.
In effect, we put a differing value on different forms of energy, with electricity at the top of the value ladder, liquid and gaseous fuels in the middle, and coal or firewood at the bottom.

태양광과 풍력 기술은 높은 가치의 전기를 즉시 생산한다는 점에서 장점이 있다.
Solar and wind technologies have an advantage in that they produce high-value electricity directly.

....

35. 다음 글에서 전체 흐름과 관계없는 문장은?
 Some forms of energy are more versatile in their usefulness than others. For example, we can use electricity for a myriad of applications, whereas the heat from burning coal is currently used mostly for stationary applications like generating power. ① When we turn the heat from burning coal into electricity, a substantial amount of energy is lost due to the inefficiency of the process. ② But we are willing to accept that loss because coal is relatively cheap, and it would be difficult and inconvenient to use burning coal directly to power lights, computers, and refrigerators. ③ Finding an economical way to use coal to produce carbon fibers will help revitalize rural communities suffering from the decline in coal production. ④ In effect, we put a differing value on different forms of energy, with electricity at the top of the value ladder, liquid and gaseous fuels in the middle, and coal or firewood at the bottom. ⑤ Solar and wind technologies have an advantage in that they produce high-value electricity directly.

정답 ③

본문이 에너지원의 활용성 차이를 설명하는 데 초점을 맞추고 있는 반면, ③은 석탄을 이용한 탄소섬유 생산이 농촌 지역 경제에 미치는 영향을 다루고 있어 주제와 관련이 없다.

carbon fiber 탄소 섬유
revitalize 활성화하다, 재활성화하다
rural communities 지역사회
decline 감소, 쇠퇴
production 생산

탄소 섬유를 생산하기 위해 석탄을 이용하는 경제적인 방법을 찾는것은 석탄 생산의 감소로부터 고통받고 있는 지역사회를 소생시키는데 도움을 줄 것이다.
③ Finding an economical way to use coal to produce carbon fibers will help revitalize rural communities suffering from the decline in coal production.

conflict 갈등
rival 라이벌, 상대
flee 도망가다
initially 처음에
sufficient 충분한

상대를 공격하는 것과 도피하는 것 사이에서 갈등하는 동물은 처음에는 즉시 결정을 내릴 수 있게 해줄 만큼 충분한 정보를 갖지 못할 수도 있다.
The animal in a conflict between attacking a rival and fleeing may initially not have sufficient information to enable it to make a decision straight away.

optimal 최적의

상대가 싸움에서 이길 것 같다면, 최적의 결정은 즉시 포기하고 부상당할 위험을 무릅쓰지 않는 것일 것이다.
① If the rival is likely to win the fight, then the optimal decision would be to give up immediately and not risk getting injured.

defeatable 이길 만한
considerable 상당한
territory 영역, 영토
stake 말뚝, 내기에 거는 돈
be at stake 성패가 달려 있다

하지만 상대가 약해서 쉽게 이길만하다면, 싸워서 영역, 암컷, 먹이 또는 성패가 달린 것은 무엇이든 얻는 것에 상당한 이익이 있을 수 있을 것이다.
② But if the rival is weak and easily defeatable, then there could be considerable benefit in going ahead and obtaining the territory, females, food or whatever is at stake.

opponent 상대
maximize 최대화하다

상대에 대한 정보를 수집하는 데 약간의 추가 시간을 들임으로써, 그 동물은 그러한 정보 없이 결정을 내리는 경우보다 이길 가능성을 최대화하는 결정에 도달할 가능성이 더 크다.
④ By taking a little extra time to collect information about the opponent, the animal is more likely to reach a decision that maximizes its chances of winning than if it takes a decision without such information.

assessment 평가
vital 매우 중요한
outcome 결과

오늘날 많은 신호들이 이러한 정보 수집 또는 '평가' 기능을 갖는 것으로 간주되어, 다양한 선택의 가능한 결과에 관한 매우 중요한 정보를 제공함으로써 의사 결정 과정의 메커니즘에 직접적으로 기여한다.
⑤ Many signals are now seen as having this information gathering or 'assessment' function, directly contributing to the mechanism of the decision-making process by supplying vital information about the likely outcomes of the various options.

....

35. 다음 글에서 전체 흐름과 관계없는 문장은?
 The animal in a conflict between attacking a rival and fleeing may initially not have sufficient information to enable it to make a decision straight away. ① If the rival is likely to win the fight, then the optimal decision would be to give up immediately and not risk getting injured. ② But if the rival is weak and easily defeatable, then there could be considerable benefit in going ahead and obtaining the territory, females, food or whatever is at stake. ③ Animals under normal circumstances maintain a very constant body weight and they eat and drink enough for their needs at regular intervals. ④ By taking a little extra time to collect information about the opponent, the animal is more likely to reach a decision that maximizes its chances of winning than if it takes a decision without such information. ⑤ Many signals are now seen as having this information gathering or 'assessment' function, directly contributing to the mechanism of the decision-making process by supplying vital information about the likely outcomes of the various options.

정답 ③

의사 결정 과정에서 사전에 대상에 대한 정보를 수집하는 것의 이점에 관해 설명하고 있는 글이므로, 보통의 상황에서 동물은 매우 일정한 체중을 유지하고 규칙적인 간격으로 필요한 만큼 충분히 먹고 마신다는 내용의 ③은 전체 흐름과 관계가 없다.

intervals 인터벌, 간격

③ 보통의 상황에서 동물은 매우 일정한 체중을 유지하며, 그들은 규칙적인 간격으로 자신들에게 필요한 만큼 충분히 먹고 마신다.
 Animals under normal circumstances maintain a very constant body weight and they eat and drink

enough for their needs at regular intervals.

※
stake의 원래 의미는 "말뚝, 막대기"이다.
이 단어는 처음에는 땅에 박는 나무나 금속 막대를 뜻했다. 이후 의미가 확장되면서 다양한 뜻을 가지게 되었다.

그들은 텐트를 나무 말뚝에 묶었다. [말뚝, 막대기]
They tied the tent to a wooden stake.
그는 그 경기에 큰 돈을 걸었다. [내기 돈, 판돈]
He put a large stake on the game.
이 결정에는 많은 것이 걸려 있다. [이해관계, 위태로운 것]
There is a lot at stake in this decision.

이처럼 stake는 "말뚝"에서 출발해 "내기에서 거는 돈"이라는 의미로 발전했고, 나아가 "어떤 일에서 잃거나 얻을 가능성이 있는 것"을 뜻하게 되었다. "be at stake"에서의 stake는 이 세 번째 의미에서 유래한 것이다.

consequence 결과, 영향
mechanical 기계적인, 물리적인
breakdown 분해, 붕괴
profound 깊은, 엄청난

요리에 의한 음식의 물리적 힘에 의한 분해의 결과는 심오하다.
The consequences of the mechanical breakdown of food by cooking are profound.

stiffness 뻣뻣함, 단단함
toughness 단단함, 질김
drastically 급격하게, 과감하게
processing 가공, 처리

음식의 단단함과 질김이 모두 급격하게 감소되어, 물리적 힘에 의한 처리가 훨씬 더 쉬워진다.
Both the stiffness and toughness of the food is drastically reduced, making mechanical processing far ① easier.

여러분의 치아가 음식을 분해하기 위해 가할 필요가 있는 힘은 더 작고, 음식은 훨씬 더 쉽게 세포의 내용물을 방출하게 된다.
The forces your teeth need to apply to break up the food are lower, and the food ② releases its cell contents far more easily.

optimal 최적의

음식을 분해하기 위한 최적의 치아 형태 또한 바뀐다.
The optimal tooth shape for breaking up the food also ③ changes.

compression 압축
*molar 어금니
pointed ends 뾰족한

질긴 재료를 갈고 단단한 것을 으깨기 위해 큰 압축력을 가할 수 있는 두껍고 평평한 판이 필요하기보다는, 더 부드러운 음식을 잘라내기 위해 뾰족한 끝을 갖고 있는 어금니를 가지는 것이 더 낫다.
Rather than needing thick, flat plates that can apply large compression forces to grind up tough materials and crush hard ones, it is better to have molars with pointed ends to cut

through the softer food.

loosen 느슨하게 하다, (결합이) 풀어지다

그것은 훨씬 더 큰(→작은) 힘에서 물러지고 훨씬 더 빨리 분해된다.
It loosens at much ④ higher(→lower) forces and breaks up far more quickly.

hunter-gatherer 수렵채집인
apes 에잎스 유인원
relatively 상대적으로

현대의 수렵채집인들은 심지어 비교적 부드러운 과일을 먹는 유인원들보다도 자신의 음식을 씹는 데 훨씬 더 적은 시간을 보낸다.
Modern hunter-gatherers spend far less time chewing their food even than apes that eat relatively soft fruit;

침팬지들이 (하루에) 대여섯 시간을 씹는 것에 비해 그들은 하루에 1시간 미만 동안 씹는다.
they chew for less than an hour a day compared with five or six hours for chimpanzees.

permanent 영구적인
***foraging** 포리징 식량 채집, 수렵

이것은 불을 살피고, 오래가는 거주지를 만들고, 도구를 만들고, 또는 식량을 더 찾아다니는 것과 같은 다른 일들을 위한 많은 시간을 이용할 수 있게 만든다.
This ⑤ frees up plenty of time for other tasks, such as looking after the fire, making a permanent camp, toolmaking, or further foraging.

....

30. 다음 글의 밑줄 친 부분 중, 문맥상 낱말의 쓰임이 적절하지 않은 것은? [3점]

The consequences of the mechanical breakdown of food by cooking are profound. Both the stiffness and toughness of the food is drastically reduced, making mechanical processing far ① easier. The forces your teeth need to apply to break up the food are lower, and the food ② releases its cell contents far more easily. The optimal tooth shape for breaking up the food also ③ changes. Rather than needing thick, flat plates that can apply large compression forces

to grind up tough materials and crush hard ones, it is better to have molars with pointed ends to cut through the softer food. It loosens at much ④ <u>higher</u> forces and breaks up far more quickly. Modern hunter-gatherers spend far less time chewing their food even than apes that eat relatively soft fruit; they chew for less than an hour a day compared with five or six hours for chimpanzees. This ⑤ <u>frees</u> up plenty of time for other tasks, such as looking after the fire, making a permanent camp, toolmaking, or further foraging.
* molar 어금니 * forage 식량을 찾아다니다

정답 ④ higher(→lower)

문맥상 조리된 음식은 더 부드러워지고 씹기 쉬워지므로, 적은 힘으로도 부서져야 한다. 하지만 "higher forces"는 더 큰 힘을 의미하므로 lower로 수정하는 것이 적절하다.

religion 종교
equator 적도
*ethnocentrism 에쓰노센트리즘 자민족 중심주의

왜 언어와 종교는 적도 주변에서 급증하며, 왜 그것의 빈도가 자민족 중심주의와 또한 관련이 있을까?
Why would languages and religions increase rapidly around the equator, and why is their frequency also related to ethnocentrism?

lie in ~에 있다
*pathogen 패쎄전 병원균, 병원체
density 밀도
tropics 열대
temperate 온대의

이 질문들에 대한 답은 병원균의 밀도가 온대 기후나 한랭 기후보다 열대 지방에서 훨씬 더 높다는 사실에 있다.
The answer to these questions lies in the fact that pathogen density is much higher in the tropics than it is in temperate and cold climates.

스웨덴에 살면, 가능성이 크다. 오백 마일 이내의 어떤 집단이든 동일한 몇 가지 병원균에 노출되었을
When you live in Sweden, chances are good that any group within five hundred miles has been exposed to the same few pathogens.

in contrast 반면에, 대조적으로
prior 이전의

반면에 여러분이 콩고에 산다면 계곡 반대편에 있는 집단은 아마 여러분이 이전에 접촉한 적이 없는 병원균에 노출되었을지도 모른다.
In contrast, when you live in the Congo, the group on the other side of the valley may well have been exposed to a pathogen with which you've had no prior contact.

interact 교류하다, 상호작용하다

이러한 이유로, 열대 지방의 사람들은 그들이 다른 집단과 교류할 때 병에 잘 걸린다는 것을 알게 되었고, 그래서 그들은 그것(교류)을 하는 것을 중단했을 것이다.
For this reason, humans in the tropics learned that when they interacted with other groups they tended to get sick, so they would have stopped doing it.

pre-scientific 과학 이전의

과학 이전의 세계에서는 자신의 병을 이웃 탓으로 돌리고 그 결과 그들을 싫어하는 것이 논리적이었다.
In a pre-scientific world, it was logical to blame their neighbors for their illness, and therefore to dislike them.

interact 교류하다. 상호작용 하다
divide 갈라지다

혐오와 두려움이 이웃을 계속 갈라놓았고, 일단 타인과 더는 교류하지 않게 되면 언어와 종교도 역시 자연스럽게 갈라지게 된다.
Dislike and fear kept neighbors apart, and once you don't interact with others anymore, your languages and religions naturally divide as well.

contribute 기여하다. 초래하다
diversification 디벌시피케이션 다양화
discouraging 낙담시키는. ~를 못하게 하다
interactions 상호작용

높은 병원균 밀도는 사람들이 이웃 집단과 교류하지 못하게 하여 언어와 종교의 다양화를 초래할 수 있다. 적도 주변 지역에서 보여진 것처럼
→ High pathogen density can contribute to the (A) diversification of languages and religions by (B) discouraging people's interactions with their neighboring groups, as was shown in the regions around the equator.

....

40. 다음 글의 내용을 한 문장으로 요약하고자 한다. 빈칸 (A), (B)에 들어갈 말로 가장 적절한 것은?

 Why would languages and religions increase rapidly around the equator, and why is their frequency also related to ethnocentrism? The answer to these questions lies in the fact that pathogen density is much higher in the tropics than it is in temperate and cold climates. When you live in Sweden, chances are good that any group within five hundred miles has been exposed to the same few pathogens. In contrast, when you live in the Congo, the group on the other side of the valley may well have been exposed to a pathogen with which you've had no prior contact. For this reason, humans in the tropics learned that when they interacted with other groups they tended to get sick, so they would have stopped doing it. In a pre-scientific world, it was logical to blame their neighbors for their illness, and therefore to dislike them.

Dislike and fear kept neighbors apart, and once you don't interact with others anymore, your languages and religions naturally divide as well.
* ethnocentrism: 자민족 중심주의 * pathogen: 병원균

→ High pathogen density can contribute to the (A) of languages and religions by (B) people's interactions with their neighboring groups, as was shown in the regions around the equator.

	(A)		(B)
①	diversification	·····	discouraging
②	extinction	·····	delaying
③	extinction	·····	expanding
④	unification	·····	discouraging
⑤	diversification	·····	expanding

정답 ①

높은 병원균 밀도는 사람들의 이웃 집단과의 상호작용을 (B) 저해함으로써 언어와 종교의 (A) 다양화에 기여할 수 있으며, 이는 적도 주변 지역에서 나타난 현상이다.
병원균 밀도가 높은 열대 지역에서는 이웃과의 접촉이 질병을 유발할 가능성이 크므로 사람들은 타 집단과의 교류를 피하게 된다. 이러한 단절로 인해 집단 간 언어와 종교가 자연스럽게 분리되며 다양성이 증가한다. 따라서 (A)에는 "diversification"이, (B)에는 "discouraging"이 들어가는 것이 적절하다.

①	diversification	다양화	·····	discouraging	저해하는
②	extinction	멸종	·····	delaying	지연하는
③	extinction	멸종	·····	expanding	확장하는
④	unification	통합	·····	discouraging	저해하는
⑤	diversification	다양화	·····	expanding	확장하는

한글 – 영어 순서가 맞다.

영양의 두개골에서, 눈구멍은 머리의 측면에 위치한다.
On an antelope's skull, the eye sockets are situated on the side of the head.

한글 의미를 아는 상태로 영어를 읽으면
각 어구의 의미와 – 영어를 하나씩 대응시키며

점차 영어 의미 구조들이 학습되지만

영어 – 한글 순은

On an antelope's skull, the eye sockets are situated on the side of the head.
영양의 두개골에서, 눈구멍은 머리의 측면에 위치한다.

영어를 읽을 때는 의미를 모르다가
한글을 읽고 글 자체의 뜻만 알게 된 채

영어 학습을 했다고 착각하고 넘어가게 되며

영어와 – 의미가 대응되지 않았다.

characteristic 특징, 특성
maintain 유지하다, 지속하다

비록 인구가 줄어들더라도 반드시 유지되어야만 하는 도시의 몇 가지 특징들은 무엇인가?
What are some characteristics of cities that must be maintained even if the population decreases?

propose 제안하다
concept 개념

만약 이 질문이 대답 될 수 있다면 그 개념에 기반하여 새로운 도시 모델이 제안될 수 있다.
If this question can be answered, a new city model can be proposed based on the concept.

productivity 생산성
diversity 다양성

여기서 우리는 도시의 특징들로 생산성과 다양성에 초점을 맞춘다.
Here, we focus on productivity and diversity as characteristics of cities.

driving force 원동력, 추진력
sustainability 지속 가능성

(B) 이는 생산성과 다양성을 보장하는 것이 지속 가능성을 위한 원동력이기 때문이다.
(B) This is because ensuring productivity and diversity is the driving force for sustainability.

accumulate 축적되다, 쌓이다

예를 들어 만약 일할 장소가 있다면, 사람들은 그곳에 모여 일을 하며 인구는 점차 축적되어 도시를 형성한다.
For example, if there is a place to work, people gather and work there, and the population gradually accumulates to form a city.

industrial structure 산업 구조
vulnerable 벌루너블 취약한, 영향을 받기 쉬운 그러나 단일 산업에 의존하는 산업 구조는 사회적 변화에 취약하다.
However, the industrial structure that depends on a single industry is vulnerable to social changes.

(A) 금광 도시들과 탄광 도시들이 흥망성쇠 해 왔던 것을 고려하면 그것들의 취약성은 분명하다.
(A) Given that gold mining cities and coal mining cities have risen and fallen, their vulnerability is obvious.

다양한 산업에 다양한 사람들이 모이는 도시는 사회적 변화에 안정적이다.
A city where various people gather in various industries is secure against social changes.

biodiversity 바이오다이벌시티 생물 다양성
species 종(생물)
sustainability 지속 가능성

자연 세계에서도 마찬가지이며, 생물 다양성의 중요성은 종의 지속 가능성에 있어서 필수적이다.
The same is true in the natural world, and the importance of biodiversity is essential for the sustainability of the species.

(C) 도시에서도 마찬가지이다.
(C) The same is true in cities.

coexist 공존하다
depend on 의존하다, 좌우되다
overcome 극복하다

모든 연령대와 소득 수준의 사람들이 함께 살고, 다양한 산업들이 서로 의존하면서 공존하는 사회에서 도시들은 인구 감소와 같은 환경적 변화를 극복하면서 계속 존재할 것이다.
In a society where people of all ages and income levels live together, and diverse industries coexist while depending on each other, cities will continue to exist overcoming environmental changes such as population decline.

36. 주어진 글 다음에 이어질 글의 순서로 가장 적절한 것을 고르시오.

 What are some characteristics of cities that must be maintained even if the population decreases? If this question can be answered, a new city model can be proposed based on the concept. Here, we focus on productivity and diversity as characteristics of cities.

(A) Given that gold mining cities and coal mining cities have risen and fallen, their vulnerability is obvious. A city where various people gather in various industries is secure against social changes. The same is true in the natural world, and the importance of biodiversity is essential for the sustainability of the species.

(B) This is because ensuring productivity and diversity is the driving force for sustainability. For example, if there is a place to work, people gather and work there, and the population gradually accumulates to form a city. However, the industrial structure that depends on a single industry is vulnerable to social changes.

(C) The same is true in cities. In a society where people of all ages and income levels live together, and diverse industries coexist while depending on each other, cities will continue to exist overcoming environmental changes such as population decline.

① (A) - (C) - (B) 　　　② (B) - (A) - (C)
③ (B) - (C) - (A) 　　　④ (C) - (A) - (B)
⑤ (C) - (B) - (A)

정답 ②

본문에서 도시가 유지되기 위해 필요한 특성을 설명한 후, 생산성과 다양성이 지속 가능성의 원동력임을 강조하는 방식으로 전개된다.

(B)에서 생산성과 다양성이 지속 가능성을 유지하는 핵심 요소라고 설명하며, 단일 산업에 의존하는 도시의 취약성을 지적하고 있다.
다음으로 (A)에서 금광이나 탄광 도시처럼 특정 산업에 의존하는 도시가 쇠퇴하는 사례를 들어 이러한 취약성을 구체적으로 설명하고 있다. 또한, 자연계에서도 생물다양성이 지속 가능성을 보장한다는 점을 언급하며 비교한다.
마지막으로 (C)에서 도시에서도 다양한 연령과 소득 수준의 사람들이 함께 살아가고 여러 산업이 공존할 때 지속 가능성이 높아진다는 결론을 제시한다.

따라서 가장 적절한 순서는 ② (B) - (A) - (C) 이다.

commonsense 상식적인
merit 장점
contradict 모순되다

상식적인 지식에 장점이 있을 수 있지만, 그것에는 약점도 있는데, 그중에서 중요한 것은 그것이 모순되는 경우가 많다는 것이다.
Although commonsense knowledge may have merit, it also has weaknesses, not the least of which is that it often contradicts itself.

flock 모이다

예를 들어, 우리는 비슷한 사람들이 서로 좋아하기 마련이라는 말 ('유유상종') 을 듣지만,
For example, we hear that people who are similar will like one another ("Birds of a feather flock together")

닮지 않은 사람들이 서로 좋아하기 마련이라는 말('정반대되는 사람들은 서로에게 끌린다')도 듣는다.
but also that persons who are dissimilar will like each other ("Opposites attract").

우리는 집단이 개인보다 더 현명하고 더 똑똑하다는 말('두 사람의 지혜가 한 사람의 지혜보다 낫다')을 듣지만,
① We are told that groups are wiser and smarter than individuals ("Two heads are better than one")

inevitably 인에비터블리 불가피하게
spoil 망치다
broth 수프

집단 작업이 불가피하게 좋지 않은 결과를 만든다는 말('요리사가 너무 많으면 수프를 망친다')도 듣는다.
but also that group work inevitably produces poor results ("Too many cooks spoil the broth").

contradictory 모순된
statement 말, 진술
hold true 사실이다, 진실이다
*aphorisms 에포리즘스 격언
insight 통찰

이런 모순된 말들 각각은 특정한 상황에서는 사실일 수 있지만, 그것이 언제 적용되는지와 언제 적용되지 않는지에 관한 명확한 진술이 없으면 격언은 사람들 사이의 관계에 대한 통찰력을 거의 제공하지 못한다.
② Each of these contradictory statements may hold true under particular conditions, but without a clear statement of when they apply and when they do not, aphorisms provide little insight into relations among people.

그것들은 우리가 결정을 내려야 하는 상황에서는 그야말로 거의 아무런 지침도 제공하지 못한다.
④ They provide even less guidance in situations where we must make decisions.

*entails 수반하다
venture 모험하다

예를 들어, 위험을 수반하는 선택에 직면할 때, '모험하지 않으면 아무것도 얻을 수 없다' 또는 '나중에 후회하는 것보다 조심하는 것이 낫다' 중에 우리는 어느 지침을 이용해야 하는가?
⑤ For example, when facing a choice that entails risk, which guideline should we use — "Nothing ventured, nothing gained" or "Better safe than sorry"?

....

35. 다음 글에서 전체 흐름과 관계 없는 문장은?

 Although commonsense knowledge may have merit, it also has weaknesses, not the least of which is that it often contradicts itself. For example, we hear that people who are similar will like one another ("Birds of a feather flock together") but also that persons who are dissimilar will like each other ("Opposites attract"). ① We are told that groups are wiser and smarter than individuals ("Two heads are better than one") but also that group work inevitably produces poor results ("Too many cooks spoil the broth"). ② Each of these contradictory statements may hold true under particular conditions, but without a clear statement of when they apply and when they do not, aphorisms provide little insight into relations among people. ③ That is why we heavily depend on aphorisms whenever we face difficulties and challenges in the long journey of our lives. ④ They provide even less guidance in situations where we must make decisions. ⑤ For example, when facing a choice that entails risk, which guideline should we use — "Nothing ventured, nothing gained" or "Better safe than sorry"?
* aphorism: 격언 * entail: 수반하다

정답 ③

상식적인 지식이 담긴 격언에는 모순되는 것이 많아 어떤 상황에서 어떤 격언이 적용되는지에 관한 명확한 설명이 없으면 아무런 도움이 되지 않는다는 것이 이 글의 요지이다. 따라서 삶의 여정에서 어려움과 도전에 직면할 때마다 격언에 의존하게 된다는 내용인 ③은 전체 흐름과 관계가 없다.

*aphorisms 에포리즘스 격언

그것이 우리가 삶의 긴 여정에서 어려움과 도전에 직면할 때마다 격언에 매우 의존하는 이유이다.
③ That is why we heavily depend on aphorisms whenever we face difficulties and challenges in the long journey of our lives.

strategy 전략, 계획

우리는 우리가 어디에 있고 어디로 가기를 원하는지를 먼저 이해하지 않고서 우리 삶을 위한 전략을 세우는 것을 시작할 수 없다.
We can't begin to build a strategy for our lives without first understanding where we are and where we want to go.

reasonable 합리적인, 타당한
assume 가정하다, 추정하다

사람들은 서로 다르기 때문에, 그들의 현재 상황이나 출발점 또한 다를 것이라고 가정하는 것이 합당하다.
Since people are different, it's reasonable to assume their current situations or starting points will be different as well.

***tout** 타우트 과대 선전하다, 장점을 내세우다
formula 공식, 방법
take into account 고려하다, 감안하다
worthless 가치 없는, 쓸모없는

그것이 바로 사람들의 서로 다른 출발점을 고려하지 않고 성공이나 개선을 위한 하나의 방식만을 권유하는 서적들이 가치가 없는 이유이다.
That's why books that tout a single formula for success or improvement, without taking into account the different places people are starting from, are worthless.

diagnose 다이아그노스 진단하다
prescription 처방전

잘못된 것이 무엇인지 진단하기 위해 어떤 질문도 하지 않거나 아무런 검사도 하지 않고 아무튼 처방 전을 발급한 의사를 신뢰하겠는가?
Would you trust a doctor who didn't ask any questions or run any tests to diagnose what was wrong, yet wrote you a prescription anyway?

***adage** 애디지 속담, 격언
malpractice 의료 과실, 위법 행위

의학에는 '진단 없는 처방은 의료 과실과도 같다.'라는 격언이 있다.
In medicine, the adage is Prescription without diagnosis equals malpractice.

전략을 '처방할' 수 있기 전에 먼저 상황, 즉 우리가 서 있는 곳, 우리가 현재 있는 곳을 진단해야 한다.
Before we can "prescribe" strategy, we first need to diagnose the situation — where we stand, where we are today.

----

20. 다음 글에서 필자가 주장하는 바로 가장 적절한 것은?
We can't begin to build a strategy for our lives without first understanding where we are and where we want to go. Since people are different, it's reasonable to assume their current situations or starting points will be different as well. That's why books that tout a single formula for success or improvement, without taking into account the different places people are starting from, are worthless. Would you trust a doctor who didn't ask any questions or run any tests to diagnose what was wrong, yet wrote you a prescription anyway? In medicine, the adage Is Prescription without diagnosis equals malpractice. Before we can "prescribe" strategy, we first need to diagnose the situation — where we stand, where we are today.
* tout 권유하다 * adage 격언

① 자신의 현재 상황을 파악한 후에 전략을 세워야 한다.
② 다른 사람의 능력을 인정하고 배울 줄 알아야 한다.
③ 상황이 바뀌어도 처음 세운 원칙을 고수해야 한다.
④ 서두르지 말고 작은 목표부터 단계별로 달성해야 한다.
⑤ 한 가지 방식만 고집하지 말고 다양한 시도를 해야 한다.

정답 ①

이유는 본문에서 전략을 세우기 전에 먼저 자신이 어디에 있는지, 즉 현재의 상황을 이해해야 한다는 점을 강조하고 있기 때문이다. 사람마다 출발점이 다르기 때문에 모두에게 동일한 성공 법칙을 적용하는 것은 무의미하며, 적절한 전략을 세우려면 먼저 자신의 위치를 진단해야 한다고 설명하고 있다. 이를 의사의 진단과 처방에 비유하면서, 상황을 분석하지 않고 전략을 세우는 것은 잘못된 접근이라고 주장하고 있다.

자신감이 있다는 것은 맘이 편하다는 것과 같지 않다.
Confident is not the same as comfortable.

misconception 오해

자신감을 갖게 되는 것에 관한 가장 큰 오해 중 하나는 그것이 두려움 없이 사는 것을 의미한다는 것이다.
One of the biggest misconceptions about becoming self-confident is that it means living fearlessly.

자신감 구축의 핵심은 오히려 그 반대이다.
The key to building confidence is quite the opposite.

willing 기꺼이 하는

이는 우리가 우리에게 중요한 일을 할 때 두려움 이 존재하도록 기꺼이 두는 것을 의미한다.
It means we are willing to let fear be present as we do the things that matter to us.

무언가에 대한 어느 정도의 자신감이 생기면 기분이 좋다.
When we establish some self-confidence in something, it feels good.

hold on to ~을 고수하다

우리는 거기에 머물러서 고수하고 싶어 한다.
We want to stay there and hold on to it.

하지만 우리가 자신감을 느끼는 곳으로만 간다면, 그런 경우 자신감은 그 이상으로 절대 확장되지 않는다.
But if we only go where we feel confident, then confidence never expands beyond that.

우리가 잘할 수 있다고 알고 있는 일만 한다면, 새롭고 미지의 것에 대한 두려움은 커지는 경향이 있다.
If we only do the things we know we can do well, fear of the new and unknown tends to grow.

inevitably 필연적으로, 불가피하게
***vulnerability 벌루너빌리티 취약성**

자신감을 키우려면 필연적으로 취약성과 친구가 되어야 하는데 그것이 한동안 자신감 없이 지낼 수 있는 유일한 방법이기 때문이다.
Building confidence inevitably demands that we make friends with vulnerability because it is the only way to be without confidence for a while.

하지만 자신감이 커질 수 있는 유일한 방법은 기꺼이 자신감 없이 지낼 때이다.
But the only way confidence can grow is when we are willing to be without it.

우리가 두려움 속으로 들어가 미지의 것과 어울릴 수 있을 때, 바닥에서부터 자신감을 쌓는 것은 바로 그렇게 하는 용기이다.
When we can step into fear and sit with the unknown, it is the courage of doing so that builds confidence from the ground up.

....

20. 다음 글에서 필자가 주장하는 바로 가장 적절한 것은?
  Confident is not the same as comfortable. One of the biggest misconceptions about becoming self-confident is that it means living fearlessly. The key to building confidence is quite the opposite. It means we are willing to let fear be present as we do the things that matter to us. When we establish some self-confidence in something, it feels good. We want to stay there and hold on to it. But if we only go where we feel confident, then confidence never expands beyond that. If we only do the things we know we can do well, fear of the new and unknown tends to grow. Building confidence inevitably demands that we make friends with vulnerability because it is the only way to be without confidence for a while. But the only way confidence can grow is when we are willing to be without it. When we can step into fear and sit with the unknown, it is the courage of doing so that builds confidence from the ground up.
* vulnerability: 취약성
① 적성을 파악하기 위해서는 자신 있는 일을 다양하게 시도해야 한다.
② 자신감을 키우기 위해 낯설고 두려운 일에 도전하는 용기를 가져야 한다.
③ 어려운 일을 자신 있게 수행하기 위해 사전에 계획을 철저히 세워야 한다.
④ 과도한 자신감을 갖기보다는 자신의 약점을 객관적으로 분석해야 한다.
⑤ 자신의 경험과 지식을 바탕으로 당면한 문제에 자신 있게 대처해야 한다.

정답 ②

자신감을 갖는다는 것이 두려움 없이 사는 것을 의미한다는 생각은 큰 오해라고 하면서, 우리가 자신감을 느끼는 곳에만 간다면 자신감은 그 이상으로 확장되지 않으므로 자신감을 키우기 위해 두려움 속으로 들어가 미지의 것과 어울릴 수 있는 용기가 필요하다는 것이 글의 중심 내용이다.

DAY 2

firefly 반딧불이
attract 끌어들이다, 유인하다
glow 빛나다, 발광하다

반딧불이는 짝의 주의를 끌기 위해서 꽁무니에 불을 밝히는 것만이 아니라, 박쥐에게 자기들을 먹지 말라고 말하기 위해 빛을 내기도 한다.
Fireflies don't just light up their behinds to attract mates, they also glow to tell bats not to eat them.

twist 반전, 곡해
trait 특징, 특성
discover 발견하다, 알아내다
colleagues 동료

반딧불이의 이름을 지어주는 특성에 대한 이야기의 이 반전은 Jesse Barber와 그의 동료들에 의해 발견되었다.
This twist in the tale of the trait that gives fireflies their name was discovered by Jesse Barber and his colleagues.

mammal 포유류

빛이 하는 경고 역할은 반딧불이와 박쥐 모두에게 유익한데, 왜냐하면 이 곤충이 그 포유동물(박쥐)에게는 역겨운 맛이 나기 때문이다.
The glow's warning role benefits both fireflies and bats, because these insects taste disgusting to the mammals.

swallow 삼키다
chemical 화학 물질
release 방출하다, 분비하다

반딧불이를 삼키면, 반딧불이가 배출하는 화학 물질 때문에 박쥐가 그것을 다시 토해내게 낸다.
(①) When swallowed, chemicals released by fireflies cause bats to throw them back up.

연구팀은 여덟 마리의 박쥐를 서너 마리의 반딧불이와, 그보다 세 배가 많은 딱정벌레와 나방을 포함한 맛이 좋은 곤충들과 함께 어두운 방에 나흘 동안 두었다.
(②) The team placed eight bats in a dark room with three or four fireflies plus three times

as many tasty insects, including beetles and moths, for four days.

첫날 밤 동안에, 모든 박쥐는 적어도 한 마리의 반딧불이를 잡았다.
(③) During the first night, all the bats captured at least one firefly.

prey 먹잇감, 포식 대상

그러나 네 번째 밤에 이르러서는, 대부분의 박쥐는 반딧불이를 피하고 대신 다른 모든 먹이를 잡는 법을 배웠다.
(④) But by the fourth night, most bats had learned to avoid fireflies and catch all the other prey instead.

organ 기관, 장기

그 팀이 반딧불이에서 빛이 나는 기관을 어둡게 칠했을 때, 새로운 한 무리의 박쥐는 그것들을 피하는 법을 배우는 데 두 배의 시간이 걸렸다.
(When the team painted fireflies' light organs dark, a new set of bats took twice as long to learn to avoid them.)

*bioluminescence 바이오루메네센스 생물 발광
*larvae 랄바 애벌레의 복수형
immature 미성숙한, 덜 자란

오랫동안 반딧불이의 생물 발광은 주로 짝짓기 신호의 역할을 한다고 생각되었지만, 새로운 연구 결과는 짝짓기를 하기에 미숙함에도 불구하고 반딧불이 애벌레 역시 빛을 내는 이유를 설명해 준다.
(⑤) It had long been thought that firefly bioluminescence mainly acted as a mating signal, but the new finding explains why firefly larvae also glow despite being immature for mating.

....

39. 글의 흐름으로 보아, 주어진 문장이 들어가기에 가장 적절한 곳을 고르시오.
When the team painted fireflies' light organs dark, a new set of bats took twice as long to learn to avoid them.

 Fireflies don't just light up their behinds to attract mates, they also glow to tell bats not to eat them. This twist in the tale of the trait that gives fireflies their name was discovered by

Jesse Barber and his colleagues. The glow's warning role benefits both fireflies and bats, because these insects taste disgusting to the mammals. (①) When swallowed, chemicals released by fireflies cause bats to throw them back up. (②) The team placed eight bats in a dark room with three or four fireflies plus three times as many tasty insects, including beetles and moths, for four days. (③) During the first night, all the bats captured at least one firefly. (④) But by the fourth night, most bats had learned to avoid fireflies and catch all the other prey instead. (⑤) It had long been thought that firefly bioluminescence mainly acted as a mating signal, but the new finding explains why firefly larvae also glow despite being immature for mating.

* bioluminescence: 생물 발광(發光) * larvae: larva(애벌레)의 복수형

정답 ⑤

반딧불이가 꽁무니에 불을 밝히는 이유는 짝짓기를 하기 위함일 뿐만 아니라, 박쥐에게 잡아 먹이지 않기 위함이기도 하다는 내용의 글이다. 주어진 문장은 한 연구팀이 반딧불이가 빛을 내는 기관을 어둡게 칠하자 새로운 한 무리의 박쥐가 반딧불이를 피하는 데 두 배의 시간이 걸렸다는 내용이므로, 반딧불이의 빛을 내는 기관을 그대로 둔 상태에서 얻은 결과 다음에 와야 한다. 따라서 주어진 문장이 들어가기에 가장 적절한 곳은 ⑤이다.

costly 비용이 많이 드는, 대가가 큰
*forage 포-리지 먹이를 찾아 다니다

놀이는 먹이를 찾아다니는 데 쓰일 수 있는 에너지와 시간을 빼앗기 때문에 대가를 치를 수 있다.
Play can be costly because it takes energy and time which could be spent foraging.

노는 동안 어린 동물은 큰 위험에 처할 수도 있다.
While playing, the young animal may be at great (A) (comfort / <u>risk</u>).

Southern fur seal 남방물개
sea lion 바다사자

예를 들어 바다사자들에게 먹힌 어린 남방물개들 중 86퍼센트가 그들이 잡힐 당시 다른 물개들과 물놀이를 하고 있었다.
For example, 86 percent of young Southern fur seals eaten by sea lions were play-swimming with others when they were caught.

propose 제안하다, 제시하다
motor 운동의, 근육 운동과 관련된
social interaction 사회적 상호작용

이러한 대가와는 반대로, 사냥 또는 싸움과 같은 다 자란 동물의 행동 및 운동과 사교 기술을 발달시키기 위한 연습을 포함하여, 놀이에 있어 많은 기능들이 제시되어 왔다.
Against these costs many functions have been proposed for play, including practice for adult behaviours such as hunting or fighting, and for developing motor and social interaction skills.

experimental 실험적인
evidence 증거

그러나 이러한 이론들에 대해 동물들에 있어 실험적 증거가 거의 없다.
However, for these theories, there is (B) (much / <u>little</u>) experimental evidence in animals.

track 추적하다, 따라가다
*juvenile 쥬베나일 성장기의, 어린

meerkats 미어캣
prove 증명하다, 입증하다
influence 영향을 미치다

예를 들면, 미어캣의 성장기 놀이와 다 자랐을 때의 행동을 추적한 세부 연구들은 싸움 놀이가 다 자랐을 때의 싸우는 능력에 영향을 주었다는 것을 증명할 수 없었다.
For example, detailed studies which tracked juvenile play and adult behaviour of meerkats couldn't prove that play-fighting influenced fighting ability as an adult.

persistence 지속성, 끈기
species 종(생물)
mystery 미스터리, 수수께끼

그러므로 아주 많은 동물들에 걸친 놀이의 지속은 미스터리로 남아 있다.
Therefore, the persistence of play across so many animal species (C) (<u>remains</u> / resloves) a mystery.

diverse 다양한
factor 요소, 요인

해답은 다양한 다수의 요인들을 포함할 것 같은데, 우리가 '놀이'라고 일컫는 것 자체가 그러하듯 여러 종들에게 있어 꽤 다를 것이다.
The answers are likely to involve diverse and multiple factors, which may be quite different in different species, as might what we call play itself.

....

30. (A), (B), (C)의 각 네모 안에서 문맥에 맞는 낱말로 가장 적절한 것은?

　　Play can be costly because it takes energy and time which could be spent foraging. While playing, the young animal may be at great (A) (comfort / risk). For example, 86 percent of young Southern fur seals eaten by sea lions were play-swimming with others when they were caught. Against these costs many functions have been proposed for play, including practice for adult behaviours such as hunting or fighting, and for developing motor and social interaction skills. However, for these theories, there is (B) (much / little) experimental evidence in animals. For example, detailed studies which tracked juvenile play and adult behaviour of meerkats couldn't prove that play-fighting influenced fighting ability as an adult. Therefore, the persistence of play across so many animal species (C) (remains / resloves) a mystery. The answers are likely to involve diverse and multiple factors, which may be quite different in different species, as might what we call play itself.

* forage: 먹이를 찾아 다니다   * juvenile: 성장기의

	(A)		(B)		(C)
①	comfort	……	little	……	remains
②	comfort	……	much	……	resolves
③	risk	……	little	……	remains
④	risk	……	much	……	remains
⑤	risk	……	little	……	resolves

정답 ③

(A)에서는 놀이하는 어린 동물이 위험에 처할 수 있다고 말하며, 특히 바다사자가 물개 새끼를 사냥하는 사례를 제시하고 있다. 따라서 risk가 적절하다.
(B)에서는 동물의 놀이가 성체가 되었을 때 실제로 어떤 영향을 미치는지에 대한 실험적 증거가 부족하다고 설명하고 있다. 따라서 little이 적절하다.
(C)에서는 다양한 동물에서 놀이가 지속되는 이유가 아직 미스터리로 남아 있다고 언급하고 있으므로, remains가 적절하다.

ingredient 성분, 재료

사람들은 흔히 합성 식품 성분이 천연 성분보다 더 해롭다고 가정하지만, 이것이 항상 그런 것은 아니다.
People often assume that synthetic food ingredients are more harmful than natural ones, but this is not always the case.

precisely 정밀하게, 정확하게
fashion 방식
composition 성분의 조합, 구성
property 특성, 성질
toxicity 독성

일반적으로 합성 성분은 정밀하게 통제된 방식으로 만들어질 수 있으며, 성분의 조합과 특성이 잘 정의되어 있어 잠재적인 독성을 주의 깊게 평가할 수 있다.
Typically, synthetic ingredients can be made in a precisely controlled fashion and have well-defined compositions and properties, allowing careful evaluation of their potential toxicity.

appreciably 상당히, 눈에 띄게
isolated 분리된, 격리된

반면에 천연 성분은 원산지, 수확된 시기, 생애 동안 경험한 기후, 토양의 질, 분리되고 저장된 방식에 따라 성분의 조합과 특성이 상당히 차이를 보이는 경우가 많다.
On the other hand, natural ingredients often vary appreciably in their composition and properties depending on their origin, the time of year they were harvested, the climate they experienced throughout their lifetime, the soil quality, and how they were isolated and stored.

variation 변동, 변화

이러한 변동성으로 인해 안전성을 테스트하기가 매우 어려울 수 있어서, 그때그때 달라질 수 있는 미세 성분들의 잠재적인 독성에 대해 결코 확신할 수 없다.
These variations can make testing their safety extremely difficult — one is never sure about the potential toxicity of minor components that may vary from time to time.

어떤 경우에는 천연 식품 성분이 수백 년 또는 수천 년 동안 명백한 건강 문제를 일으키지 않고 섭취되었으므로 안전하다고 가정될 수 있다.

In some cases, a natural food component has been consumed for hundreds or thousands of years without causing any obvious health problems and can, therefore, be assumed to be safe.

하지만 여전히 매우 주의해야 한다.
However, one must still be very careful.

variability 변동성, 변화 가능성
assumption 가정, 추정
*synthetic 합성의

→ 합성 식품 성분 생산 과정의 통제 가능성과 천연 식품 성분의 변동성은 천연 성분이 더 안전하다는 사람들의 일반적인 가정에 이의를 제기할 수도 있다.
The (A) <u>controllability</u> of the production process for synthetic food ingredients and the variability of natural food ingredients may (B) <u>challenge</u> people's commonly held assumption that the natural ingredients are more secure.

....

40. 다음 글의 내용을 한 문장으로 요약하고자 한다. 빈칸 (A), (B)에 들어갈 말로 가장 적절한 것은?
People often assume that synthetic food ingredients are more harmful than natural ones, but this is not always the case. Typically, synthetic ingredients can be made in a precisely controlled fashion and have well-defined compositions and properties, allowing careful evaluation of their potential toxicity. On the other hand, natural ingredients often vary appreciably in their composition and properties depending on their origin, the time of year they were harvested, the climate they experienced throughout their lifetime, the soil quality, and how they were isolated and stored. These variations can make testing their safety extremely difficult — one is never sure about the potential toxicity of minor components that may vary from time to time. In some cases, a natural food component has been consumed for hundreds or thousands of years without causing any obvious health problems and can, therefore, be assumed to be safe. However, one must still be very careful.
* synthetic 합성의

→ The (A) of the production process for synthetic food ingredients and the variability of natural food ingredients may (B) people's commonly held assumption that the natural ingredients are more secure.

	(A)		(B)		(A)		(B)
①	controllability	······	challenge	②	predictability	······	support
③	manageability	······	intensify	④	affordability	······	reverse
⑤	accessibility	······	question				

정답 ①

사람들이 천연 성분이 합성 성분보다 더 안전하다고 가정하는 것과는 달리 합성 성분은 그 생산이 정밀하게 통제되며, 오히려 천연 성분이 다양한 요인에 의해 변동성이 크다는 내용의 글이다. 따라서 요약문의 빈칸 (A), (B)에 들어갈 말로 가장 적절한 것은 ① '통제 가능성 – 이의를 제기할'이다.

	(A)			(B)	
①	controllability	통제 가능성	······	challenge	이의를 제기할
②	predictability	예측 가능성	······	support	지지할
③	manageability	관리 가능성	······	intensify	강화할
④	affordability	구입 가능성	······	reverse	뒤바꿀
⑤	accessibility	접근 가능성	······	question	의심할

principle 원칙, 법칙
sunk cost 매몰 비용
fallacy 오류, 착각

경제학에서 '매몰 비용 오류'라고 알려진 원리가 있다.
In economics, there is a principle known as the sunk cost fallacy.

ownership 소유권
overvalue 과대평가하다

여러분이 어떤 것에 투자하고 소유권을 가지면, 그것을 지나치게 중시한다는 생각이다.
The idea is that when you are invested and have ownership in something, you overvalue that thing.

path 길, 방향
pursuit 추구, 활동
abandon 포기하다, 버리다

(B) 이것은 사람들이 분명히 그만두어야 하는 경로를 계속 따르거나 추구를 계속하게 한다.
(B) This leads people to continue on paths or pursuits that should clearly be abandoned.

relationship 관계
invested 투자한, 쏟아부은

예를 들어, 사람들은 그저 자신의 많은 것을 그 관계에 투여했기 때문에 자주 끔찍한 관계에 남아 있다.
For example, people often remain in terrible relationships simply because they've invested a great deal of themselves into them.

pour 쏟아붓다

또는, 누군가는 시장에서 분명히 나쁜 아이디어인 사업에 계속 돈을 쏟아부을지도 모른다.
Or someone may continue pouring money into a business that is clearly a bad idea in the market.

(A) 때로는 한 사람이 할 수 있는 가장 현명한 일은 중지하는 것이다.
(A) Sometimes, the smartest thing a person can do is quit.

played-out 진부해진, 낡아빠진
argument 주장, 논리

이것이 진실이더라도, 그것은 또한 식상하고 효력이 떨어진 주장이 될 수 있다.
Although this is true, it has also become a tired and played-out argument.

sunk 침몰한, 가라앉은

매몰 비용이 언제나 나쁜 것이 틀림없는 것은 아니다.
Sunk cost doesn't always have to be a bad thing.

leverage 레버리지 활용하다, 이용하다
tendency 경향, 성향

(C) 실제로, 여러분은 이 인간적인 경향을 여러분에게 득이 되도록 이용할 수 있다.
(C) Actually, you can leverage this human tendency to your benefit.

ensure 보장하다, 확실하게 하다
follow through 끝까지 해내다
commitment 헌신, 약속
up front 미리, 선불로
stay on the path 길을 유지하다, 지속하다

확실히 자신이 자신의 약속을 끝까지 완수하기 위해 많은 돈을 개인 트레이너에게 투자하는 사람처럼, 여러분 또한 여러분이 있고 싶은 경로에 확실히 있기 위해 선지급으로 많은 것[돈]을 투자할 수 있다.
Like someone invests a great deal of money in a personal trainer to ensure they follow through on their commitment, you, too, can invest a great deal up front to ensure you stay on the path you want to be on.

37. 다음 글에 이어지는 순서로 옳은 것을 고르시오.

In economics, there is a principle known as the sunk cost fallacy. The idea is that when you are invested and have ownership in something, you overvalue that thing.

(A) Sometimes, the smartest thing a person can do is quit. Although this is true, it has also become a tired and played-out argument. Sunk cost doesn't always have to be a bad thing.
(B) This leads people to continue on paths or pursuits that should clearly be abandoned. For example, people often remain in terrible relationships simply because they've invested a great deal of themselves into them. Or someone may continue pouring money into a business that is clearly a bad idea in the market.
(C) Actually, you can leverage this human tendency to your benefit. Like someone invests a great deal of money in a personal trainer to ensure they follow through on their commitment, you, too, can invest a great deal up front to ensure you stay on the path you want to be on. [3점]

* leverage 이용하다

① (A) — (C) — (B)　　　　② (B) — (A) — (C)
③ (B) — (C) — (A)　　　　④ (C) — (A) — (B)
⑤ (C) — (B) — (A)

정답 ②

매몰 비용 오류를 소개한 주어진 글 다음에, 매몰 비용의 문제점과 그 구체적 사례를 언급한 (B)가 이어져야 한다. 그다음으로 매몰 비용 오류에 대처하는 방법은 중지하는 것이지만 매몰 비용도 긍정적 측면이 있다고 언급한 (A)가 뒤따르고, 그에 대한 구체적 사례를 제시한 (C)로 이어지는 것이 자연스럽다. 따라서 주어진 글 다음에 이어질 글의 순서로 가장 적절한 것은 ② '(B)-(A)-(C)'이다.

lawyer 변호사, 법률가
argument 논증, 주장
principle 원칙, 법칙
conclusion 결론

변호사와 과학자는 어떤 결론으로 이어지는 증거와 원리의 요약을 의미하는 논거를 사용한다.
Lawyers and scientists use argument to mean a summary of evidence and principles leading to a conclusion;

하지만 과학적 논거는 법적인 논거와 다르다.
however, a scientific argument is different from a legal argument.

prosecuting 프로시큐팅 기소하다
attorney 변호사
prosecuting attorney 기소 검사
construct 구성하다, 만들다
persuade 설득하다
judge 판사
jury 배심원
accused 피고인, 피의자
guilty 유죄의

기소 검사는 피고가 유죄라고 판사나 배심원을 설득하기 위한 논거를 구성한다.
A prosecuting attorney constructs an argument to persuade the judge or a jury that the accused is guilty;

defense attorney 변호인
trial 재판, 심리

동일한 재판의 피고 측 변호사는 동일한 판사나 배심원을 정반대의 결론으로 설득하기 위한 논거를 구성한다.
a defense attorney in the same trial constructs an argument to persuade the same judge or jury toward the opposite conclusion.

prosecutor 검사, 기소자
defender 변호인, 방어자
obliged to ~할 의무가 있는

respective 각각의, 개별적인

검찰관과 피고 측 변호사 중 그 어느 누구도 자신들 각자의 입장을 약화시키는 것을 고려해야 할 의무는 없다.
Neither prosecutor nor defender is obliged to consider anything that weakens their respective cases.

aspect 측면, 양상

그와는 반대로, 과학자는 자기 자신의 생각을 검증해 보고 자연의 어떤 측면에 대해 정확한 설명을 하고 싶어 하기 때문에 논거를 구성한다.
On the contrary, scientists construct arguments because they want to test their own ideas and give an accurate explanation of some aspect of nature.

claim 주장, 요구
fundamental 기본적인, 근본적인
hypothesis 하이포쎄시스 가설, 추측

과학자는 자신의 주장을 뒷받침하는 증거나 가설을 포함시킬 수 있으나, 전문적인 과학의 한 가지 근본적인 규칙을 지켜야 한다.
Scientists can include any evidence or hypothesis that supports their claim, but they must observe one fundamental rule of professional science.

그들은 모든 알려진 증거와 이전에 제시된 모든 가설들을 포함시켜야 한다.
They must include all of the known evidence and all of the hypotheses previously proposed.

explicitly 익스플리시틀리 명확하게, 분명히
account for 설명하다, 고려하다

변호사들과 달리 과학자들은 자신들이 틀릴 수도 있다는 가능성을 명시적으로 설명해야 한다.
Unlike lawyers, scientists must explicitly account for the possibility that they might be wrong

utilize 활용하다, 이용하다

→ 자신들의 논거를 뒷받침하기 위해 정보를 선택적으로 활용하는 변호사들과는 달리, 과학자들은 정보 중 일부가 자신들의 논거를 강화시키지 않을 것 같다 하더라도 모든 정보를 포함시켜야 한다.
Unlike lawyers, who utilize information (A) <u>selectively</u> to support their arguments, scientists must include all information even if some of it is unlikely to (B) <u>strengthen</u> their arguments.

40. 다음 글의 내용을 한 문장으로 요약하고자 한다. 빈칸 (A), (B)에 들어갈 말로 가장 적절한 것은?

Lawyers and scientists use argument to mean a summary of evidence and principles leading to a conclusion; however, a scientific argument is different from a legal argument. A prosecuting attorney constructs an argument to persuade the judge or a jury that the accused is guilty; a defense attorney in the same trial constructs an argument to persuade the same judge or jury toward the opposite conclusion. Neither prosecutor nor defender is obliged to consider anything that weakens their respective cases. On the contrary, scientists construct arguments because they want to test their own ideas and give an accurate explanation of some aspect of nature. Scientists can include any evidence or hypothesis that supports their claim, but they must observe one fundamental rule of professional science. They must include all of the known evidence and all of the hypotheses previously proposed. Unlike lawyers, scientists must explicitly account for the possibility that they might be wrong Unlike lawyers, who utilize information (A) to support their arguments, scientists must include all information even if some of it is unlikely to (B) their arguments.

	(A)	(B)
①	objectively	weaken
②	objectively	support
③	accurately	clarify
④	selectively	strengthen
⑤	selectively	disprove

정답 ④

검사나 피고 측 변호사는 자신들의 변론에 유리한 정보만을 선별적으로 선택하여 논거를 구성하지만 과학자는 자신의 가설이나 논거에 상관없이 모든 정보를 논거에 포함시켜야 한다는 내용의 글이므로, 요약문의 빈칸에 들어갈 말로 ④ '선택적으로 - 강화시키다'가 가장 적절하다.

①	objectively	객관적으로	…… weaken	약화시키다
②	objectively	객관적으로	…… support	뒷받침하다
③	accurately	정확하게	…… clarify	분명하게 하다
④	selectively	선택적으로	…… strengthen	강화시키다
⑤	selectively	선택적으로	…… disprove	틀렸음을 입증하다

commanding 커맨딩 웅장한, 눈길을 끄는
vast 광대한, 거대한

우주에서 보았을 때 지구의 가장 인상적인 특징들 중 하나는 드넓은 바다의 푸르름이다.
When viewed from space, one of the Earth's most commanding features is the blueness of its vast oceans.

large body of water 거대한 수역

적은 양의 물은 이러한 많은 양의 물의 색을 나타내지 않고,
Small amounts of water do not indicate the color of these large bodies of water;

깨끗한 식수가 유리잔 속에서 검사될 때 그것은 맑고 무색인 것처럼 보인다.
when pure drinking water is examined in a glass, it appears clear and colorless.

relatively 상대적으로
reveal 드러내다, 나타내다

파란색을 드러내기 위해서는 분명 비교적 많은 양의 물이 필요하다. 왜 그런 것일까?
Apparently a relatively large volume of water is required to reveal the blue color. Why is this so?

*penetrate 침투하다, 통과하다
absorption 흡수
scattering 산란

빛이 물을 관통할 때 그것은 흡수와 산란 둘 다를 겪는다.
When light penetrates water, it experiences both absorption and scattering.

molecule 몰레큘 분자
*infrared 적외선
to a lesser degree 더 적은 정도로

물 분자는 적외선을 강하게 흡수하고 더 적은 정도로 붉은빛을 흡수한다.
Water molecules strongly absorb infrared and, to a lesser degree, red light.

wavelength 파장

동시에 물 분자는 더 짧은 파장을 산란시키기에 충분히 작아서 물에 청록색을 부여한다.
At the same time, water molecules are small enough to scatter shorter wavelengths, giving water its blue-green color.

long-wavelength absorption 장파장 흡수

장파장 흡수의 양은 수심의 작용이다.
The amount of long-wavelength absorption is a function of depth;

즉, 물이 더 깊을수록 더 많은 붉은 빛이 흡수된다.
the deeper the water, the more red light is absorbed.

intensity 강도, 세기
original value 원래 값
fall to zero 0으로 떨어지다

15미터 수심에서는 붉은빛의 강도가 기존 값의 25%로 떨어지고 30미터 이상의 수심에서는 0으로 떨어진다.
At a depth of 15m, the intensity of red light drops to 25% of its original value and falls to zero beyond a depth of 30m.

inhabitant 거주 생물, 거주자

이 수심에서 보이는 모든 물체는 청록빛 내에서 보인다.
Any object viewed at this depth is seen in a blue-green light.

이러한 이유로 바닷가재와 게와 같은 바다의 붉은색 서식 동물들은 램프를 들고 있지 않은 잠수부들에게는 검게 보인다.
For this reason, red inhabitants of the sea, such as lobsters and crabs, appear black to divers not carrying a lamp.

....

24. 다음 글의 제목으로 가장 적절한 것은?
  When viewed from space, one of the Earth's most commanding features is the blueness of its

vast oceans. Small amounts of water do not indicate the color of these large bodies of water; when pure drinking water is examined in a glass, it appears clear and colorless. Apparently a relatively large volume of water is required to reveal the blue color. Why is this so? When light penetrates water, it experiences both absorption and scattering. Water molecules strongly absorb infrared and, to a lesser degree, red light. At the same time, water molecules are small enough to scatter shorter wavelengths, giving water its blue-green color. The amount of long-wavelength absorption is a function of depth; the deeper the water, the more red light is absorbed. At a depth of 15m, the intensity of red light drops to 25% of its original value and falls to zero beyond a depth of 30m. Any object viewed at this depth is seen in a blue-green light. For this reason, red inhabitants of the sea, such as lobsters and crabs, appear black to divers not carrying a lamp.

* penetrate: 관통하다 * infrared: 적외선

① We Should Go Green with the Ocean Exploration
② Various Tones of Water Our Deceptive Eyes Show Us
③ How Deep-Sea Microorganisms Affect the Ocean's Color
④ Why So Blue: The Science Behind the Color of Earth's Oceans
⑤ The Bigger Volume Water Has, the Lower Temperature It Gets

정답 ④

왜 그렇게 파란가: 지구 바다색의 과학
Why So Blue: The Science Behind the Color of Earth's Oceans

이유는 본문이 지구의 바다가 푸르게 보이는 과학적 이유를 설명하는 내용이기 때문이다. 물이 어떻게 빛을 흡수하고 산란시키는지, 그리고 깊이에 따라 색이 어떻게 달라지는지를 다루고 있다. 특히, 물 분자가 적외선과 적색광을 강하게 흡수하고 짧은 파장을 산란시켜 푸른빛을 띠게 된다는 점을 강조하고 있다.

① 우리는 바다 탐험에서 친환경적인 접근을 해야 한다
We Should Go Green with the Ocean Exploration
② 우리의 기만적인 눈이 보여주는 다양한 물의 색조
Various Tones of Water Our Deceptive Eyes Show Us
③ 심해 미생물이 바다의 색에 미치는 영향
How Deep-Sea Microorganisms Affect the Ocean's Color
⑤ 물의 부피가 클수록 온도가 낮아진다
The Bigger Volume Water Has, the Lower Temperature It Gets

initial 초기의, 처음의
attraction 끌림, 매력

파트너 사이의 균형이나 조화는 관계에서 시간이 지남에 따라 분명히 발전하지만, 그것은 파트너에 대한 초기 매력과 관심의 요인이기도 하다.
Although a balance or harmony between partners clearly develops over time in a relationship, it is also a factor in initial attraction and interest in a partner.

extent 정도, 범위
verbal 언어적인

즉, 두 사람이 첫 만남에서 비슷한 언어적 그리고 비언어적 습관을 공유하는 정도까지 그들은 서로 더 편안할 것이다.
That is, to the extent that two people share similar verbal and nonverbal habits in a first meeting, they will be more comfortable with one another.

expressive 표현력이 풍부한

예를 들어, 속도가 빠른 사람들은 빠르게 말을 하고 움직이며 더 표현력이 있는 반면, 속도가 느린 사람들은 다른 속도를 가지고 표현력이 덜 하다.
For example, fast-paced individuals talk and move quickly and are more expressive, whereas slow-paced individuals have a different tempo and are less expressive.

interaction 상호작용
continuum 컨티뉴엄 연속체, 범위

이러한 연속체의 반대쪽 끝에 있는 사람들 간의 초기 상호 작용은 유사한 유형 간의 그것들보다 더 어려울 수 있다.
Initial interactions between people at opposite ends of such a continuum may be more difficult than those between similar types.

pursue 추구하다, 계속하다

대조적인 유형의 경우 사람들은 그들이 상호작용 유형에 있어서 유사한 경우보다 관계를 추구하는 것에 관심이 적을 수 있다.

In the case of contrasting styles, individuals may be less interested in pursuing a relationship than if they were similar in interaction styles.

click 잘 맞다, 통하다

그러나 비슷한 유형의 사람들은 더 편안하고 그들이 단지 서로 '즉시 마음이 통하는' 것 같다는 것을 느낀다.
Individuals with similar styles, however, are more comfortable and find that they just seem to "click" with one another.

coordination 조정
initiation 시작, 개시

따라서 행동 조정은 관계의 시작을 위한 선택 필터를 제공할 수 있다.
Thus, (behavioral coordination) may provide a selection filter for the initiation of a relationship.

⋯⋯⋯

31. 다음 빈칸에 들어갈 말로 가장 적절한 것을 고르시오.

 Although a balance or harmony between partners clearly develops over time in a relationship, it is also a factor in initial attraction and interest in a partner. That is, to the extent that two people share similar verbal and nonverbal habits in a first meeting, they will be more comfortable with one another. For example, fast-paced individuals talk and move quickly and are more expressive, whereas slow-paced individuals have a different tempo and are less expressive. Initial interactions between people at opposite ends of such a continuum may be more difficult than those between similar types. In the case of contrasting styles, individuals may be less interested in pursuing a relationship than if they were similar in interaction styles. Individuals with similar styles, however, are more comfortable and find that they just seem to "click" with one another. Thus, (   ) may provide a selection filter for the initiation of a relationship.

① information deficit
② cultural adaptability
③ meaning negotiation
④ behavioral coordination
⑤ unconditional acceptance

정답 ④

이유는 본문에서 사람들이 비슷한 말투나 비언어적 습관을 가질수록 더 편안함을 느끼고 관계 형성이 쉬워진다는 점을 설명하고 있기 때문이다. 즉, 두 사람이 얼마나 유사한 행동 패턴을 보이는지가 관계 형성에 영향을 미친다는 것이다.

① information deficit 정보 부족
② cultural adaptability 문화적 적응력
③ meaning negotiation 의미 협상
④ behavioral coordination 행동 조정(협응)
⑤ unconditional acceptance는 무조건적인 수용

viewing ~ as ~ ~을 ~로 바라보다
transform 변화시키다, 바꾸다
*physiology 생리학, 생리 작용

스트레스 반응을 자원으로 보는 것은 두려움이라는 생리 기능을 용기라는 생명 작용으로 바꿀 수 있다.
Viewing the stress response as a resource can transform the physiology of fear into the biology of courage.

threat 위협, 위험

그것은 위협을 도전으로 바꿀 수 있고 여러분이 압박감 속에서도 최선을 다하도록 도울 수 있다.
It can turn a threat into a challenge and can help you ① do your best under pressure.

even when ~일지라도
transform into ~로 변화시키다

불안감의 경우에서처럼 스트레스가 도움이 되지 않는다고 느껴질 때조차도 그것을 기꺼이 받아들이는 것은 그것을 도움이 되는 것, 즉, 더 많은 에너지, 더 많은 자신감, 그리고 더 기꺼이 행동을 취하려는 마음으로 바꿀 수 있다.
Even when the stress doesn't feel helpful — as in the case of anxiety — welcoming it can transform ② it into something that is helpful: more energy, more confidence, and a greater willingness to take action.

strategy 전략, 방법

스트레스의 징후를 알아차릴 때마다 이 전략을 여러분의 삶에 적용할 수 있다.
You can apply this strategy in your own life anytime you notice signs of stress.

breath quickening 숨이 가빠지는 것

여러분의 심장 박동이나 호흡이 빨라지는 것을 느낄 때 그것은 여러분에게 더 많은 에너지를 주려고 노력하는 여러분의 몸의 방식이라는 것을 깨달아야 한다.
When you feel your heart beating or your breath quickening, ③ realizing(→realize) that it is your body's way of trying to give you more energy.

여러분의 몸에서 긴장을 감지한다면 스트레스 반응이 여러분에게 자신의 힘을 이용할 기회를 준다는 점을 상기하라.
If you notice tension in your body, remind yourself ④ that the stress response gives you access to your strength.

palms 손바닥

손바닥에 땀이 나는가? 첫 데이트에 나갔을 때 어떤 기분이었는지를 기억하라.
Sweaty palms? Remember what it felt like ⑤ to go on your first date —

즉, 여러분이 원하는 것에 가까이 있을 때 손바닥에 땀이 난다.
palms sweat when you're close to something you want.

....

29. 다음 글의 밑줄 친 부분 중, 어법상 틀린 것은?
 Viewing the stress response as a resource can transform the physiology of fear into the biology of courage. It can turn a threat into a challenge and can help you ① do your best under pressure. Even when the stress doesn't feel helpful — as in the case of anxiety — welcoming it can transform ② it into something that is helpful: more energy, more confidence, and a greater willingness to take action. You can apply this strategy in your own life anytime you notice signs of stress. When you feel your heart beating or your breath quickening, ③ realizing that it is your body's way of trying to give you more energy. If you notice tension in your body, remind yourself ④ that the stress response gives you access to your strength. Sweaty palms? Remember what it felt like ⑤ to go on your first date — palms sweat when you're close to something you want. *physiology 생리 기능

정답 ③

③ When이 이끄는 부사절 다음에 주절이 이어지는데, realizing 뒤에 다른 술어 동사가 없으므로, 명령문이 주절이 될 수 있도록 realizing을 realize로 고쳐야 한다.

① help에 이어지는 목적격 보어로는 to부정사나 동사원형이 둘 다 가능하므로 do는 어법상 적절하다.
② 앞에 있는 the stress를 가리키는 대명사 it은 어법상 적절하다.
④ remind의 직접목적어인 명사절을 이끌고 있으므로 접속사 that은 어법상 적절하다.
⑤ it은 형식상의 주어이고 to go on your first date가 내용상의 주어에 해당하는 부분이므로 to go는 어법상 적절하다.

puzzling 난해한, 이해하기 어려운
aspect 측면, 양상
innovation 혁신
lip service 입에 발린 말, 말뿐인 찬사

아마도 혁신의 가장 당혹스러운 측면은 우리가 그것에 대해서 내놓는 모든 입에 발린 말에 비해 그것이 정말 인기가 없다는 것이다.
Perhaps the most puzzling aspect of innovation is how unpopular it is, for all the lip service we pay to it.

abundant 풍부한, 많은
evidence 증거, 근거
transform 변화시키다, 변혁하다
innumerable 셀 수 없이 많은
kneejerk reaction 반사적인 반응, 즉각적인 반응
disgust 혐오감, 역겨움

그것이 무수한 방식으로 거의 모든 사람의 삶을 더욱 나은 쪽으로 바꿔왔다는 많은 증거에도 불구하고, 어떤 새로운 것에 대한 대부분의 사람들의 반사적인 반응은 흔히 걱정이며 때로는 심지어 혐오감이다.
Despite the abundant evidence that it has transformed almost everybody's lives for the better in innumerable ways, the kneejerk reaction of most people to something new is often worry, sometimes even disgust.

obvious 명백한, 분명한
consequence 결과, 영향

그것이 우리 자신에게 명백히 쓸모 있지 않은 한, 우리는 발생할지 모를 나쁜 결과를 좋은 결과 보다 훨씬 더 많이 상상하는 경향이 있다.
Unless it is of obvious use to ourselves, we tend to imagine the bad consequences that might occur far more than the good ones.

obstacle 장애물, 방해물
innovator 혁신가
vested 부여된
vested interest 기득권
status quo 현재 상태, 현상 유지

그리고 우리는 투자자, 관리자, 피고용인을 막론하고 현 상태에 기득권을 가진 사람들을 대신하여 혁신하려는 사람을 방해한다.
And we throw obstacles in the way of innovators, on behalf of those with a vested interest in the status quo: investors, managers and employees alike.

delicate 연약한, 섬세한
vulnerable 취약한, 상처받기 쉬운
underfoot 발밑에, 짓밟혀
regrow 다시 자라다, 재생하다

역사는 혁신이 연약하고 상처 입기 쉬운 꽃이며 쉽게 발로 짓밟혀 뭉개지지만, 상황이 허락하면 빨리 재성장함을 보여준다.
History shows that innovation is a delicate and vulnerable flower, easily crushed underfoot, but quick to regrow if conditions allow.

....

21. 밑줄 친 innovation is a delicate and vulnerable flower, easily crushed underfoot이 다음 글에서 의미하는 바로 가장 적절한 것은?

Perhaps the most puzzling aspect of innovation is how unpopular it is, for all the lip service we pay to it. Despite the abundant evidence that it has transformed almost everybody's lives for the better in innumerable ways, the kneejerk reaction of most people to something new is often worry, sometimes even disgust. Unless it is of obvious use to ourselves, we tend to imagine the bad consequences that might occur far more than the good ones. And we throw obstacles in the way of innovators, on behalf of those with a vested interest in the status quo: investors, managers and employees alike. History shows that innovation is a delicate and vulnerable flower, easily crushed underfoot, but quick to regrow if conditions allow.
* kneejerk: 반사적인 * status quo: 현 상태

① Innovation comes from the need for solving deficiency.
② Innovative people are usually very sensitive to criticism.
③ Innovation is often faced with disapproval and opposition.
④ A single misstep in planning could ruin innovation entirely.
⑤ Innovative ideas need a series of revision and refinement.

정답은 ③

③ 혁신은 자주 저항과 반대를 자주 마주한다.
Innovation is often faced with disapproval and opposition.

이유는 본문에서 새로운 혁신이 사람들에게 흔히 걱정이나 거부감을 불러일으키며, 기존 체제에 이해관계를 가진 사람들로 인해 방해받는다고 설명하고 있기 때문이다. 또한, 혁신은 연약하고 쉽게 짓밟힐 수 있지만, 적절한 조건이 주어지면 다시 성장할 수 있다고 말하고 있다. 이는 혁신이 저항과 반대를 자주 마주한다는 의미와 가장 잘 연결된다.

deficiency 결핍

① 혁신이 결핍을 해결하기 위한 필요에서 비롯된다.
Innovation comes from the need for solving deficiency.
② 혁신적인 사람들이 비판에 민감하다.
Innovative people are usually very sensitive to criticism.
④ 계획상의 실수가 혁신을 망칠 수 있다.
A single misstep in planning could ruin innovation entirely.

revision 개정
refinement 개선

⑤ 혁신적인 아이디어는 여러 번의 수정과 개선을 거쳐야 한다.
Innovative ideas need a series of revision and refinement.

DAY 3

vice principal 교감 선생님

학생 여러분, 좋은 아침입니다. 저는 Morris 교감입니다.
Good morning, students. This is your vice principal, Ms. Morris.

each class period 각 교시
reduce 줄이다, 단축하다

다음 주 화요일에는 각 수업 시간이 50분에서 40분으로 줄어들 것임을 여러분에게 알려 드립니다.
I want to inform you that each class period will be reduced from 50 minutes to 40 minutes next Tuesday.

parent-teacher conference 학부모-교사 상담
be held 열리다, 개최되다

그날 열릴 학부모-교사 협의회로 인해, 학교가 평소보다 한 시간 일찍 마칠 예정입니다.
Due to the parent-teacher conferences that will be held on that day, school will end one hour earlier than usual.

여러분은 그날 평소에 받는 똑같은 수업을 그대로 받게 될 것입니다.
You'll still take the same classes that you normally would on that day.

수업 시작종과 종료종은 줄어든 수업 시간표에 맞춰 울릴 것입니다.
The starting and ending bells will ring according to the reduced class time schedule.

다시 한 번 말하자면, 다음 주 화요일 수업 시간이 각각 10분씩 단축될 예정이라는 점을 기억해 주세요. 감사합니다.
Once again, please keep in mind that next Tuesday's class periods will be shortened by 10 minutes each. Thank you.

1. 다음을 듣고, 여자가 하는 말의 목적으로 가장 적절한 것을 고르시오.

Good morning, students. This is your vice principal, Ms. Morris. I want to inform you that each class period will be reduced from 50 minutes to 40 minutes next Tuesday. Due to the parent-teacher conferences that will be held on that day, school will end one hour earlier than usual. You'll still take the same classes that you normally would on that day. The starting and ending bells will ring according to the reduced class time schedule. Once again, please keep in mind that next Tuesday's class periods will be shortened by 10 minutes each. Thank you.

① 학교 종소리 교체 계획을 알리려고
② 학교 수업 시간 단축을 공지하려고
③ 등교 시간 변경을 안내하려고
④ 학부모 상담 신청서 제출을 독려하려고
⑤ 학교 행사 후 교실 정리 정돈을 당부하려고

정답 ②

game 사냥, 사냥감
reindeer 순록

유럽 최초의 '호모 사피엔스'는 주로 큰 사냥감, 특히 순록을 먹고 살았다.
Europe's first Homo sapiens lived primarily on large game, particularly reindeer.

uncertain 불확실한

심지어 이상적인 상황에서도, 이런 빠른 동물을 창이나 활과 화살로 사냥하는 것은 불확실한 일이다.
Even under ideal circumstances, hunting these fast animals with spear or bow and arrow is an
①uncertain task.

*exploit 익스플로잇 이용하다, 악용하다

그러나 순록에게는 인류가 인정사정없이 이용할 약점이 있었는데, 그것은 순록이 수영을 잘 못한다는 것이었다.
The reindeer, however, had a ②weakness that mankind would mercilessly exploit:

uniquely 독특하게
vulnerable 벌루너블 취약한
antlers 앤틀러스 뿔
struggle 애쓰다

순록은 물에 떠 있는 동안, 코를 물 위로 내놓으려고 애쓰면서 가지진 뿔을 높이 쳐들고 천천히 움직이기 때문에,
유례없이 공격받기 쉬운 상태가 된다.
it swam poorly. While afloat, it is uniquely ③vulnerable, moving slowly with its antlers held
high as it struggles to keep its nose above water.

어느 시점에선가, 석기 시대의 한 천재가 수면 위를 미끄러지듯이 움직일 수 있음으로써 자신이 얻을 엄청난 사냥
의 이점을 깨닫고 최초의 배를 만들었다.
At some point, a Stone Age genius realized the enormous hunting ④advantage he would gain
by being able to glide over the water's surface, and built the first boat.

laboriously 라보리어슬리 힘들게
overtaken 추격하여 잡은

*hauled 하얼드 끌어올린
aboard 배에 타고
tribal 부족의

힘들게 (→쉽게) 따라잡아서 도살한 먹잇감을 일단 배 위로 끌어 올리면, 사체를 부족이 머무는 곳으로 가지고 가는 것은 육지에서보다는 배로 훨씬 더 쉬웠을 것이다.
Once the ⑤laboriously (→easily) overtaken and killed prey had been hauled aboard, getting its body back to the tribal camp would have been far easier by boat than on land.

인류가 이런 장점을 다른 물품에 적용하는 데는 긴 시간이 걸리지 않았을 것이다.
It would not have taken long for mankind to apply this advantage to other goods.

....

30. 다음 글의 밑줄 친 부분 중, 문맥상 낱말의 쓰임이 적절하지 않은 것은?
Europe's first Homo sapiens lived primarily on large game, particularly reindeer. Even under ideal circumstances, hunting these fast animals with spear or bow and arrow is an ①uncertain task. The reindeer, however, had a ②weakness that mankind would mercilessly exploit: it swam poorly. While afloat, it is uniquely ③vulnerable, moving slowly with its antlers held high as it struggles to keep its nose above water. At some point, a Stone Age genius realized the enormous hunting ④advantage he would gain by being able to glide over the water's surface, and built the first boat. Once the ⑤laboriously overtaken and killed prey had been hauled aboard, getting its body back to the tribal camp would have been far easier by boat than on land. It would not have taken long for mankind to apply this advantage to other goods.
* exploit: 이용하다 * haul: 끌어당기다

정답 ⑤

순록이 물에 떠 있는 동안에는 천천히 움직이기 때문에 공격받기 쉬운 상태가 되고 쉽게 따라잡힌다는 맥락이므로, ⑤의 laboriously를 easily와 같은 낱말로 고쳐야 한다.

locust 메뚜기

사막 메뚜기는 식량원의 입수 가능성과 지역 메뚜기 개체군의 밀도에 따라 현저히 다른 두 가지 방식으로 산다.
The desert locust lives in two remarkably different styles depending on the availability of food sources and the density of the local locust population.

scarce 부족한
habitat 서식지
*camouflage 캐모플라지 위장
solitary 혼자의

그들이 원래 사는 사막의 서식지에서 보통 그렇듯 식량이 부족할 때는 메뚜기들이 위장을 위해 고안된 색채를 갖고 태어나며 혼자 살아간다.
When food is scarce, as it usually is in their native desert habitat, locusts are born with coloring designed for camouflage and lead (A) (solitary / social) lives.

vegetation 초목

그러나 드물긴 하지만 상당량의 비가 내리는 기간이 와서 초목이 크게 성장하게 되면, 모든 것이 변한다.
But when rare periods of significant rain produce major vegetation growth, everything changes.

loners 혼자, 외톨이
insufficient 부족한
abundant 풍부한

처음에는 그 메뚜기들이 그저 풍부한 식량 공급량을 맘껏 먹어 치우면서 계속 혼자 산다.
At first, the locusts continue to be loners, just feasting off the (B) (insufficient / abundant) food supply.

crowded 밀집한

그러나 그 여분의 초목이 죽어 없어지기 시작하면, 메뚜기들은 자신들이 (수가 많아져서) 서로 혼잡하게 있다는 것을 알게 된다.
But as the extra vegetation starts to die off, the locusts find themselves crowded together.

company 동료

갑자기, 밝은 색을 띠고 함께 있기를 선호하는 새끼 메뚜기들이 태어난다.
Suddenly, baby locusts are born with bright colors and a preference for company.

inactivity 활동하지 않음
gather 모이다
overwhelm 압도하다
overestimate 과대평가하다

서로를 피하고 위장과 무활동을 통해 포식자들로부터 몸을 숨기는 대신 이 메뚜기들은 거대한 떼를 짓고, 함께 먹으며, 순전히 숫자를 통해 자기네 포식자들을 압도한다.
Instead of avoiding one another and hiding from predators through camouflage and inactivity, these locusts gather in vast groups, feed together, and (C) (<u>overwhelm</u> / overestimate) their predators simply through numbers.

....

29. (A), (B), (C)의 각 네모 안에서 문맥에 맞는 낱말로 가장 적절한 것은?
The desert locust lives in two remarkably different styles depending on the availability of food sources and the density of the local locust population. When food is scarce, as it usually is in their native desert habitat, locusts are born with coloring designed for camouflage and lead (A) (solitary / social) lives. But when rare periods of significant rain produce major vegetation growth, everything changes. At first, the locusts continue to be loners, just feasting off the (B)(insufficient / abundant) food supply. But as the extra vegetation starts to die off, the locusts find themselves crowded together. Suddenly, baby locusts are born with bright colors and a preference for company. Instead of avoiding one another and hiding from predators through camouflage and inactivity, these locusts gather in vast groups, feed together, and (C) (overwhelm / overestimate) their predators simply through numbers.
* camouflage 위장

	(A)	(B)	(C)
①	solitary	insufficient	overwhelm
②	solitary	abundant	overwhelm
③	solitary	insufficient	overestimate
④	social	abundant	overwhelm
⑤	social	insufficient	overestimate

정답 ②

(A) solitary는 '혼자의'라는 뜻이고, social은 '사회생활을 하는'이라는 뜻이다. 이어지는 문장 그다음에서 the locusts continue to be loners라고 했으므로 (A)에 가장 적절한 낱말은 solitary이다.
(B) insufficient는 '불충분한'이라는 뜻이고, abundant는 '풍부한'이라는 뜻이다. 앞에서 when rare periods of significant rain produce major vegetation growth라고 언급했으므로 (B)에 가장 적절한 낱말은 abundant이다.
(C) overwhelm은 '압도하다'라는 뜻이고, overestimate는 '과대평가하다'라는 뜻이다. 메뚜기들이 거대한 떼를 지어 자기네 포식자들을 압도한다는 의미가 되어야 문맥이 자연스러우므로 (C)에 가장 적절한 낱말은 overwhelm이다.

molecule 분자
adenosine 아데노신

낮 동안에 아데노신이라고 불리는 분자가 어러분의 뇌에 쌓인다.
During the day, a molecule called adenosine builds up in your brain.

bind 결합하다, 붙다
receptor 수용체
nerve cell 신경 세포
neuron 뉴런, 신경 단위
*drowsy 드라우지 졸린, 나른한

아데노신은 신경 세포들, 다시 말해 뉴런들의 수용체들과 결합해 그것들의 활동을 늦추고 여러분이 나른함을 느끼게 한다.
Adenosine binds with receptors on nerve cells, or neurons, slowing down their activity and making you feel drowsy.

fire 발화하다, 활성화되다
alert 깨어 있는, 경계하는

그러나 카페인 역시 이 수용체들과 결합할 수 있고, 그렇게 함으로써 그것이 아데노신의 효과를 차단하여 뉴런을 더 활성화시키고 여러분이 깨어 있도록 유지시킨다.
But caffeine is also able to bind with these receptors, and by doing so it blocks adenosine's effect, making your neurons fire more and keeping you alert.

*gland 분비선, 샘

카페인은 또한 뇌 기저부의 분비선을 활성화시킨다.
Caffeine also activates a gland at the base of your brain.

*adrenal gland 부신(신장 위의 내분비샘)
kidney 신장, 콩팥
adrenaline 아드레날린

이것은 신장에 있는 부신이 아드레날린을 생산하도록 하는 호르몬을 분비시켜 여러분의 심장을 더욱 빨리 뛰게 하고 혈압이 올라가게 한다.
This releases hormones that tell the adrenal glands on your kidneys to produce adrenaline, causing your heart to beat faster and your blood pressure to rise.

intake 섭취량, 흡입
consistent 일관된, 지속적인

하지만 여러분의 하루 카페인 섭취량이 일정하다면 뇌가 이에 적응할 것이다.
If, however, your daily caffeine intake is consistent, your brain will adapt to it.

여러분의 뇌는 이와 같다. '그래, 매일 아침 나는 이 수용체들과 결합해서 아데노신이 그것들과 결합하는 것을 막는 이 카페인을 섭취하고 있군.'
Your brain is like, 'Okay, every morning I'm getting this caffeine that's binding to these receptors and blocking adenosine from binding to them.'

그래서 여러분의 뇌는 아데노신에게 그것들(수용체)과 결합하여 평소의 효과를 낼 더 많은 기회를 수기 위해 추가의 수용체들을 만들어 낸다.
So your brain creates extra receptors to give adenosine more of an opportunity to bind with them and have its usual effect.

counteract 대응하다, 상쇄하다

그리고 카페인에 대응하기 위해 더 많은 아데노신이 또한 생성된다.
And more adenosine is also produced to counteract the caffeine.

그것이 같은 효과를 내기 위해서 점점 더 많은 카페인이 필요한 이유다.
That's why it takes more and more caffeine to have the same effect.

....

23. 다음 글의 주제로 가장 적절한 것은?
　During the day, a molecule called adenosine builds up in your brain. Adenosine binds with receptors on nerve cells, or neurons, slowing down their activity and making you feel drowsy. But caffeine is also able to bind with these receptors, and by doing so it blocks adenosine's effect, making your neurons fire more and keeping you alert. Caffeine also activates a gland at

the base of your brain. This releases hormones that tell the adrenal glands on your kidneys to produce adrenaline, causing your heart to beat faster and your blood pressure to rise. If, however, your daily caffeine intake is consistent, your brain will adapt to it. Your brain is like, 'Okay, every morning I'm getting this caffeine that's binding to these receptors and blocking adenosine from binding to them.' So your brain creates extra receptors to give adenosine more of an opportunity to bind with them and have its usual effect. And more adenosine is also produced to counteract the caffeine. That's why it takes more and more caffeine to have the same effect.

* drowsy 나른한 * gland (분비)선

① what your brain does for regular hormone production
② consequences of sleep deprivation caused by caffeine
③ connection between brain health and hormone balance
④ efforts to overcome the constant temptation of caffeine
⑤ how your brain adapts to a steady caffeine consumption

정답은 ⑤

⑤ 당신의 뇌가 지속적인 카페인 섭취에 적응하는 방식
how your brain adapts to a steady caffeine consumption

이유는 본문이 카페인이 뇌에서 작용하는 방식과, 지속적인 섭취에 따라 뇌가 어떻게 적응하는지를 설명하고 있기 때문이다. 아데노신이 졸음을 유도하는 과정, 카페인이 이를 차단하는 역할, 그리고 지속적인 카페인 섭취에 대한 뇌의 적응 방식(수용체 증가와 아데노신 추가 생성)이 단계적으로 설명되고 있다.

deprivation 데프리베이션 **결핍, 박탈**
temptation 유혹

① 당신의 뇌가 정상적인 호르몬 생산을 위해 하는 일
what your brain does for regular hormone production
② 카페인으로 인해 발생하는 수면 부족의 결과
consequences of sleep deprivation caused by caffeine
③ 뇌 건강과 호르몬 균형의 연결
connection between brain health and hormone balance
④ 지속적인 카페인의 유혹을 극복하려는 노력
efforts to overcome the constant temptation of caffeine

distinct 뚜렷이 구별되는, 별개의

흥미롭게도, 다른 누군가가 지켜보고 있다는 것은 수행에 두 가지 매우 상이한 영향을 미친다.
Interestingly, being observed has two quite distinct effects on performance.

어떤 경우에는, 수행이 저하되어 심지어 수행 결과가 아예 없는 지경에까지 이른다.
In some cases, performance is decreased, even to the point of non-existence.

stage fright 무대 공포증

이것의 극단적인 예는 대중 앞에서 공연하기를 갑자기 두려워하는 무대 공포증이다.
The extreme of this is stage fright, the sudden fear of public performance.

instance 사례, 경우
in mid-career 도중에서

(B) 연기 인생 도중에 무대 공포증이 생겨서 공연을 전혀 할 수 없게 된 유명한 연기자들의 많은 사례가 있다.
(B) There are many instances of well-known actors who, in mid-career, develop stage fright and simply cannot perform.

enhance 향상시키다, 높이다

반대의 극단적인 예로는 다른 누군가가 지켜보고 있을 때 수행 능력이 높아지는 것인데, 사람들은 다른 사람들이 보고 있다는 것을 알 때 그 일이 무엇이든 더 잘한다.
The other extreme is that being observed enhances performance, people doing whatever it might be better when they know that others are watching.

(C) 일반적으로 어떤 사람이 새롭거나 처음으로 하는 일을 할 때는 그 일을 하는 동안 다른 사람이 지켜보는 것이 수행 능력을 저하시키는 것 같다.
(C) The general rule seems to be that if one is doing something new or for the first time, then being observed while doing it decreases performance.

engage in ~에 참여하다, 종사하다

이와 반대로, 잘 알고 있거나 많이 연습한 과제를 하거나 활동을 할 때 다른 사람이 지켜보는 것은 수행 능력을 향상시키는 경향이 있다.

On the other hand, being observed while doing some task or engaging in some activity that is well known or well practiced tends to enhance performance.

(A) 따라서 여러분이 새로운 스포츠를 배울 때는 혼자 그것을 시작하는 것이 낫지만, 그것에 숙달되면, 관중이 있을 때 아마도 더 질힐 것이다.

(A) So, if you are learning to play a new sport, it is better to begin it alone, but when you become skilled at it, then you will probably perform better with an audience.

....

36. 주어진 글 다음에 이어질 글의 순서로 가장 적절한 것을 고르시오.

Interestingly, being observed has two quite distinct effects on performance. In some cases, performance is decreased, even to the point of non-existence. The extreme of this is stage fright, the sudden fear of public performance.

(A) So, if you are learning to play a new sport, it is better to begin it alone, but when you become skilled at it, then you will probably perform better with an audience.

(B) There are many instances of well-known actors who, in mid-career, develop stage fright and simply cannot perform. The other extreme is that being observed enhances performance, people doing whatever it might be better when they know that others are watching.

(C) The general rule seems to be that if one is doing something new or for the first time, then being observed while doing it decreases performance. On the other hand, being observed while doing some task or engaging in some activity that is well known or well practiced tends to enhance performance.

① (A) — (C) — (B)　　　　② (B) — (A) — (C)
③ (B) — (C) — (A)　　　　④ (C) — (A) — (B)
⑤ (C) — (B) — (A)

정답 ③

무대 공포증에 대해 이야기한 주어진 글 다음에, 이어서 무대 공포증에 대해 설명한 (B)가 오고, 처음 배우는 것과 숙달된 것을 하는 경우에 대해 일반적으로 설명한 (C)가 온 다음, 스포츠라는 구체적인 예를 들어서 처음 배우는 경우와 숙달된 경우를 나누어 설명한 (A)가 마지막에 오는 것이 가장 적절하다.

eyes-on-the-prize 목표 지향적인
mentality 사고방식, 태도

자기 목표에 몰두하는 사고방식이 잘못일 수 있다고 우려할 이유가 있다.
There's reason to worry that an eyes-on-the-prize mentality could be a mistake.

over-confident 지나치게 자신감 있는
self-disciplined 자기 절제하는

많은 연구에 따르면, 우리는 자기 훈련이 된다는 것이 얼마나 쉬운지에 관해 과신하는 경향이 있다.
Lots of research shows that we tend to be over-confident about how easy it is to be self-disciplined.

optimistically 낙관적으로
*crumb 부스러기

이것이 우리 중 매우 많은 사람이 낙관적으로 방문당 이용료를 내는 것이 더 저렴할 텐데도 값비싼 체육관 회원권을 사고, 다 끝내지도 못할 온라인 강좌에 등록하며, 우리의 한 달 치 간식 예산을 줄이기 위해 할인하는 대형 과자를 사서 결국 앉은 자리에서 한 번에 마지막 부스러기까지 다 먹는 이유이다.
This is why so many of us optimistically buy expensive gym memberships when paying per-visit fees would be cheaper, register for online classes we'll never complete, and purchase family-size chips on discount to trim our monthly snack budget, only to consume every last crumb in a single sitting.

temptation 유혹, 충동

우리는 '미래의 내'가 좋은 선택을 할 수 있을 거라고 생각하지만, 너무나 자주 '현재의 나'는 유혹에 굴복한다.
We think "future me" will be able to make good choices, but too often "present me" gives in to temptation.

remarkable 놀라운, 주목할 만한

사람들에게는 자신의 실패를 무시하는 놀라운 능력이 있다.
People have a remarkable ability to (ignore) their own failures.

*flounder 플라운더 허우적거리다, 실패하다, 가자미
rosy 낙관적인, 장밋빛의
optimism 낙관주의, 긍정적인 태도

거듭 실패하면서도 우리 중 많은 사람은 우리의 과거의 실수로부터 배우기보다는 다음에는 더 잘할 거라는 우리의 능력에 관해 장밋빛 낙관주의를 용케 유지한다.
Even when we flounder again and again, many of us manage to maintain a rosy optimism about our ability to do better next time rather than learning from our past mistakes.

cling to ~에 집착하다, 고수하다
*upbeat 긍정적인, 희망적인

우리는 새로운 시작과 낙관적인 태도를 유지할 다른 이유들에 매달리고, 그것이 아침에 우리가 침대에서 일어나는 데 도움이 될지는 모르지만 가능한 가장 영리한 방식으로 우리가 변화에 접근하는 것을 막을 수 있다.
We cling to fresh starts and other reasons to stay upbeat, which may help us get out of bed in the morning but can prevent us from approaching change in the smartest possible way.

···

31. 다음 빈칸에 들어갈 말로 가장 적절한 것을 고르시오.

 There's reason to worry that an eyes-on-the-prize mentality could be a mistake. Lots of research shows that we tend to be over-confident about how easy it is to be self-disciplined. This is why so many of us optimistically buy expensive gym memberships when paying per-visit fees would be cheaper, register for online classes we'll never complete, and purchase family-size chips on discount to trim our monthly snack budget, only to consume every last crumb in a single sitting. We think "future me" will be able to make good choices, but too often "present me" gives in to temptation. People have a remarkable ability to _____ their own failures. Even when we flounder again and again, many of us manage to maintain a rosy optimism about our ability to do better next time rather than learning from our past mistakes. We cling to fresh starts and other reasons to stay upbeat, which may help us get out of bed in the morning but can prevent us from approaching change in the smartest possible way.
* crumb 부스러기 * flounder 실패하다 * upbeat 낙관적인

① criticize   ② remind   ③ ignore
④ detect   ⑤ overestimate

정답 ③

이유는 본문에서 사람들이 자신의 실패를 반복하면서도 낙관적인 태도를 유지하며 과거의 실수를 교훈으로 삼지 않는 경향을 설명하고 있기 때문이다.

사람들은 헬스장 회원권을 충동적으로 구매하거나, 다 먹지 않을 것처럼 대용량 과자를 사지만 결국 모든 과자를 한 번에 먹어 버린다. 또한, 자신의 자제력이 좋다고 믿지만 현실에서는 유혹을 쉽게 이기지 못한다. 이처럼 과거의 실패를 통해 배우지 않고 자신의 실패를 무시하는 태도를 보이기 때문에 빈칸에 들어갈 말로 ignore가 가장 적절하다.

④ detect 감지하다
⑤ overestimate 과대평가하다

attentive 주의 깊은
moral 도덕적인
*legislation 레지슬레이션 입법

역사적으로, 조세 입법 입안자들은 경제학과 역사 문제에 주의를 기울이고 도덕적 질문에는 주의를 덜 기울인다.
Historically, drafters of tax legislation are attentive to questions of economics and history, and less attentive to moral questions.

controversial 논란이 되는
irrelevant 관련 없는

도덕성에 관한 질문은 종종 입법 토론에서 옆으로 밀려나면서, 너무 논란이 많거나, 답변하기 너무 어렵거나, 아니면 최악의 경우, 계획과 무관한 것으로 분류된다.
Questions of morality are often pushed to the side in legislative debate, labeled too controversial, too difficult to answer, or, worst of all, irrelevant to the project.

하지만, 사실, 조세의 도덕적 문제는 세법을 만드는 핵심에 있다.
But, in fact, the moral questions of taxation are at the very heart of the creation of tax laws.

fundamental 근본적인
*imposition 부과

무관한 것이 아니라, 도덕적 질문은 세금 부과에 근본적이다.
Rather than irrelevant, moral questions are fundamental to the imposition of tax.

distributive 디스트리뷰티브 분배의

세금은 사회의 분배 정의 이론을 적용한 것이다.
Tax is the application of a society's theories of distributive justice.

vacuum 진공 상태

경제학은 입법부가 특정 세법이 특정 목표를 달성하는 데 도움이 될지를 결정하는 것을 돕는 것에 큰 도움이 될 수 있지만, 경제학만으로는 목표를 규명할 수 없다.

Economics can go a long way towards helping a legislature determine whether or not a particular tax law will help achieve a particular goal, but economics cannot, in a vacuum, identify the goal.

ethics 윤리학

조세 정책을 만드는 것은 도덕적 목표를 규명하는 것을 요구하는데, 그것은 윤리학과 도덕적 분석을 수반해야 하는 과업이다.
Creating tax policy requires identifying a moral goal, which is a task that must involve ethics and moral analysis.

⋯⋯⋯

22. 다음 글의 요지로 가장 적절한 것은?

 Historically, drafters of tax legislation are attentive to questions of economics and history, and less attentive to moral questions. Questions of morality are often pushed to the side in legislative debate, labeled too controversial, too difficult to answer, or, worst of all, irrelevant to the project. But, in fact, the moral questions of taxation are at the very heart of the creation of tax laws. Rather than irrelevant, moral questions are fundamental to the imposition of tax. Tax is the application of a society's theories of distributive justice. Economics can go a long way towards helping a legislature determine whether or not a particular tax law will help achieve a particular goal, but economics cannot, in a vacuum, identify the goal. Creating tax policy requires identifying a moral goal, which is a task that must involve ethics and moral analysis.
* legislation 입법 * imposition 부과

① 분배 정의를 실현하려면 시민 단체의 역할이 필요하다.
② 사회적 합의는 민주적인 정책 수립의 선행 조건이다.
③ 성실한 납세는 안정적인 정부 예산 확보의 기반이 된다.
④ 경제학은 세법을 개정할 때 이론적 근거를 제공한다.
⑤ 세법을 만들 때 도덕적 목표를 설정하는 것이 중요하다.

정답 ⑤

조세 정책을 입법할 때 도덕적 질문에 주의를 기울이지 않는 경향이 있지만, 윤리학과 도덕적 분석을 통해 조세 정책의 도덕적 목표를 규명하는 것이 필요하다는 내용의 글이다. 따라서 글의 요지로 가장 적절한 것은 ⑤이다.

finite 한정된, 유한한
utterance 어터런스 발화, 표현

언어를 습득하는 과정에서 아이들은 유한한 발화에만 노출된다.
In the course of acquiring a language, children are exposed to only a finite set of utterances.

하지만 그들은 무한한 문장들을 사용하고 이해하게 된다.
Yet they come to use and understand an infinite set of sentences.

(C) 이것은 언어 사용의 창조적인 측면으로 일컬어져 왔다.
(C) This has been referred to as the creative aspect of language use.

이 '창조성'은 시 나 소설을 쓸 수 있는 능력이라기보다는 이전에 결코 말하거나 듣지 못한 새로운 문장을 무한히 만들어내고 이해할 수 있는 능력을 말한다.
This 'creativity' does not refer to the ability to write poetry or novels but rather the ability to produce and understand an unlimited set of new sentences never spoken or heard previously.

precise 정확한, 정밀한

아이들이 받는 정확한 언어적 입력은 아이들마다 다르며,
The precise linguistic input children receive differs from child to child;

두 아이가 정확히 똑같은 발화에 노출되는 경우는 없다.
no two children are exposed to exactly the same set of utterances.

(A) 하지만 그들은 모두 거의 동일한 문법에 도달한다.
(A) Yet, they all arrive at pretty much the same grammar.

*haphazard 햅해저드 무작위의, 우연한
caretaker 보호자, 양육자
illustrate 설명하다, 예시하다

돌봐주는 사람들이 문법의 특정한 점을 예를 들어 보여주기 위해 자신의 아이들에게 말하지는 않는다는 점에서 아이들이 받는 입력은 무작위적이다.

The input that children get is haphazard in the sense that caretakers do not talk to their children to illustrate a particular point of grammar.

systematic 체계적인, 조직적인

하지만 모든 아이들은 언어에 대한 체계적인 지식을 발달시킨다.
Yet, all children develop systematic knowledge of a language.

limitation 제한, 한계
variation 변이, 차이
circumstance 환경, 상황
rich 풍부한, 다양한
uniform 통일된, 균일한
linguistic 언어의, 언어학적인

(B) 따라서, 아이들이 받는 입력에서의, 그리고 또한 그들의 개인적인 상황에서의 극심한 한계와 변동에도 불구하고, 그들 모두는 언어 지식의 풍부하고 동일한 세계를 빌딜시킨다.
(B) Thus, despite the severe limitations and variation in the input children receive, and also in their personal circumstances, they all develop a rich and uniform system of linguistic knowledge.

attain 획득하다, 달성하다

습득된 지식은 다양한 방식으로 그 입력을 넘어선다.
The knowledge attained goes beyond the input in various ways.

....

37. 주어진 글 다음에 이어질 글의 순서로 가장 적절한 것을 고르시오.
 In the course of acquiring a language, children are exposed to only a finite set of utterances. Yet they come to use and understand an infinite set of sentences.

(A) Yet, they all arrive at pretty much the same grammar. The input that children get is haphazard in the sense that caretakers do not talk to their children to illustrate a particular point of grammar. Yet, all children develop systematic knowledge of a language.

(B) Thus, despite the severe limitations and variation in the input children receive, and also in their personal circumstances, they all develop a rich and uniform system of linguistic knowledge. The knowledge attained goes beyond the input in various ways.

(C) This has been referred to as the creative aspect of language use. This 'creativity' does not refer to the ability to write poetry or novels but rather the ability to produce and understand an unlimited set of new sentences never spoken or heard previously. The precise linguistic input children receive differs from child to child; no two children are exposed to exactly the same set of utterances. [3점]
* haphazard 무작위적인, 되는 대로의

① (A) - (C) - (B)   ② (B) - (A) - (C)
③ (B) - (C) - (A)   ④ (C) - (A) - (B)
⑤ (C) - (B) - (A)

정답 ④

이유는 본문이 아이들이 제한된 언어 입력을 받으면서도 무한한 문장을 이해하고 사용할 수 있게 되는 과정을 설명하는 흐름을 따르기 때문이다.

먼저 C에서는 이러한 현상을 창의적 언어 사용(creative aspect of language use)이라고 정의하며, 아이들이 이전에 들어본 적 없는 문장도 이해하고 생성할 수 있다는 점을 강조한다. 또한, 아이들이 받는 언어 입력이 각기 다르다는 점을 언급한다.

다음으로 A에서는 아이들이 각기 다른 언어 입력을 받지만 결과적으로 유사한 문법을 습득한다는 점을 설명한다. 즉, 부모나 보호자가 특정한 문법 규칙을 가르치지 않아도 모든 아이가 체계적인 언어 지식을 형성하게 된다는 것이다.

마지막으로 B에서는 이러한 현상을 정리하며, 제한적이고 개인차가 있는 언어 입력에도 불구하고 아이들은 일관된 언어 체계를 형성하며, 이는 단순히 입력된 언어를 그대로 학습하는 것을 넘어서는 현상이라고 결론을 내린다.

따라서 가장 적절한 순서는 ④ (C) - (A) - (B)이다.

assume 가정하다, 추정하다

우리는 더 많은 시간을 얻는 방법은 속도를 내는 것이라고 추정하는 경향이 있다.
We tend to assume that the way to get more time is to speed up.

하지만 속도를 내는 것은 실제로 우리의 속도를 늦출 수 있다.
But speeding up can actually slow us down.

rush 서두르다, 급히 움직이다

급하게 집을 나가다가 결국 열쇠와 지갑을 식탁에 두고 온 것을 깨닫게 된 적이 있는 사람이라면 누구나 이러한 것을 너무나도 잘 알고 있다.
Anyone who has ever rushed out of the house only to realize that their keys and wallet are sitting on the kitchen table knows this only too well.

그리고 줄어드는 것은 비단 효율성만이 아니다.
And it's not just our efficiency that is reduced.

aware 인식하는, 알고 있는
mindful 주의 깊은, 신경 쓰는

우리가 의식을 덜하거나 '유념을' 덜 하게 되어 경험의 질도 또한 악화된다.
The quality of the experience suffers too, as we become less aware or 'mindful.'

entire 전체의, 완전한

아무 것도 맛을 느끼지 못한 채 식사 전체를 끝내 본 적이 있는가?
Have you ever eaten an entire meal without tasting any of it?

서두르는 것은 우리에게 더 적은 시간을 제공할 뿐만 아니라 우리가 진짜로 가지고 있는 그 시간으로부터 즐거움과 혜택을 또한 빼앗아 갈 수 있다.
Hurrying up doesn't just give us less time, it can also steal the pleasure and benefit from the time that we do have.

우리 중 많은 사람에게 서두름은 삶의 한 방식이다.
For many of us, hurrying is a way of life.

thrill 스릴, 짜릿함
unacceptable 받아들일 수 없는, 용납할 수 없는

우리 중 몇몇은 그것(서두름)이 우리에게 제공하는 긴장감(스릴)을 즐기는 반면 다른 사람들은 끊임없는 압박으로 미칠 지경이 되고 받아들일 수 없는 정도까지 자신의 삶의 속도가 올라가고 있다고 느낀다.
Some of us enjoy the thrill that it gives us while others are driven crazy by the constant pressure and feel that their lives are speeding up to an unacceptable degree.

어느 쪽이든, 약간 천천히 가는 행동에 의해 향상될 수 있는 삶의 영역이 거의 틀림없이 있다.
Either way, there are almost certainly areas of our life that could be.

....

31. 다음 빈칸에 들어갈 말로 가장 적절한 것을 고르시오.
 We tend to assume that the way to get more time is to speed up. But speeding up can actually slow us down. Anyone who has ever rushed out of the house only to realize that their keys and wallet are sitting on the kitchen table knows this only too well. And it's not just our efficiency that is reduced. The quality of the experience suffers too, as we become less aware or 'mindful.' Have you ever eaten an entire meal without tasting any of it? Hurrying up doesn't just give us less time, it can also steal the pleasure and benefit from the time that we do have. For many of us, hurrying is a way of life. Some of us enjoy the thrill that it gives us while others are driven crazy by the constant pressure and feel that their lives are speeding up to an unacceptable degree. Either way, there are almost certainly areas of our life that could be. [3점]

① affected by temporary sufferings
② disturbed by inconsistent behaviors
③ enhanced by a little go-slow behavior
④ complicated by slow-but-steady actions
⑤ dominated by a little speedy decision making

정답 ③

③ 약간 천천히 가는 행동에 의해 향상될
enhanced by a little go-slow behavior

급하게 서둘러서 일을 처리하다 보면 오히려 일의 처리 속도가 느려지는 경우가 있고 거기서 느낄 수 있는 즐거움
을 빼앗기는 경우도 있다는 내용의 글이므로 ③ '약간 천천히 가는 행동에 의해 향상될'이 빈칸에 들어갈 말로 가
장 적절하다.

① 일시적인 수난에 의해 영향을 받을
affected by temporary sufferings
② 일관성이 없는 행동에 의해 방해를 받을
disturbed by inconsistent behaviors
④ 느리지만 꾸준한 행동에 의해 복잡해질
complicated by slow-but-steady actions
⑤ 약간 빠른 의사 결정에 의해 지배당할
dominated by a little speedy decision making

privilege 특권, 영광

지난 4년간 이 회사에서 근무한 것은 영광이었습니다.
 It has been a privilege to serve in this company for the past four years.

insight 통찰력, 식견
invaluable 매우 귀중한

안전 관리자로서 제가 얻었던 경험과 통찰력은 귀중했었습니다.
The experiences and insights I have gained as a safety manager have been invaluable.

consideration 고려, 숙고

하지만 신중한 고려 후에 저는 다른 회사에서 직책을 수락하였고, Lewis Ltd.를 떠날 것입니다.
However, after careful consideration, I have accepted a position at another company and will be leaving Lewis Ltd.

 이것이 내리기 쉬운 결정은 아니었지만, 저는 저의 새로운 역할이 제 미래의 목표에 도움이 될 거라 확신합니다.
This was not an easy decision to make, but I am confident that my new role will help me with my future goals.

제 마지막 근무일은 4월 30일이 될 것입니다.
My last day of work will be on April 30th.

smooth transfer 원활한 인수인계
duty 업무, 직무

매끄러운 인수인계를 돕기 위해 제가 할 수 있는 모든 것을 다 할 것입니다.
I will do all I can to assist in a smooth transfer of duties.

저는 당신과 Lewis Ltd. 모두에게 행운이 가득하기를 빕니다.
I wish both you and Lewis Ltd. every good fortune.

18. 다음 글의 목적으로 가장 적절한 것은?

 It has been a privilege to serve in this company for the past four years. The experiences and insights I have gained as a safety manager have been invaluable. However, after careful consideration, I have accepted a position at another company and will be leaving Lewis Ltd. This was not an easy decision to make, but I am confident that my new role will help me with my future goals. My last day of work will be on April 30th. I will do all I can to assist in a smooth transfer of duties. I wish both you and Lewis Ltd. every good fortune.

① 업무에 대한 조언을 구하려고
② 다른 부서로의 이동을 요청하려고
③ 신규 채용 조건에 대해 안내하려고
④ 구직자를 위한 프로그램을 홍보하려고
⑤ 다른 회사로 이직하게 되었음을 알리려고

정답 ⑤

이유는 본문에서 작성자가 현재 회사에서의 경험이 소중했음을 언급한 후, 다른 회사에서 새로운 직책을 맡기로 결정했으며, 4월 30일에 퇴사할 것임을 알리고 있기 때문이다. 또한, 원활한 업무 인수를 위해 최선을 다하겠다고 밝히며, 회사와 동료들에게 행운을 기원하고 있다. 이는 명확하게 퇴사를 알리는 목적에 부합한다.

DAY 4

concern 관련되다, 관계가 있다
in regard to ~에 관하여
law firm 법률 회사

관계자 분께, 저는 당신의 법률 회사에 인턴십을 지원한 Sona Lee와 관련하여 이 편지를 씁니다.
To whom it may concern, I am writing this letter in regard to Sona Lee applying for an internship in your law firm.

get to know 알게 되다, 친숙해지다

저는 지난 한 해 동안 계약법 수업의 학생으로 그녀를 알게 되었습니다.
I have gotten to know her over the past year, as a student in my Contracts course.

assignment 과제, 임무
demonstrate 보여주다, 입증하다
thorough 쏘로우 철저한, 면밀한

그녀가 완성한 과제들은 훌륭했고, 계약법에 대한 완전한 이해를 보여주었습니다.
The assignments she completed were excellent, and demonstrated a thorough understanding of contract law.

remarkable 놀라운, 주목할 만한
interpersonal skills 대인 관계 능력

그녀는 또한 놀라운 에너지와 대인 관계 능력을 지니고 있습니다.
She also has remarkable energy and interpersonal skills.

represent 대표하다, 대변하다
student council 학생회
responsibility 책임, 임무
spirit 열정, 의욕
interact with ~와 소통하다, 교류하다
effectively 효과적으로

그녀는 이 법학 전문 대학원의 학생회에서 그녀의 반을 대표하고 있고 학생들과 효과적으로 상호 작용하며 활기차게 이 책임을 맡아 왔습니다.
She represents her class on the law school's student council and has taken on this responsibility with spirit, interacting with students effectively.

application 지원서, 신청서
wholeheartedly 진심으로, 전적으로

저는 그녀의 지원을 진심으로 지지합니다.
I support her application wholeheartedly.

....

18. 다음 글의 목적으로 가장 적절한 것은?
To whom it may concern,

 I am writing this letter in regard to Sona Lee applying for an internship in your law firm. I have gotten to know her over the past year, as a student in my Contracts course. The assignments she completed were excellent, and demonstrated a thorough understanding of contract law. She also has remarkable energy and interpersonal skills. She represents her class on the law school's student council and has taken on this responsibility with spirit, interacting with students effectively. I support her application wholeheartedly.

Sincerely yours,
Conan Stevenson

① 계약 절차에 대한 이의를 제기하려고
② 우수한 학생을 인턴 채용에 추천하려고
③ 학생회장 선거 운영 방법을 문의하려고
④ 법률 회사의 유능한 변호사를 소개하려고
⑤ 법학 전문 대학원의 교육 과정을 안내하려고

정답 ②

이유는 본문에서 작성자가 Sona Lee라는 학생을 법률 회사의 인턴십 후보자로 추천하고 있기 때문이다. 학생이 계약법 과목에서 우수한 성과를 보였으며, 학생회 활동에서도 뛰어난 리더십과 대인관계를 발휘했다고 설명하며, 그녀의 인턴십 지원을 전적으로 지지한다고 밝히고 있다.

enhanced 향상된, 강화된
light-gathering 빛을 모으는

고양이의 눈이 어둠 속에서 빛난다는 사실은 그것의 강화된 집광 효율성의 일부인데,
The fact that cats' eyes glow in the dark is part of their enhanced light-gathering efficiency;

reflective 반사하는, 반사적인
retina 망막

망막 뒤에는 반사 층이 있어서 빛이 눈에 들어올 때나 망막 뒤에서 반사될 때 그것이 망막에 닿을 수 있다.
there is a reflective layer behind the retina, so light can hit the retina when it enters the eye, or when it is reflected from behind the retina.

ghostly 유령 같은, 희미한

망막을 어떤 식으로든 벗어난 빛은 눈을 빠져나와 그 유령 같은 빛을 만들어 낸다.
(①) Light that manages to miss the retina exits the eye and creates that ghostly glow.

*rod (시신경의) 간상체
predator 포식자
exceptionally 예외적으로, 대단히

고양이의 집광 능력이 고양이의 눈 속 매우 많은 간상체의 개체 수와 결합 될 때, 그 결과는 어둠 속에서 유난히 잘 볼 수 있는 포식자이다.
(②) When cats' light-gathering ability is combined with the very large population of rods in their eyes, the result is a predator that can see exceptionally well in the dark.

accuracy 정확성
inability 무능력, 불가능

고양이는 덜 정확한 주간 시력과 가까운 물체에 초점을 못 맞추는 것으로 이러한 야간의 정확성에 대한 '대가를 지불한다.'
(Cats 'pay' for this nighttime accuracy with less accurate daytime vision and an inability to focus on close objects.)

counterproductive 역효과를 내는

이것은 비생산적으로 보일 수 있는데,
(③) This may seem counterproductive;

만약 고양이가 그 마지막, 아슬아슬한 순간에 그것(쥐)에 초점을 맞출 수 없다면 어둠 속에서 쥐를 보는 것이 무슨 의미가 있을까?
what is the point of seeing a mouse in the dark if, in that final, close moment, the cat can't focus on it?

*tactile 택타일 촉각의, 촉감의

이때 촉각 정보가 작용하기 시작하는데,
(④) Tactile information comes into play at this time;

*whisker (고양이의) 수염
grasp 붙잡음, 움켜쥠

고양이들은 콧수염을 앞으로 움직여서 그들의 턱으로 물 수 있는 범위 내의 물체들에 대한 정보를 얻는 데 사용할 수 있다.
cats can move their whiskers forward and use them to get information about objects within the grasp of their jaws.

surplus 과잉, 초과

그러므로 다음번에 여러분이 밝은 햇빛 속에서, 눈이 반쯤 감긴 채로, 낮잠을 자고 있는 것처럼 보이는 고양이를 보면, 그것이 단순히 과도한 빛으로부터 망막을 보호하고 있을 뿐일 수도 있다는 것을 기억하라.
(⑤) So the next time you see a cat seeming to nap in the bright sunlight, eyes half-closed, remember that it may simply be shielding its retina from a surplus of light.

39. 글의 흐름으로 보아, 주어진 문장이 들어가기에 가장 적절한 곳을 고르시오.

Cats 'pay' for this nighttime accuracy with less accurate daytime vision and an inability to focus on close objects.

 The fact that cats' eyes glow in the dark is part of their enhanced light-gathering efficiency; there is a reflective layer behind the retina, so light can hit the retina when it enters the eye, or when it is reflected from behind the retina. (①) Light that manages to miss the retina exits the eye and creates that ghostly glow. (②) When cats' light-gathering ability is combined with the very large population of rods in their eyes, the result is a predator that can see exceptionally well in the dark. (③) This may seem counterproductive; what is the point of seeing a mouse in the dark if, in that final, close moment, the cat can't focus on it? (④) Tactile information comes into play at this time; cats can move their whiskers forward and use them to get information about objects within the grasp of their jaws. (⑤) So the next time you see a cat seeming to nap in the bright sunlight, eyes half-closed, remember that it may simply be shielding its retina from a surplus of light. [3점]
* rod (시신경의) 간상체(杆狀體) * tactile 촉각의 * whisker (고양이의) 수염

정답 ③

주어진 문장은 "Cats 'pay' for this nighttime accuracy with less accurate daytime vision and an inability to focus on close objects."이며, 이는 고양이가 야간 시력을 강화하는 대신 낮 동안의 시력이 떨어지고 가까운 물체에 초점을 맞추기 어렵다는 내용을 담고 있다.

글의 흐름을 보면, ①~②에서는 고양이의 눈이 어두운 곳에서 빛나는 이유와 빛을 효율적으로 모으는 방식에 대해 설명하고 있다. ③에서는 이러한 능력이 고양이의 야간 시력에 큰 이점을 준다고 강조한다. 이어지는 ④에서는 "This may seem counterproductive;"라고 하며, 앞에서 설명한 내용과 대조되는 점을 언급하고 있다. 이는 고양이가 밤에 사물을 잘 볼 수 있지만 가까운 물체에 초점을 맞추기 어렵다는 내용과 연결된다.

따라서 주어진 문장은 ③번 자리에 들어가는 것이 가장 적절하다.

genetic 유전적인
variation 변이

진화 과정은 이용 가능한 유전적 변이에 작용한다.
The evolutionary process works on the genetic variation that is available.

natural selection 자연 선택
unlikely 가능성이 적은

따라서 자연 선택이 완벽하고 '최대로 적합한' 개체의 진화로 이어질 가능성은 작다.
It follows that natural selection is unlikely to lead to the evolution of perfect, 'maximally fit' individuals.

organisms 유기체
fittest 가장 적합한

그보다, 생물체는 '가능한 가장 적합한' 또는 '아직은 가장 적합한' 상태로 환경에 맞춰지게 되는데,
Rather, organisms come to match their environments by being 'the fittest available' or 'the fittest yet':

즉 그들이 '상상할 수 있는 가장 좋은 것'은 아니다.
they are not 'the best imaginable'.

properties 속성
originated 기원한

적합성 결여의 일부는 생물체가 가진 현재의 특성 모두가 그 생물체가 현재 살고 있는 환경과 모든 면에서 유사한 환경에서 유래한 것이 아니기 때문에 발생한다.
Part of the lack of fit arises because the present properties of an organism have not all originated in an environment similar in every respect to the one in which it now lives.

remote 먼
ancestors 조상
baggage 짐

constrain 제한하다

진화 역사의 과정에서, 생물체의 먼 조상들은 후속적으로 미래의 진화를 제약하는 일련의 특성들, 즉 진화적 '짐'을 진화시켰을 수도 있다.
Over the course of its evolutionary history, an organism's remote ancestors may have evolved a set of characteristics — evolutionary 'baggage' — that subsequently constrain future evolution.

*vertebrates 벌터브랫츠 척추동물
vertebral column 벌터브럴 컬럼 척추

수백만 년 동안 척추동물의 진화는 척추를 가진 생물체에 의해 달성될 수 있는 것으로 제한되어 왔다.
For many millions of years, the evolution of vertebrates has been limited to what can be achieved by organisms with a vertebral column.

게다가, 현재 생물체와 그 환경 간의 정확한 일치로 보이는 것의 대부분은 제약으로도 볼 수 있는데,
Moreover, much of what we now see as precise matches between an organism and its environment may equally be seen as constraints:

foliage 폴리에지 잎(한 나무의 나뭇잎이나, 나뭇잎과 줄기를 총칭)
perspective 관점

코알라는 유칼립투스 잎으로 성공적으로 생활하지만, 다른 관점에서는 코알라는 유칼립투스 잎 없이는 살 수 없다.
koala bears live successfully on Eucalyptus foliage, but, from another perspective, koala bears cannot live without Eucalyptus foliage.

adaptability 적응력

→ 한 생물체가 현재 가지고 있는 생존 특성은 그 생물체가 환경에서 발생하는 변화에 대처하는 상황에 있을 때 적응성에 장애물이 될 수 있다.
The survival characteristics that an organism currently carries may act as a(n) (A) <u>obstacle</u> to its adaptability when the organism finds itself coping with changes that arise in its (B) <u>surroundings.</u>

40. 다음 글의 내용을 한 문장으로 요약하고자 한다. 빈칸 (A)와 (B)에 들어갈 말로 가장 적절한 것은?

 The evolutionary process works on the genetic variation that is available. It follows that natural selection is unlikely to lead to the evolution of perfect, 'maximally fit' individuals. Rather, organisms come to match their environments by being 'the fittest available' or 'the fittest yet': they are not 'the best imaginable'. Part of the lack of fit arises because the present properties of an organism have not all originated in an environment similar in every respect to the one in which it now lives. Over the course of its evolutionary history, an organism's remote ancestors may have evolved a set of characteristics — evolutionary 'baggage' — that subsequently constrain future evolution. For many millions of years, the evolution of vertebrates has been limited to what can be achieved by organisms with a vertebral column. Moreover, much of what we now see as precise matches between an organism and its environment may equally be seen as constraints: koala bears live successfully on Eucalyptus foliage, but, from another perspective, koala bears cannot live without Eucalyptus foliage.

* vertebrate: 척추동물

→ The survival characteristics that an organism currently carries may act as a(n) (A) to its adaptability when the organism finds itself coping with changes that arise in its (B).

	(A)	(B)		(A)	(B)
①	improvement	...... diet	②	obstacle	...... surroundings
③	advantage	...... genes	④	regulator	...... mechanisms
⑤	guide	...... traits			

정답 ②

진화의 과정에서 생물체는 진화적 짐에 의해 미래의 진화에 제약받으며, 유칼립투스 잎으로 성공적으로 생활하지만 유칼립투스 잎이 없이는 살 수 없는 코알라의 사례가 보여주듯이, 현재 환경과의 상호 작용에서 이점을 제공하는 생존 특성이 변화하는 환경에서는 적응을 어렵게 한다는 내용이다. 따라서 요약문의 빈칸 (A), (B)에 들어갈 말로 가장 적절한 것은 ② '장애물 – 환경'이다.

① improvement 개선   ······ diet 먹거리
② obstacle 장애물   ······ surroundings 환경
③ advantage 장점   ······ genes 유전자
④ regulator 조절 장치   ······ mechanisms 메커니즘
⑤ guide 길잡이   ······ traits 특성

*forager 포리저 수렵 채집인
seasonal 계절적인

고대 농부와 수렵 채집인 모두 계절에 따른 식량 부족을 겪었다.
Both ancient farmers and foragers suffered seasonal food shortages.

이 기간 동안 어린이와 어른 모두 어떤 날에는 배가 고픈 채 잠자리에 들었을 것이며 모두가 지방과 근육을 잃었을 것이다.
During these periods children and adults alike would go to bed hungry some days and everyone would lose fat and muscle.

severe 심각한, 혹독한
existential 존재에 관한, 생존을 위협하는
threatening 위협적인
famine 기근, 굶주림

(C) 그러나 더 오랜 기간 동안 농경 사회는 수렵 채집인보다 심각하고, 존재적으로 위협적인 기근에 시달릴 가능성이 훨씬 더 높았다.
(C) But over longer periods of time farming societies were far more likely to suffer severe, existentially threatening famines than foragers.

productive 생산적인, 효율적인
yield 산출량, 수확량
risky 위험한, 불확실한

수렵 채집이 농업보다 훨씬 덜 생산적이고 훨씬 더 낮은 에너지 생산량을 발생시킬지 모르지만 그것은 또한 훨씬 덜 위험하다.
Foraging may be much less productive and generate far lower energy yields than farming but it is also much less risky.

impose 부과하다, 강요하다
*staple 주요한
harsh 가혹한, 혹독한
align with ~에 맞추다, 조화시키다

(B) 이는 첫째, 수렵채집인이 자신들의 환경에 의해 부과된 자연적 한계 내에서 잘 사는 경향이 있었기 때문이고, 둘째, 농부는 보통 한두 가지 주요한 작물에 의존했던 데 반하여, 심지어 가장 가혹한 환경에 있는 수렵채집인은 수십 가지의 다른 식량원에 의존했고, 그래서 변화하는 상황에 대한 생태계 자체의 역동적인 반응에 맞추기 위해 보통 자신들의 식단을 조정할 수 있었기 때문이다.
(B) This is firstly because foragers tended to live well within the natural limits imposed by their environments, and secondly because where farmers typically relied on one or two staple crops, foragers in even the harshest environments relied on dozens of different food sources and so were usually able to adjust their diets to align with an ecosystem's own dynamic responses to changing conditions.

ecosystem 생태계
inevitably 불가피하게

(A) 일반적으로 복잡한 생태계에서 한 해 날씨가 한 집단의 식물 종에게 적합하지 않다고 판명될 때, 그것은 거의 필연적으로 다른 것들에게 적합하다.
(A) Typically, in complex ecosystems when weather one year proves unsuitable for one set of plant species, it almost inevitably suits others.

*catastrophe 카타스트로피 재앙, 대참사
harvest 수확, 추수
sustained 지속적인
drought 가뭄

그러나 농업 사회에서 예를 들어 지속적인 가뭄의 결과로 수확이 실패할 때, 그러면 참사가 일어난다.
But in farming societies when harvests fail as a result of, for example, a sustained drought, then catastrophe emerges.

....

37. 주어진 글 다음에 이어질 글의 순서로 가장 적절한 것을 고르시오.
 Both ancient farmers and foragers suffered seasonal food shortages. During these periods children and adults alike would go to bed hungry some days and everyone would lose fat and muscle.

(A) Typically, in complex ecosystems when weather one year proves unsuitable for one set of plant species, it almost inevitably suits others. But in farming societies when harvests fail as a result of, for example, a sustained drought, then catastrophe emerges.

(B) This is firstly because foragers tended to live well within the natural limits imposed by their environments, and secondly because where farmers typically relied on one or two staple crops, foragers in even the harshest environments relied on dozens of different food sources and so were usually able to adjust their diets to align with an ecosystem's own dynamic responses to changing conditions.
(C) But over longer periods of time farming societies were far more likely to suffer severe, existentially threatening famines than foragers. Foraging may be much less
productive and generate far lower energy yields than farming but it is also much less risky. [3점]
* forager: 수렵 채집인 * catastrophe: 참사 * staple: 주요한

① (A) - (C) - (B)　　　　② (B) - (A) - (C)
③ (B) - (C) - (A)　　　　④ (C) - (A) - (B)
⑤ (C) - (B) - (A)

정답 ⑤

주어진 문장은 고대 농부와 수렵 채집인이 계절적 식량 부족을 겪었으며, 이로 인해 배고픔을 경험하고 체중이 감소했다는 내용을 설명하고 있다. 이어질 글의 논리적 흐름을 분석하면 다음과 같다.

(C) 단기적으로는 농업과 수렵 채집 모두 식량 부족을 겪었지만, 장기적으로 보면 농경 사회가 훨씬 심각한 기근을 겪을 가능성이 높았음을 설명한다. 농업은 생산성이 높지만, 수렵 채집보다 위험성이 크다는 점을 강조한다.

(B) 수렵 채집인이 기근에 덜 취약했던 이유를 설명한다. 그들은 자연의 한계를 벗어나지 않는 범위에서 생활했고, 특정 작물에 의존하는 농부들과 달리 다양한 식량원을 활용할 수 있었기 때문에 환경 변화에 적응할 수 있었다.

(A) 농경 사회의 취약점을 강조한다. 자연 생태계에서는 특정 기후가 한 작물에는 부적합해도 다른 작물에는 적합할 가능성이 높지만, 농경 사회에서는 극심한 가뭄 같은 재해가 발생하면 주 작물의 수확이 실패하여 심각한 기근으로 이어질 수 있다.

이러한 흐름을 고려할 때 가장 적절한 순서는 (C) → (B) → (A)이며, 정답은 ⑤이다.

contingency 콘틴전시 우연, 우발, 임시
contingency pricing 승소 시 보수 약정

결과 기반 가격 책정 중 가장 일반적으로 일러진 형태는 변호사가 사용하는 '승소 시 보수 약징'이라고 불리는 관행이다.
The most commonly known form of results-based pricing is a practice called contingency pricing, used by lawyers.

(C) 승소 시 보수 약정은 개인 상해 및 특정 소비자 소송에 대해 비용이 청구되는 주요 방식이다.
(C) Contingency pricing is the major way that personal injury and certain consumer cases are billed.

settle 해결하다, 합의를 보다

이 방식에서 변호사는 소송이 해결될 때까지 수수료나 지불금을 받지 않는데, 그 때 그들은 의뢰인이 받는 금액의 일정 비율을 받는다.
In this approach, lawyers do not receive fees or payment until the case is settled, when they are paid a percentage of the money that the client receives.

compensate 보수[급여]를 지불하다

(A) 따라서 의뢰인에게 유리한 결과에만 보수가 지불된다.
(A) Therefore, only an outcome in the client's favor is compensated.

intimidate 겁을 주다

의뢰인의 관점에서 보면, 이러한 소송의 의뢰인 대부분이 법률 사무소에 익숙하지 않고 아마도 겁을 먹을 수 있다는 부분적인 이유로 그 가격 책정은 타당하다.
From the client's point of view, the pricing makes sense in part because most clients in these cases are unfamiliar with and possibly intimidated by law firms.

그들의 가장 큰 두려움은 해결하는 데 몇 년이 걸릴 수 있는 소송에 대한 높은 수수료이다.
Their biggest fears are high fees for a case that may take years to settle.

settlement 합의금

(B) 승소 시 보수 약정을 사용함으로써 의뢰인은 합의금을 받을 때까지 수수료를 지불하지 않도록 보장받는다.
(B) By using contingency pricing, clients are ensured that they pay no fees until they receive a settlement.

승소 시 보수 약정의 이런 경우와 여타 경우에서 서비스의 경제적 가치는 서비스 전에 결정하기 어렵고, 공급자는 구매자에게 가치를 전달하는 위험과 보상을 그들이 나눌 수 있게 하는 가격을 전달한다.
In these and other instances of contingency pricing, the economic value of the service is hard to determine before the service, and providers develop a price that allows them to share the risks and rewards of delivering value to the buyer.

....

37. 주어진 글 다음에 이어질 글의 순서로 가장 적절한 것을 고르시오.
The most commonly known form of results-based pricing is a practice called contingency pricing, used by lawyers.

(A) Therefore, only an outcome in the client's favor is compensated. From the client's point of view, the pricing makes sense in part because most clients in these cases are unfamiliar with and possibly intimidated by law firms. Their biggest fears are high fees for a case that may take years to settle.
(B) By using contingency pricing, clients are ensured that they pay no fees until they receive a settlement. In these and other instances of contingency pricing, the economic value of the service is hard to determine before the service, and providers develop a price that allows them to share the risks and rewards of delivering value to the buyer.
(C) Contingency pricing is the major way that personal injury and certain consumer cases are billed. In this approach, lawyers do not receive fees or payment until the case is settled, when they are paid a percentage of the money that the client receives. [3점]
* intimidate: 위협하다

① (A) — (C) — (B) 　　　② (B) — (A) — (C)
③ (B) — (C) — (A) 　　　④ (C) — (A) — (B)
⑤ (C) — (B) — (A)

정답 ④

주어진 문장에서 언급된 승소 시 보수 약정을 구체적으로 설명하는 (C)가 주어진 문장 다음에 바로 이어지고, (A)의 첫 문장 '의뢰인에게 유리한 결과만 보수가 지불된다.'는 (C)에서 언급된 승소 시 보수 약정의 수수료 지급 방식으로 인한 결과이므로 (A)가 (C) 다음에 이어져야 하며, 의뢰인의 관점에서 승소 시 보수 약정이 타당하다는 (A)에 이어서, 공급자의 입장에서 승소 시 보수 약정을 설명하는 (B)가 마지막에 와야한다. 따라시 주어진 글 다음에 이어질 글의 순서로 가장 적절한 것은 ④ '(C) ─ (A) ─ (B)'이다.

Regression effect 회귀 효과
- 어떤 값이 극단적인 상태일 때, 시간이 지나면서 그 값이 평균으로 돌아가는 경향. 예를 들어 한 학생의 성적이 우연히 극단적으로 떨어졌을 때, 다음 시험에서 원래의 성적으로 돌아가는 경향

Regression fallacy 회귀 오류
- 사건이나 현상이 원래의 평균으로 돌아가는 자연스러운 경향을 잘못 해석하는 오류. 주로 회귀 효과를 이해하지 못한 채, 이를 다른 원인에 의해 발생한 변화로 잘못 간주할 때 발생

회귀 오류는 이 자연스러운 현상을 외부 요인, 예를 들어 특정 교육 방법이나 특별한 조치 덕분에 학생이 더 잘했다고 잘못 해석하는 경우. 즉, 학생의 점수가 평범한 수준으로 돌아간 것을 "특별한 방법" 덕분으로 오해하는 것.

regression fallacy 회귀 오류
causal reasoning 인과적 추론
fluctuate 플럭츄에이트 변동하다, 오르내리다
typically 일반적으로, 보통

회귀의 오류는 어떻게 상황이 일반적으로 어떤 평균적인 상태 주변에서 무작위로 변동하는 지를 고려하지 못하여 발생하는 인과 추론의 실수이다.
Regression fallacy is a mistake of causal reasoning due to the failure to consider how things fluctuate randomly, typically around some average condition.

intense 극심한, 강렬한
exceptional 예외적인, 뛰어난
***subdued** 서브듀드 약해진, 가라앉은
natural fluctuation 내츄럴 플럭츄에이션 자연적 변동

심한 통증, 스포츠에서의 특출한 활약 그리고 높은 주가는 결국 자연스러운 변동 때문에 더 약화된 상태가 뒤따를 가능성이 있다.
Intense pain, exceptional sports performance, and high stock prices are likely to be followed by more subdued conditions eventually due to natural fluctuation.

(B) 이 사실을 인식하지 못하는 것은 인과관계에 대한 잘못된 결론으로 이어질 수 있다.
(B) Failure to recognize this fact can lead to wrong conclusions about causation.

예를 들어, 어떤 사람이 가끔 요통으로 고통 받고 있는데 어떤 것도 그 문제를 완전히 해결할 수 없는 것처럼 보

인다.
For example, someone might suffer from back pain now and then but nothing seems to solve
the problem completely.

recognize 인식하다, 깨닫다
causation 커제이션 인과관계
alternative therapy 대체 요법

(A) 매우 심한 통증이 있는 기간 동안, 환자는 등에 자석 패치를 붙이는 것과 같은 대체 의학 요법을 시도하기로
결정했다.
(A) During a period of very intense pain, the patient decided to try alternative therapy like
putting a magnetic patch on his back.

conclude 결론짓다

그는 이후에 통증을 덜 느꼈으며 패치가 효과가 있었다는 결론을 내렸다.
He felt less pain afterward and concluded that the patch worked.

하지만 이것은 단지 회귀의 결과일 수 있다.
But this could just be the result of regression.

lessen 줄어들다, 완화되다
natural cycle 자연적 순환

(C) 만약 그가 통증이 매우 심했을 때 치료법을 시도 했다면, 통증이 이미 절정에 도달했으며 어쨌든 자연스러운
주기의 일부로 줄었을 가능성이 꽤 있다.
(C) If he sought treatment when the pain was very intense, it is quite possible that the pain
has already reached its peak and would lessen in any case as part of the natural cycle.

infer 추론하다, 결론을 내리다
ignore 무시하다, 간과하다
relevant 관련 있는, 적절한

패치가 효과가 있었다고 추론하는 것은 타당한 다른 설명을 무시한 것이다.
Inferring that the patch was effective ignored a relevant alternative explanation.

36. 주어진 글 다음에 이어질 글의 순서로 가장 적절한 것을 고르시오.

Regression fallacy is a mistake of causal reasoning due to the failure to consider how things fluctuate randomly, typically around some average condition. Intense pain, exceptional sports performance, and high stock prices are likely to be followed by more subdued conditions eventually due to natural fluctuation.

(A) During a period of very intense pain, the patient decided to try alternative therapy like putting a magnetic patch on his back. He felt less pain afterward and concluded that the patch worked. But this could just be the result of regression.

(B) Failure to recognize this fact can lead to wrong conclusions about causation. For example, someone might suffer from back pain now and then but nothing seems to solve the problem completely.

(C) If he sought treatment when the pain was very intense, it is quite possible that the pain has already reached its peak and would lessen in any case as part of the natural cycle. Inferring that the patch was effective ignored a relevant alternative explanation.

* subdued: 약화된

① (A) - (C) - (B)　　　② (B) - (A) - (C)
③ (B) - (C) - (A)　　　④ (C) - (A) - (B)
⑤ (C) - (B) - (A)

정답 ②

주어진 문장은 회귀 오류(regression fallacy)가 어떤 현상이 자연적으로 평균 수준으로 되돌아가는 것을 고려하지 않고 인과관계를 잘못 해석하는 오류라고 설명하고 있다. 이어질 글의 흐름을 분석하면 다음과 같다.

(B) 회귀 오류를 인식하지 못하면 인과관계를 잘못 해석할 수 있음을 지적하면서, 허리 통증을 예시로 들어 설명을 시작한다.

(A) 허리 통증이 심할 때 환자가 대체 요법(자석 패치)을 사용했고, 이후 통증이 감소하자 효과가 있었다고 결론을 내렸다는 사례를 제시한다.

(C) 그러나 이 통증 감소는 단순히 통증이 최고조에 이른 뒤 자연적으로 완화되는 과정일 가능성이 크며, 환자가 자석 패치의 효과를 과대평가했을 수 있음을 지적한다.

이러한 논리적 흐름을 고려할 때 가장 적절한 순서는 (B) → (A) → (C)이며, 정답은 ② 이다.

열과 온도는 쉽게 혼동될 수 있는 두 가지 양(量)이다.
Heat and temperature are two quantities that can be easily confused.

닭고기 수프를 아주 큰 솥에 담아 스토브 위에 올려놓고 요리하는 것을 상상해보라.
Imagine cooking a very large pot of chicken soup on the stove.

꽤 뜨거운 온도인 섭씨 95도가 될 때까지 그 수프를 가열한다고 가정해보자.
Let's suppose you heat the soup until it is 95°C, quite hot.

여러분은 숟가락을 움켜잡고는 맛을 보기 위해 한 숟가락의 수프를 뜬다.
(①) You grab a spoon and take out a spoonful of soup to taste.

솥에서 수프 한 숟가락을 떠낼 때, 그것(한 숟가락의 수프)은 더 큰 샘플(솥에 담긴 수프)과 같은 온도를 지니고 있다.
(②) As you remove the spoonful of soup from the pot, it has the same temperature as the larger sample.

bare 맨, 드러난

운이 나쁘게도, 여러분이 그 수프를 맛보려고 입으로 가져올 때, 숟가락이 손에서 미끄러지면서 맨발에 (숟가락에 담겨있던) 내용물이 쏟아지게 된다.
(③) Unfortunately, as you bring the soup towards your mouth to taste it, the spoon slips from your hand, pouring its contents on your bare foot.

여러분의 발에 떨어진 섭씨 95도의 수프 한 숟가락은 고통을 주지만, 여러분이 뜻하지 않게 섭씨 95도의 수프가 담긴 솥 전체를 발에 쏟을 때만큼 심하지는 않다.
(The spoonful of 95°C soup hitting your foot hurts, but not as badly as it would if you accidentally spilled the entire pot of 95°C soup on your foot.)

come in contact with ~와 접촉하다

수프 한 숟가락과 수프로 가득 찬 솥 둘 다 같은 온도를 지니고 있다면, 왜 더 큰 샘플이 피부에 닿을 때 더 큰 피해를 줄까?
(④) If both the spoonful and the pot full of soup have the same temperature, why would

the larger sample cause more damage if it came in contact with your skin?

lie in ~에 있다, ~에 놓여 있다

그 문제에 대한 해답은 온도와 열의 차이에 있다.
(⑤) The answer to the question lies in the difference between temperature and heat.

....

38. 글의 흐름으로 보아, 주어진 문장이 들어가기에 가장 적절한 곳을 고르시오.
The spoonful of 95°C soup hitting your foot hurts, but not as badly as it would if you accidentally spilled the entire pot of 95°C soup on your foot.

Heat and temperature are two quantities that can be easily confused. Imagine cooking a very large pot of chicken soup on the stove. Let's suppose you heat the soup until it is 95°C, quite hot. (①) You grab a spoon and take out a spoonful of soup to taste. (②) As you remove the spoonful of soup from the pot, it has the same temperature as the larger sample. (③) Unfortunately, as you bring the soup towards your mouth to taste it, the spoon slips from your hand, pouring its contents on your bare foot. (④) If both the spoonful and the pot full of soup have the same temperature, why would the larger sample cause more damage if it came in contact with your skin? (⑤) The answer to the question lies in the difference between temperature and heat.

정답 ④

섭씨 95도의 수프 한 숟가락이 발에 떨어져 고통을 주지만, 그 고통은 같은 온도의 수프가 담긴 솥 전체를 발에 쏟을 때만큼 심하지는 않다는 내용의 주어진 문장 앞에는 한 숟가락의 수프가 발에 쏟아지는 상황이 제시되어야 한다. 또한, 주어진 문장 다음에는 왜 그런 고통(피해)의 차이가 생기는지에 대한 설명이 이어져야 자연스럽다. 따라서 주어진 문장의 위치로 ④가 가장 적절하다.

urban 도시의
make contact with ~와 접촉하다

도시 환경은 일반적으로 우리이 피부와 접촉하지 않도록 설게된다.
The urban environment is generally designed so as not to make contact with our skin.

push through 헤치고 나아가다
bush 덤불, 관목

우리는 우리가 학교 혹은 직장에 가는 길에 덤불을 통과하지 않는다.
We do not push through bushes on our way to school or work.

sidewalk 보도, 인도
kept clear of ~을 없애다, 깨끗이 유지하다
obstacle 장애물, 방해물

길과 보도는 장애물이 없도록 유지된다.
Roads and sidewalks are kept clear of obstacles.

materiality 메테리얼리티 물질성, 실체
unexpected 예상치 못한
branch 나뭇가지
curb 연석, 도로 경계석

우리가 예상치 못한 나뭇가지에 스치는 것을 느끼거나 연석에 거의 넘어질 뻔할 때처럼, 우리는 오직 이따금 한 번씩 환경의 물질성에 대해 떠올리게 된다.
Only once in a while are we reminded of the materiality of the environment, as when we feel the brush of an unexpected tree branch or nearly fall over a curb.

우리 시간의 대부분은 심지어 밖에서 보내지지 않는다.
Most of our time is not even spent outside.

보통 '외부'는 단지 우리가 '내부'에 가기 위해 거쳐 가는 공간일 뿐이다.
"Outside" is often just a space we go through to get "inside."

architecture 건축, 건축물
*collude 결탁하다
tactile 촉각의, 촉감의
stimulation 자극

우리의 시간은 주로 실내에서 보내지고 그곳에서 건축술과 설계가 가능한 한 촉각적 자극이 결여된 환경을 제공하기 위해 결탁한다.
Our time is largely spent indoors, where architecture and design collude to provide an environment as lacking as possible in tactile stimulation.

corridor 코리도얼 복도, 통로
still 정적인, 움직이지 않는
neutral 중립적인, 변화 없는
effortlessly 쉽게, 수월하게

현대의 대학 혹은 사무실 건물에서 바닥과 벽은 평평하고 매끈하며 복도는 깨끗하고 공기는 바람 한 점 없으며 온도는 중간이고 승강기는 사람을 한 층에서 다른 층으로 수월하게 실어 나른다.
In the modern university or office building, floors and walls are flat and smooth, corridors are clear, the air is still, the temperature is neutral, and elevators carry one effortlessly from one level to another.

assume 가정하다, 생각하다
best served 가장 적절한 상태가 되다
tactile environment 촉각 환경

(우리가 그 존재를 거의 알아차리지 않을) 때 우리의 촉각 환경에 의해 우리가 최고의 편의를 제공받는다고 흔히 여겨진다.
It is commonly assumed that we are best served by our tactile environment when (we scarcely notice its presence.)

....

32. 다음 빈칸에 들어갈 말로 가장 적절한 것을 고르시오.
The urban environment is generally designed so as not to make contact with our skin. We do not push through bushes on our way to school or work. Roads and sidewalks are kept clear of obstacles. Only once in a while are we reminded of the materiality of the environment, as when we feel the brush of an unexpected tree branch or nearly fall over a curb. Most of our

time is not even spent outside. "Outside" is often just a space we go through to get "inside." Our time is largely spent indoors, where architecture and design collude to provide an environment as lacking as possible in tactile stimulation. In the modern university or office building, floors and walls are flat and smooth, corridors are clear, the air is still, the temperature is neutral, and elevators carry one effortlessly from one level to another. It is commonly assumed that we are best served by our tactile environment when (____).

* collude: 결탁하다

① we accept its harsh elements
② we scarcely notice its presence
③ it does not hinder social interactions
④ we experience it using all the senses
⑤ its design reflects the natural environment

정답 ②

본문은 현대 도시 환경이 촉각적 자극을 최소화하도록 설계되어 있으며, 우리가 환경과의 직접적인 접촉을 거의 경험하지 않는다고 설명하고 있다. 마지막 문장에서 "we are best served by our tactile environment"라는 표현이 나오는데, 앞서 환경이 촉각적 요소를 최소화하도록 설계되었다는 내용을 고려하면, 우리가 그것의 존재를 거의 인식하지 못할 때가 가장 적절하다. 따라서 정답은 ② we scarcely notice its presence

hinder 방해하다

① 우리가 그것의 가혹한 요소를 받아들일 때
we accept its harsh elements
③ 그것이 사회적 상호작용을 방해하지 않을 때
it does not hinder social interactions
④ 우리가 모든 감각을 사용하여 그것을 경험할 때
we experience it using all the senses
⑤ 그것의 디자인이 자연 환경을 반영할 때
its design reflects the natural environment

시간 속에 거리는 공간 속에 거리와 같다.
Distance in time is like distance in space.

사람들이 수천 마일 떨어져서 살더라도 그들은 중요하다.
People matter even if they live thousands of miles away.

likewise 마찬가지로, 똑같이
hence 이후에, 앞으로

마찬가지로, 그들이 지금부터 수천 년 후에 살더라도 그들은 중요하다.
Likewise, they matter even if they live thousands of years hence.

unreality 비현실성

두 경우 모두, 거리를 비현실성으로 칙긱하고 우리가 볼 수 있는 것의 한계를 세상의 한계로 취급하기 쉽다.
In both cases, it's easy to mistake distance for unreality, to treat the limits of what we can see as the limits of the world.

doorstep 문간, 현관 앞
border 국경, 경계

하지만 세상이 우리의 문 앞이나 우리 국가의 경계에서 멈추지 않는 것처럼, 그것은 우리의 세대나 다음 세대에서 멈추지 않는다.
But just as the world does not stop at our doorstep or our country's borders, neither does it stop with our generation, or the next.

이러한 생각들은 상식이다.
These ideas are common sense.

proverb 속담, 격언
shade 그늘

한 유명한 속담은 "사회는 노인들이 그 그늘에 결코 앉지 못할 나무를 심을 때 크게 성장한다."라고 한다.
A popular proverb says, "A society grows great when old men plant trees under whose shade they will never sit."

dispose of 처리하다, 없애다
*radioactive 방사성의
century 세기, 100년

우리가 방사성 폐기물을 버릴 때, 우리는 "이것이 지금으로부터 수백 년 후의 사람들을 해치든 누가 상관하겠는가?"라고 말하지 않는다.
When we dispose of radioactive waste, we don't say, "Who cares if this poisons people centuries from now?"

climate change 기후 변화
pollution 오염, 공해
solely 오로지, 단독으로
for the sake of ~을 위해서

비슷하게, 기후 변화나 오염에 신경 쓰는 우리들 중 단지 오늘날 살아 있는 사람들을 위해서 그렇게 하는 사람은 거의 없다.
Similarly, few of us who care about climate change or pollution do so solely for the sake of people alive today.

우리는 대대로 지속되기를 바라는 박물관과 공원과 다리를 만들고,
We build museums and parks and bridges that we hope will last for generations;

우리는 학교와 장기적인 과학 프로젝트에 투자하고, 우리는 그림, 전통, 언어를 보존하고, 우리는 아름다운 장소를 보호한다.
we invest in schools and longterm scientific projects; we preserve paintings, traditions, languages; we protect beautiful places.

in play 영향을 미치고 있는, 고려되고 있는

많은 경우, 우리는 현재와 미래에 대한 우리의 걱정 사이에 명확한 선을 긋지 않는다 — 둘 다 영향을 끼친다.
In many cases, we don't draw clear lines between our concerns for the present and the future — both are in play.

24. 다음 글의 제목으로 가장 적절한 것은?

 Distance in time is like distance in space. People matter even if they live thousands of miles away. Likewise, they matter even if they live thousands of years hence. In both cases, it's easy to mistake distance for unreality, to treat the limits of what we can see as the limits of the world. But just as the world does not stop at our doorstep or our country's borders, neither does it stop with our generation, or the next. These ideas are common sense. A popular proverb says, "A society grows great when old men plant trees under whose shade they will never sit." When we dispose of radioactive waste, we don't say, "Who cares if this poisons people centuries from now?" Similarly, few of us who care about climate change or pollution do so solely for the sake of people alive today. We build museums and parks and bridges that we hope will last for generations; we invest in schools and longterm scientific projects; we preserve paintings, traditions, languages; we protect beautiful places. In many cases, we don't draw clear lines between our concerns for the present and the future — both are in play.
* radioactive 방사선의

① How to Be Present: Discover the Benefits of Here and Now
② The Power of Time Management: The Key to Success
③ Why Is Green Infrastructure Eventually Cost-Effective?
④ Solving Present-Day Problems from Past Experiences
⑤ How We Act Beyond the Bounds of Time

정답 ⑤

⑤ 우리가 시간을 초월하여 행동하는 방법
How We Act Beyond the Bounds of Time

이 글은 시간적 거리와 공간적 거리가 인간의 관심에서 동일한 역할을 한다는 점을 강조하며, 미래 세대에 대한 고려가 현재의 행동에 영향을 미쳐야 한다는 주장을 펼치고 있다. 저자는 방사성 폐기물 처리, 기후 변화 대응, 문화와 자연 보호 등의 사례를 들어 미래를 고려하는 것이 보편적이며 상식적인 태도임을 보여주고 있다.
글의 핵심은 우리가 현재와 미래를 분리해서 생각할 것이 아니라, 미래 세대 또한 고려해야 한다는 것이다. 이를 통해 저자는 시간적 거리로 인해 미래의 사람들을 소홀히 여기는 것은 잘못된 태도임을 강조하고 있다.

Infrastructure 인프라스트럭쳐 **인프라, 하부구조**

① How to Be Present: Discover the Benefits of Here and Now
현재에 존재하는 방법: 여기와 지금의 이점을 발견하다

② The Power of Time Management: The Key to Success
시간 관리의 힘: 성공의 열쇠
③ Why Is Green Infrastructure Eventually Cost-Effective?
왜 녹색 인프라는 결국 비용 효율적인가?
④ Solving Present-Day Problems from Past Experiences
과거의 경험으로 현재의 문제를 해결하다

hypothesis 가설
conduct 수행하다, 실행하다
objectively 객관적으로
subjective 주관적인
outcome 결과

과학 실험은 자신의 가설이 틀렸다는 것을 보여 주도록 설계되어야 하고, 결과에 대해 있을 법한 그 어떤 주관적 영향도 없이 완벽하게 객관적으로 수행되어야 한다.
Scientific experiments should be designed to show that your hypothesis is wrong and should be conducted completely objectively with no possible subjective influence on the outcome.

유감스럽게도 있다 하더라도 진정으로 객관적인 과학자는 거의 없는데 이는 그들이 흔히 실험이 시작되기 오래전에 어떤 결과가 나왔으면 좋겠는지 결정했기 때문이다.
① Unfortunately few, if any, scientists are truly objective as they have often decided long before the experiment is begun what they would like the result to be.

bias 편향, 편견
unintentionally 무의식적으로, 의도치 않게
introduce 도입하다, 유입하다
procedure 절차, 과정
interpretation 해석, 설명

이것은 매우 빈번히 편견이 실험, 실험 절차 혹은 결과의 해석에 (무심코) 더해진다는 것을 의미한다.
② This means that very often bias is (unintentionally) introduced into the experiment, the experimental procedure or the interpretation of results.

justify 정당화하다, 합리화하다
expectation 기대, 예상
ignore 무시하다, 간과하다

자신의 기대와 어긋나는 실험이 왜 무시되어야 하는지, 그리고 자신이 '기대했던' 결과를 가져다주는 실험이 왜 옳은 것인지를 자신에게 정당화하기는 너무나 쉽다.
③ It is all too easy to justify to yourself why an experiment which does not fit with your expectations should be ignored, and why one which provides the results you 'hoped for' is the right one.

partly 부분적으로
blinded (실험에서) 눈가림한, 맹검 처리된

이것은 여러분이 '앞을 예측하지 않고서' 실험을 하고 다른 사람들에게 여러분의 데이터를 점검하거나 실험을 되풀이해 보라고 요청함으로써 어느 정도 피할 수 있다.
⑤ This can be partly avoided by conducting experiments 'blinded' and by asking others to check your data or repeat experiments.

....

39. 다음 글에서 전체 흐름과 관계 없는 문장은?
Scientific experiments should be designed to show that your hypothesis is wrong and should be conducted completely objectively with no possible subjective influence on the outcome. ① Unfortunately, few, if any, scientists are truly objective as they have often decided long before the experiment is begun what they would like the result to be. ② This means that very often bias is (unintentionally) introduced into the experiment, the experimental procedure, or the interpretation of results. ③ It is all too easy to justify to yourself why an experiment which does not fit with your expectations should be ignored and why one which provides the results you 'hoped for' is the right one. ④ It is important to draw a meaningful result from the experiment on peer group activities. ⑤ This can be partly avoided by conducting experiments 'blinded' and by asking others to check your data or repeat experiments.

정답 ④

meaningful 의미 있는
peer group 동료 집단

또래 집단 활동에 관한 실험에서 의미 있는 결과를 도출하는 것이 중요하다.
④ It is important to draw a meaningful result from the experiment on peer group activities.

이 글의 중심 내용은 과학 실험을 수행할 때 실험자 자신의 기대나 편견에서 벗어나 객관성을 유지해야 한다는 것이다. 따라서 또래 집단 활동에 관한 실험에서 의미 있는 결과를 도출하는 것이 중요하다는 ④는 글의 흐름과 무관하다.

DAY 5

suffer 겪다, 고통받다
overdramatically 지나치게 극적으로
exclusively 오로지, 독점적으로
Islamic world 이슬람 세계

서기 8세기부터 12세기까지 유럽이 아마도 지나치게 극적인 이름이 붙여진 '암흑시대'를 겪고 있던 시기에, 지구상의 과학은 거의 오로지 이슬람 세계에서만 발견될 수 있었다.
From the 8th to the 12th century CE, while Europe suffered the perhaps overdramatically named Dark Ages, science on planet Earth could be found almost ① <u>exclusively</u> in the Islamic world.

exactly 정확히, 바로
*antecedent 엔테시던트 선행하는, 앞서는
nonetheless 그럼에도 불구하고
aim at ~을 목표로 하다

이 과학이 오늘날 우리의 과학과 똑같지는 않았지만, 그것(이 과학)은 확실히 그것(우리의 과학)에 선행했고, 그러기는 했지만 세계에 대해 아는 것을 목표로 한 활동이었다.
This science was not exactly like our science today, but it was surely antecedent to ② <u>it</u> and was nonetheless an activity aimed at knowing about the world.

ruler 통치자
grant 주다, 부여하다
tremendous 엄청난, 거대한
observatory 천문대

무슬림 통치자들은 엄청난 물자를 도서관, 천문대, 병원과 같은 과학 기관에 주었다.
Muslim rulers granted scientific institutions tremendous resources, such as libraries, observatories, and hospitals.

scholar 학자

근동 아랍과 북아프리카(와 심지어 스페인까지)에 걸친 모든 도시의 훌륭한 학교는 여러 세대의 학자들을 훈련시켰다.
Great schools in all the cities ③ <u>covering</u> the Arabic Near East and Northern Africa (and even into Spain) trained generations of scholars.

*lexicon 어휘, 사전
prefix 접두사
owe 기원을 두다, 빚지다
algorithm 알고리즘
alchemy 연금술
alkali 알칼리
algebra 대수학

접두사 'al'로 시작하는 현대 과학 어휘 목록의 거의 모든 단어, 즉 알고리즘, 연금술, 알코올, 알칼리, 대수학은 이슬람 과학에 그 기원을 두고 있다.
Almost every word in the modern scientific lexicon that begins with the prefix "al" ④ owes its origins to Islamic science — algorithm, alchemy, alcohol, alkali, algebra.

grind to a halt 서서히 멈추다
apparent 명백한, 분명한
*give or take 대략
unmistakably 틀림없이, 명백히

그리고 그것이 시작된 지 막 400년이 넘었던 그때, 그것은 서서히 멈춘 것 같았고, 대략 몇 백년 후에 우리가 오늘날 과학이라고 확실히 인식하게 될 것이 갈릴레오, 케플러, 그리고 조금 후에 뉴턴과 함께 유럽에서 출현했다.
And then, just over 400 years after it started, it ground to an apparent halt, and it would be a few hundred years, give or take, before ⑤ that(→what) we would today unmistakably recognize as science appeared in Europe — with Galileo, Kepler, and, a bit later, Newton.

....

29. 다음 글의 밑줄 친 부분 중, 어법상 틀린 것은? [3점]
 From the 8th to the 12th century CE, while Europe suffered the perhaps overdramatically named Dark Ages, science on planet Earth could be found almost ① exclusively in the Islamic world. This science was not exactly like our science today, but it was surely antecedent to ② it and was nonetheless an activity aimed at knowing about the world. Muslim rulers granted scientific institutions tremendous resources, such as libraries, observatories, and hospitals. Great schools in all the cities ③ covering the Arabic Near East and Northern Africa (and even into Spain) trained generations of scholars. Almost every word in the modern scientific lexicon that begins with the prefix "al" ④ owes its origins to Islamic science — algorithm, alchemy, alcohol, alkali, algebra. And then, just over 400 years after it started, it ground to an apparent halt, and it would be a few hundred years, give or take, before ⑤ that we would today unmistakably recognize as science appeared in Europe — with Galileo, Kepler, and, a bit later, Newton.

* antecedent 선행하는 * lexicon 어휘 (목록) * give or take 대략

정답 ⑤ that(→what)

접속사 before 뒤에 오는 절에서 recognize의 목적어 역할을 하면서 appeared의 주어 역할을 하는 명사절이 필요하므로 that을 선행사를 포함한 관계사인 what으로 바꿔야 한다.

① exclusively 부사
문장 "science on planet Earth could be found almost exclusively in the Islamic world."
exclusively는 부사로, "could be found"(수동태 동사구)를 수식하고 있다.
부사 exclusively는 동사를 수식하는 역할을 하므로 적절하다.
"almost exclusively"는 "거의 전적으로"라는 의미로, 과장 없이 대부분이 그랬음을 나타내는 표현이다.

② it 대명사
문장 "This science was not exactly like our science today, but it was surely antecedent to it and was nonetheless an activity aimed at knowing about the world."
"This science"와 "our science today"는 서로 다른 과학을 의미한다.
"it"는 앞 문장에서 언급된 "our science today"를 가리키는 대명사로, 적절하게 사용되었다.

③ covering 현재분사
문장 "Great schools in all the cities covering the Arabic Near East and Northern Africa (and even into Spain) trained generations of scholars."
"covering the Arabic Near East and Northern Africa (and even into Spain)"는 앞의 "cities"를 수식하는 현재분사구이다.
현재분사 "covering"은 "cities"를 설명하는 역할을 하며, 해당 지역을 포함하고 있다는 의미를 전달하므로 문법적으로 적절하다.

④ owes 단수형
문장 "Almost every word in the modern scientific lexicon that begins with the prefix 'al' owes its origins to Islamic science — algorithm, alchemy, alcohol, alkali, algebra."
주어: "Almost every word" (단수명사) → 동사 "owes"는 단수형이므로 일치한다.
"owes A to B" 구조는 "A는 B 덕분이다"라는 의미로 적절하게 사용되었다.

arguably 알규어블리 아마도, 논쟁의 여지가 있지만

동물은 거의 틀림없이 예술을 만든다.
Animals arguably make art.

bowerbird 바우어새 (화려한 둥지를 만드는 새)
dedicate 헌신하다, 바치다
fraction 부분, 일부
elaborate 정교한, 공들인
structure 구조물
twig 잔가지

뉴기니와 오스트레일리아의 수컷 바우어새는 나뭇가지, 꽃, 딸기류, 딱정벌레 날개 그리고 심지어 다채로운 잡동사니로부터 정교한 구조물을 만드는 데 그들의 시간과 에너지의 큰 부분을 바친다.
The male bowerbirds of New Guinea and Australia dedicate huge fractions of their time and energy to creating elaborate structures from twigs, flowers, berries, beetle wings, and even colorful trash.

backdrop 배경
mating dance 구애 춤
acrobatic 곡예적인, 기교적인
imitation 모방, 흉내

이것들은 그들의 복잡한 짝짓기 춤을 위한 배경이며, 그 춤은 곡예 동작과 심지어 다른 종들의 모방까지 포함한다.
These are the backdrops to their complex mating dances, which include acrobatic moves and even imitations of other species.

construct 만들다, 조립하다
stereotyped 정형화된, 틀에 박힌
beehive 벌집
hummingbird 벌새

그들이 지은 탑과 '바우어'의 가장 놀라운 점은 그것들이 벌집이나 벌새 둥지처럼 정형화되어 있지 않다는 것이다.
What's most amazing about the towers and "bowers" they construct is that they aren't stereotyped like a beehive or hummingbird nest.

각각의 것은 다르다.
Each one is different.

artistic 예술적인
craftsbirdship (조어) 새의 공예적 기술

새의 정교한 장인 정신과 함께 예술적 기술은 암컷에 의해 보상받는다.
Artistic skill, along with fine craftsbirdship, is rewarded by the females.

gauge 게이지 평가하다, 측정하다, 계량기
cognitive 코그니티브 인지의, 인식의
mate 짝, 배우자
Darwin 다윈 (진화론자)

많은 연구자들은 이 과시가 자신의 잠재적 짝의 인지적 능력을 측정하기 위해서 암컷에 의해 이용된다고 말하지만, 다윈은 암컷이 실제로 그것들의 '아름다움'에 끌렸다고 생각했다.
Many researchers suggest these displays are used by the females to gauge the cognitive abilities of her potential mates, but Darwin thought that she was actually attracted to their beauty.

다시 말해, 바우어는 (단순히 짝의 자질의 신호만인 것은 아니다.)
In other words, the bowers (aren't simply signals of mate quality;)

bouquet 꽃다발

그것들은 우리가 그림이나 봄꽃 한 다발을 감상하는 것처럼 그 자체의 목적을 위해 감상된다.
they are appreciated by the females for their own sake, much as we appreciate a painting or a bouquet of spring flowers.

2013년의 한 연구는 인지 검사에서 더 잘했던 바우어새가 짝을 유혹하는 데 더 성공적이었는지를 살펴보았다.
A 2013 study looked at whether bowerbirds that did better on cognitive tests were more successful at attracting mates.

straightforward 직접적인, 단순한

그들은 그러지 않았고, 이것은 암컷이 찾는 것이 무엇이든지 그것이 인지 능력의 직접적인 지표는 아니라는 것을 시사한다.

They were not, suggesting whatever the females are looking for, it isn't a straightforward indicator of cognitive ability.

....

31. 다음 빈칸에 들어갈 말로 가장 적절한 것을 고르시오.

 Animals arguably make art. The male bowerbirds of New Guinea and Australia dedicate huge fractions of their time and energy to creating elaborate structures from twigs, flowers, berries, beetle wings, and even colorful trash. These are the backdrops to their complex mating dances, which include acrobatic moves and even imitations of other species. What's most amazing about the towers and "bowers" they construct is that they aren't stereotyped like a beehive or hummingbird nest. Each one is different. Artistic skill, along with fine craftsbirdship, is rewarded by the females. Many researchers suggest these displays are used by the females to gauge the cognitive abilities of her potential mates, but Darwin thought that she was actually attracted to their beauty. In other words, the bowers (   ) ; they are appreciated by the females for their own sake, much as we appreciate a painting or a bouquet of spring flowers. A 2013 study looked at whether bowerbirds that did better on cognitive tests were more successful at attracting mates. They were not, suggesting whatever the females are looking for, it isn't a straightforward indicator of cognitive ability.

① block any possibility of reproduction
② aren't simply signals of mate quality
③ hardly sustain their forms long enough
④ don't let the mating competition overheat
⑤ can be a direct indicator of aggressiveness

정답 ②

단순히 짝의 질을 나타내는 신호가 아니다
aren't simply signals of mate quality.

주어진 문장에서 빈칸 앞까지의 내용은 수컷 바우어새들이 정교한 구조물을 만들어 구애 행동을 하며, 암컷들이 이를 평가한다는 점을 설명하고 있다. 이어서 다윈은 암컷이 단순히 수컷의 인지 능력을 평가하는 것이 아니라, 그 구조물 자체의 아름다움에 끌린다고 보았다. 즉, 바우어새의 구조물은 단순히 짝짓기를 위한 신호가 아니라 그 자체로 가치가 있는 예술적 표현이라는 의미이다.

또한 마지막 문장에서 2013년 연구 결과가 소개되는데, 인지 능력이 높은 바우어새가 더 많은 짝을 얻는 것이 아니라는 점이 밝혀졌다. 이는 바우어새의 구조물이 단순한 짝의 질을 나타내는 신호가 아니라는 해석과 연결된다.

reproduction 번식
sustain 유지하다
aggressiveness 공격성

① 번식의 가능성을 차단하다
block any possibility of reproduction
③ 그 형태를 충분히 오래 유지하지 못하다
hardly sustain their forms long enough
④ 짝짓기 경쟁이 과열되지 않게 하다
don't let the mating competition overheat
⑤ 공격성의 직접적인 지표가 될 수 있다
can be a direct indicator of aggressiveness

wildfire 산불
phenomenon 현상

산불은 호주의 많은 환경에서 자연스러운 현상이다.
Wildfire is a natural phenomenon in many Australian environments.

intentional 의도적인
setting 방화, 놓기
landscape 경관, 풍경
practise 실행하다, 실천하다
Aboriginal people 애보리지널 피플 원주민
millennia 수천 년

경관을 관리하기 위해 의도적으로 불을 지르는 일은 수천 년 동안 호주 원주민들에 의해 행해졌다.
The intentional setting of fire to manage the landscape was practised by Aboriginal people for millennia.

stockman 목동, 목축업자
introduce 도입하다, 시작하다
*regime 레짐- 체제, 방식

(A) 하지만 목축업자들이 도입한 불 지르기 방식은 이전 양식과는 달랐다.
(A) However, the pattern of burning that stockmen introduced was unlike previous regimes.

여건이 허락되면, 그들은 겨울에 자신들의 가축을 외부로 이동시켜 경관에 불을 지르곤 했다.
When conditions allowed, they would set fire to the landscape as they moved their animals out for the winter.

vegetation 식물, 초목
stimulate 자극하다, 촉진하다
recolonize 다시 정착하다, 재생되다

이는 숲이 우거진 초목을 없애는 역할을 했고, 또한 이듬해 봄에 새로운 식물의 성장을 촉진했다.
This functioned to clear woody vegetation and also stimulated new plant growth in the following spring.

young shoot 새싹, 어린 줄기
food source 식량원

(C) 어린 새싹은 그들의 동물들이 돌아왔을 때 준비된 먹을 수 있는 식량원이었다.
(C) The young shoots were a ready food source for their animals when they returned.

reinforce 강화하다, 보강하다
*scrubby 덤불(관목)이 우거진

하지만, 그 관행은 또한 통제하고자 했던 우거진 관목의 성장을 강화하는 경향도 있었다.
However, the practice also tended to reinforce the scrubby growth it was intended to control.

succeed 뒤를 잇다, 계승하다
shrub 관목, 덤불
strategy 전략, 방안
prevent 막다, 방지하다
regrowth 재성장, 다시 자람
consequence 결과, 영향

(B) 불에 탄 지역에 다시 대량 서식한 첫 번째 식물류는 풀이었지만, 목본성 식물과 관목이 곧 그것들의 뒤를 이었다. 그러한 재성장을 막기 위한 거의 유일한 전략은 불을 더 지르는 것이었는데, 본질적으로는 불을 사용하여 불을 사용한 결과를 통제하는 것이었다.
(B) Although grasses were the first kinds of plants to recolonize the burnt areas they were soon succeeded by further woody plants and shrubs. About the only strategy to prevent such regrowth was further burning — essentially using fire to control the consequences of using fire.

....

36. 주어진 글 다음에 이어질 순서로 알맞은 것을 고르시오.
 Wildfire is a natural phenomenon in many Australian environments. The intentional setting of fire to manage the landscape was practised by Aboriginal people for millennia.

(A) However, the pattern of burning that stockmen introduced was unlike previous regimes. When conditions allowed, they would set fire to the landscape as they moved their animals out for the winter. This functioned to clear woody vegetation and also stimulated new plant growth in the following spring.
(B) Although grasses were the first kinds of plants to recolonize the burnt areas they were soon

succeeded by further woody plants and shrubs. About the only strategy to prevent such regrowth was further burning — essentially using fire to control the consequences of using fire. (C) The young shoots were a ready food source for their animals when they returned. However, the practice also tended to reinforce the scrubby growth it was intended to control.
* regime: 양식 * scrubby: 관목이 우거진

① (A) - (C) - (B)   ② (B) - (A) - (C)
③ (B) - (C) - (A)   ④ (C) - (A) - (B)
⑤ (C) - (B) - (A)

정답 ①

호주 원주민들이 수천 년 동안 경관을 관리하기 위해 의도적으로 불을 지른다는 내용의 주어진 글 다음에는, 목축업자들은 겨울에는 가축을 외부로 이동시켜 경관에 불을 지르곤 했다는 내용의 (A)가 이어져야 한다. 그다음에는 그 동물들이 돌아왔을 때 어린 새싹이 식량원이었으나, 그 관행이 관목을 우거지게 했다는 내용의 (C)가 오고, 마지막으로 (A)에서 언급한 초목의 재성장을 막기 위해 불을 더 사용해 불의 결과를 통제했다는 내용의 (B)가 나와야 한다. 따라서 주어진 글 다음에 이어질 글의 순서로 가장 적절한 것은 ①이다.

seemingly 겉보기에는, 외견상
straightforward 단순한, 쉬운
individual 개인, 개체
*disperse 디스펄스 흩어지다, 분산하다
compete 경쟁하다
satisfy 충족시키다, 만족시키다

텃새들의 서식지 선택은 흩어지는 어린 개체가 생존을 위한 필요를 충족시키기 위해 성공적으로 경쟁할 수 있는 장소를 찾을 때까지 옮겨 다니는, 외견상 간단한 과정이다.
Resident-bird habitat selection is seemingly a straightforward process in which a young dispersing individual moves until it finds a place where it can compete successfully to satisfy its needs.

shelter 보호, 피난처

처음에는 이러한 필요에 음식과 은신처만 포함된다.
(①) Initially, these needs include only food and shelter.

identify 식별하다, 알아보다
settle 정착하다, 자리 잡다
survivorship 생존율
reproductive 번식의, 생식의

그러나 궁극적으로 그 어린 새는 생존뿐만 아니라 번식을 위한 필요조건도 충족시켜 주는 서식지를 찾고, 확인하고, 거기에 정착해야 한다.
(②) However, eventually,the young must locate, identify, and settle in a habitat that satisfies not only survivorship but reproductive needs as well.

capacity 능력, 용량
requirement 요구 조건, 필요 요소

일부의 경우, 번식기에만 특별히 요구되는 조건들 때문에 생존을 위한 최고의 기회를 제공하는 서식지가 최고의 번식 능력을 가능하게 해주는 서식지와 동일한 곳이 아닐 수도 있다.
(③) In some cases, the habitat that provides the best opportunity for survival may not be the same habitat as the one that provides for highest reproductive capacity because of requirements specific to the reproductive period.

resident 거주하는
confronted 직면한
fitness 적합성
nonbreeding 비번식의
remaining 남다
habitat 서식지

따라서 많은 텃새 종의 개체들은 다산에 유리한 번식지를 장악하는 것이 갖는 합목적성에서 오는 이득과 마주하면, 가장 높은 번식 성공이 일어나는 특정 서식지에 머물러 있음으로써 더 낮은 비번식기 생존율의 형태로 대가의 균형을 맞추도록 강요당할 수도 있다.
(Thus, individuals of many resident species, confronted with the fitness benefits of control over a productive breeding site, may be forced to balance costs in the form of lower nonbreeding survivorship by remaining in the specific habitat where highest breeding success occurs.)

migrant 이동하는, 철새의
*optimal 최적의
nonbreeding 번식하지 않는

그러나 철새들은 번식기가 아닌 동안에는 생존을 위한 최적의 서식지를, 번식기 동안에는 번식을 위한 최적의 서식지를 자유롭게 선택한다.
(④) Migrants, however, are free to choose the optimal habitat for survival during the nonbreeding season and for reproduction during the breeding season.

opposed to ~와 대조적으로, 반대되는
closely related 밀접하게 관련된

이와 같이 서로 다른 시기 동안의 서식지 선택은, 심지어 생물학적으로 밀접하게 관련이 있는 종들 사이에서조차도, 텃새들과는 달리 철새들에게 있어서 상당히 다를 수 있다.
(⑤) Thus, habitat selection during these different periods can be quite different for migrants as opposed to residents, even among closely related species.

···

38. 글의 흐름으로 보아, 주어진 문장이 들어가기에 가장 적절한 곳을 고르시오.
Thus, individuals of many resident species, confronted with the fitness benefits of control over a productive breeding site, may be forced to balance costs in the form of lower nonbreeding survivorship by remaining in the specific habitat where highest breeding success occurs.

Resident-bird habitat selection is seemingly a straightforward process in which a young dispersing individual moves until it finds a place where it can compete successfully to satisfy its needs. (①) Initially, these needs include only food and shelter. (②) However, eventually,the young must locate, identify, and settle in a habitat that satisfies not only survivorship but reproductive needs as well. (③) In some cases, the habitat that provides the best opportunity for survival may not be the same habitat as the one that provides for highest reproductive capacity because of requirements specific to the reproductive period. (④) Migrants, however, are free to choose the optimal habitat for survival during the nonbreeding season and for reproduction during the breeding season. (⑤) Thus, habitat selection during these different periods can be quite different for migrants as opposed to residents, even among closely related species.

* disperse: 흩어지다 * optimal: 최적의

정답 ④

④의 앞 문장에서 가장 최적의 서식지와 최적의 번식지가 다를 수 있다는 내용이 나왔으므로, 텃새는 번식에 가장 적합한 장소에 사는 대신 서식에 불리한 대가를 치르게 된다는 내용의 주어진 문장이 ④에 들어가는 것이 가장 적절하다. 주어진 문장은 ④의 뒤 문장에서 텃새와는 달리 철새는 서식 최적지와 번식 최적지를 오간다는 내용과도 잘 이어진다.

물 분자는 증발로 인해 대기 중을 순환한다. 물 분자가 대기 중 높은 곳으로 올라가면, 태양광의 영향을 받아 수소와 산소라는 화학적 원소로 분해될 수 있다. 훨씬 무거운 산소는 대기 중에 남거나 지구 표면에 붙잡히는 반면, 수소는 너무 가벼워서 지구의 중력이 이를 붙잡지 못하고 우주로 빠져나간다. 대기 중에 수소가 우주로 빠져나가는 과정은 자유 산소가 거의 없을 때까지 계속되었을 것이다. 그러나 지구 표면에 있는 대부분의 철과 같은 물질들이 자유 산소와 결합하면서 대기 중에 자유 산소가 충분히 나타나기 시작했다. 자유 산소가 나타나자마자, 그것은 대부분의 자유 수소를 잡아 물 분자를 다시 형성하여 수소의 손실을 줄였다. 시간이 지나면서 이 과정은 지구에 물을 유지하는 데 도움을 주었고, 동시에 대기 중 산소의 등장에도 기여했다.

molecule 분자
evaporation 증발

물 분자는 증발의 결과로 대기를 순환한다.
Water molecules circulate through the atmosphere as a result of evaporation.

atmosphere 대기, 공기
split up into ~으로 분해[분리]되다
constituent 구성 요소, 성분
under the influence of ~의 영향을 받아

물 분자가 대기 중으로 높이 상승하면, 그것은 햇빛의 영향을 받아 그것을 구성하는 화학 원소인 수소와 산소로 분해될 수도 있다.
(①) As water molecules rise high up in the atmosphere, they may split up into their constituent chemical elements, hydrogen and oxygen, under the influence of sunlight.

whereas 반면에
capture 포획하다, 붙잡다
escape 빠져나가다, 탈출하다
retain 유지하다, 보존하다

훨씬 더 무거운 산소가 대기 중에 남아 있거나 지구 표면에 붙들리는 반면에, 수소는 우주로 빠져나가는 경향이 있는데, 수소가 너무 가벼워서 지구 중력이 그것을 붙잡아 둘 수 없기 때문이다.
(②) Whereas the much heavier oxygen either remains in the atmosphere or is captured on the Earth's surface, the hydrogen tends to escape into space, because it is so light that Earth's gravity cannot retain it.

free oxygen 유리 산소
cosmos 우주
unhindered 방해받지 않은, 자유로운

수소가 우주로 빠져나가기 전에 수소를 붙잡아 둘 수 있는 유리 산소가 대기 중에 거의 없거나 전혀 없는 한, 이 과정은 방해받지 않고 계속되었을 것이다.
(③) As long as there was little or no free oxygen in the atmosphere that could capture hydrogen before it escaped into the cosmos, this process would have continued unhindered.

material 물질, 재료
surface 표면
combine 결합하다, 합쳐지다
sizable 사이저블 상당한, 꽤 많은
quantity 양, 수량

그러나 대부분이 철인 지구 표면의 이용 가능한 모든 물질이 유리 산소와 결합한 후, 그것은 대기 중에 꽤 많은 양으로 모습을 드러내기 시작했다.
(However, after all the available materials on the Earth's surface, mostly iron, had combined with the free oxygen, it began to appear in the atmosphere in sizable quantities.)

form 형성하다, 만들다

이런 일이 일어나자마자 유리 산소는 다시 물 분자를 형성함으로써 대부분의 유리 수소를 붙들어 두어 그 결과 수소 손실을 늦추었을 것이다.
(④) As soon as this happened, the free oxygen would have captured most of the free hydrogen by forming water molecules again, thus slowing down the loss of hydrogen.

over the course of time 시간이 흐르면서
help to ~하는 데 도움을 주다
emergence 출현, 발생

시간이 지남에 따라, 이 과정은 지구에 물을 보유하는 데 도움을 주었을 것이고, 동시에 대기 중의 산소 발생에도 기여했다.
(⑤) Over the course of time, this process would have helped to retain water on Earth, while it also contributed to the emergence of oxygen in the atmosphere.

38. 글의 흐름으로 보아, 주어진 문장이 들어가기에 가장 적절한 곳을 고르시오.

However, after all the available materials on the Earth's surface, mostly iron, had combined with the free oxygen, it began to appear in the atmosphere in sizable quantities.

Water molecules circulate through the atmosphere as a result of evaporation. (①) As water molecules rise high up in the atmosphere, they may split up into their constituent chemical elements, hydrogen and oxygen, under the influence of sunlight. (②) Whereas the much heavier oxygen either remains in the atmosphere or is captured on the Earth's surface, the hydrogen tends to escape into space, because it is so light that Earth's gravity cannot retain it. (③) As long as there was little or no free oxygen in the atmosphere that could capture hydrogen before it escaped into the cosmos, this process would have continued unhindered. (④) As soon as this happened, the free oxygen would have captured most of the free hydrogen by forming water molecules again, thus slowing down the loss of hydrogen. (⑤) Over the course of time, this process would have helped to retain water on Earth, while it also contributed to the emergence of oxygen in the atmosphere.

정답 ④

주어진 문장은 "그러나 지구 표면의 모든 사용 가능한 물질, 주로 철이 자유 산소와 결합한 후에야, 대기 중에 상당한 양의 산소가 나타나기 시작했다."라는 의미이다. 이 문장은 자유 산소가 대기 중에 축적되기 시작한 시점을 강조하고 있으며, 산소가 수소를 포획하여 수분을 형성하는 과정과 관련이 있다.
④번 문장은 "이 일이 발생하자마자, 자유 산소가 대부분의 자유 수소를 다시 물 분자로 형성함으로써 포획했고, 따라서 수소의 손실을 늦추었다."라고 설명하고 있다. 이는 주어진 문장에서 언급된 "산소가 대기 중에 축적되기 시작한 시점"과 직접 연결되므로, 주어진 문장이 가장 적절하게 들어갈 곳은 ④번 이다.

wind direction 풍향
measure 측정하다
*vane 풍향계

풍향은 보통 단순한 풍향계를 사용하여 측정한다.
Wind direction is usually measured through the use of a simple vane.

paddle 날개, 노
mount 장착하다, 설치하다
*spindle 축, 회전축

이것은 단순히 회전축에 고정된 일종의 노 모양의 물체로,
(①) This is simply a paddle of some sort mounted on a spindle;

catch the wind 바람을 받다
obstruction 방해, 장애물

바람을 받으면 바람이 방해받지 않고 지나가도록 돌아간다.
when it catches the wind, it turns so that the wind passes by without obstruction.

breezy 바람이 부는
variation 변화, 변동

방향은 기록되지만, 만약 여러분이 산들바람이 부는 날에 바람 풍향계를 볼 기회가 있다면, 여러분은 바람의 흐름 방향에 많은, 그야말로 많은 변화가 있다는 것을 보게 될 것이다!
(②) The direction is recorded, but if you ever have a chance to watch a wind vane on a breezy day, you will notice that there is a lot of variation in the direction of wind flow — a lot!

virtually 사실상, 거의

때때로 바람은 1~2분 이내에 거의 모든 방향에서 불어올 수 있다.
(③) Sometimes the wind can blow from virtually every direction within a minute or two.

make sense 이해하다, 의미를 찾다
calculate 계산하다

이것을 어느 정도 이해하기 위해, 때때로 한 시간에 걸친 평균적인 풍향을 계산하거나, 때때로 그 한 시간 동안 바람이 가장 많이 불어온 방향을 기록한다.
(In order to make some sense of this, an average wind direction over an hour is sometimes calculated, or sometimes the direction that the wind blew from the most during the hour is recorded.)

generalization 일반화, 개괄적 설명

어느 쪽이든, 그것은 일반화된 것이고, 데이터에는 많은 변화가 있을 수 있다는 것을 기억하는 것이 중요하다.
(④) Either way, it is a generalization, and it's important to remember that there can be a lot of variation in the data.

weather station 기상 관측소
indication 표시, 징후
prevail 만연하다, 지배적이다
some distance 일정 거리 떨어진

기상 관측소에서 기록되는 데이터는 한 지역에서의 우세한 상태를 나타내지만 기상 관측소로부터 어느 정도 떨어진 지형의 상태와 정확하게 같지는 않을 것임을 기억하는 것도 중요하다.
(⑤) It's also important to remember that the data recorded at a weather station give an indication of conditions prevailing in an area but will not be exactly the same as the conditions at a landscape some distance from the weather station.

....

38. 글의 흐름으로 보아, 주어진 문장이 들어가기에 가장 적절한 곳을 고르시오.
In order to make some sense of this, an average wind direction over an hour is sometimes calculated, or sometimes the direction that the wind blew from the most during the hour is recorded.

Wind direction is usually measured through the use of a simple vane. (①) This is simply a paddle of some sort mounted on a spindle; when it catches the wind, it turns so that the wind passes by without obstruction. (②) The direction is recorded, but if you ever have a chance to watch a wind vane on a breezy day, you will notice that there is a lot of variation in the direction of wind flow — a lot! (③) Sometimes the wind can blow from virtually every direction within a minute or two. (④) Either way, it is a generalization, and it's important to remember that there can be a lot of variation in the data. (⑤) It's also important to remember that the data recorded at a weather station give an indication of conditions prevailing in an area but will not be exactly the same as the conditions at a landscape some distance from the weather station.

* vane 풍향계   * spindle 회전축

정답 ④

주어진 문장은 "이것을 이해하기 위해, 때때로 한 시간 동안의 평균 풍향이 계산되거나, 그 시간 동안 바람이 가장 많이 불어온 방향이 기록된다."라는 의미이다. 이는 바람의 방향이 시시각각 변하기 때문에 이를 보다 의미 있는 데이터로 만들기 위한 방법을 설명하는 내용이다.

③번 문장은 "때때로 바람은 1~2분 안에 사실상 모든 방향에서 불 수 있다."라고 설명하고 있어, 바람의 방향이 일정하지 않다는 점을 강조한다. 주어진 문장은 이러한 불규칙성을 다루기 위한 방법을 설명하므로, 자연스럽게 ③번 문장 다음에 배치되는 것이 가장 적절하다. 정답은 ④번

피의자   범죄를 저지른 혐의를 받는 사람
피고인   재판을 받는 사람, 범죄를 저지른 혐의로 법원에 서 있는 사람
용의자   범죄와 관련된 혐의를 받고 있으나 아직 범죄가 확정되지 않은 사람

사법   법률과 관련된 업무, 법을 다루는 제도
사법부   법을 해석하고 적용하는 기관으로 주로 법원으로 구성, 법률에 따라 판결을 내리는 역할을 한다.

기소   범죄 혐의로 법원에 사건을 송치하는 일
검찰   범죄를 수사하고 기소하는 기관, 검사의 집단

범죄 사법의 실행에서 인간적인 대우의 원칙은 중요한 제약을 가진다. 범죄 사법은 국가가 운영하는 과정으로, 그 과정에 휘말린 사람은 큰 해를 입을 위험이 있다. 용의자와 피고인은 가장 큰 위험에 처해 있다. 절차적 규칙은 용의자에게 법적 조언과 지원을 제공하여 법정에서 자신의 사건을 준비하고 제시할 수 있도록 한다. 증거 규칙은 피고인에게 공정한 기회를 제공하여 그들이 기소된 내용을 답변할 수 있게 하고, 동시에 그들이 침묵할 권리를 존중하여 변호인을 통해 기소를 입증하도록 한다. 이와 다른 범죄 절차 및 증거 규칙은 피고인에게 사고하고 느끼는 인간으로서 존중과 배려를 제공하며, 그들이 자신의 복지에 직접적이고 심각한 영향을 미칠 수 있는 절차에 적극적으로 참여할 기회를 가질 자격이 있음을 인정한다.

humane 인간적인, 인도적인
exert 행사하다, 가하다
constraint 제한, 제약
administration 집행, 관리
criminal justice 형사 사법
state-run 국가 운영의
caught up in ~에 휘말리다
*snare 덫, 올가미

인도적 대우의 원칙은 형사법 집행에 중요한 제약을 가하는데, 이는 그 덫에 걸리는 누구에게나 매우 큰 피해를 줄 가능성을 가진 국가 운영 과정이다.
The principle of humane treatment exerts an important constraint on the administration of criminal justice, a state-run process which has the potential to do very great harm to anybody who becomes caught up in its snares.

suspect 용의자, 의심하다
accused 피고, 고소당한 사람
jeopardy 제펄디 위험, 위기

가장 명백히 위험에 처해 있는 자들은 피의자와 피고인이다.
Suspects and the accused are the ones most obviously in jeopardy.

procedural 프로씨쥬럴 절차적인
legal 법률의, 합법적인
assistance 도움, 지원
present 제출하다, 발표하다
court 법정, 법원

소송 절차 규정은 논거를 준비해서 법정에서 개진하기 위한 법적 조언과 지원을 제공함으로써 피의자에 대한 인도적 대우에 공헌한다.
Procedural rules contribute to suspects' humane treatment by providing them with legal advice and assistance to prepare and present their cases in court.

evidence 증거
afford 제공하다, 허용하다
charge 혐의, 기소
whilst 와일스트 ~하는 동안에, 반면에
counsel 변호인, 상담
*prosecution 프로씨큐션 기소, 검찰 측
proof 증명, 입증하다

증거 규정은 피고인이 잠자코 있기로 선택하고 검찰 측이 입증하도록 한다면 묵비권을 행사할 권리를 존중해 주면서 동시에 피고인에게 자신에 대한 혐의에 대응할 공정한 기회를 제공함으로써 유사한 기능을 수행한다.
Rules of evidence perform a similar function by affording accused persons fair opportunity to answer the charges against them, whilst at the same time respecting their right to remain silent if they choose to keep their counsel and put the prosecution to proof.

procedure 절차, 과정
subject 대상, 주체
entitled to ~할 자격이 있는
play a part 역할을 하다
catastrophic 재앙적인, 치명적인
welfare 복지, 안녕

이런 것들과 형사상의 증거와 소송 절차에 관한 다른 규정들은 피고인을 공적인 배려와 존중의 대상이 되는, 생각하고, 느끼고, 인간적인 대상으로 대우하는데, 그들은 자신의 안녕에 직접적이고도 어쩌면 파멸적일 수 있는 영향력을 지닌 소송 절차에서 적극적인 역할을 할 수 있는 기회를 제공받을 권리를 부여받게 된다.
These and other rules of criminal evidence and procedure treat the accused as thinking, feeling, human subjects of official concern and respect, who are entitled to be given the opportunity to play an active part in procedures with a direct and possibly catastrophic impact on their welfare.

....

23. 다음 글의 주제로 가장 적절한 것은?
The principle of humane treatment exerts an important constraint on the administration of criminal justice, a state-run process which has the potential to do very great harm to anybody who becomes caught up in its snares. Suspects and the accused are the ones most obviously in jeopardy. Procedural rules contribute to suspects' humane treatment by providing them with legal advice and assistance to prepare and present their cases in court. Rules of evidence perform a similar function by affording accused persons fair opportunity to answer the charges against them, whilst at the same time respecting their right to remain silent if they choose to keep their counsel and put the prosecution to proof. These and other rules of criminal evidence and procedure treat the accused as thinking, feeling, human subjects of official concern and respect, who are entitled to be given the opportunity to play an active part in procedures with a direct and possibly catastrophic impact on their welfare.
＊ snare 덫 ＊ prosecution 검찰 측

① correlations between crime rates and social welfare
② efforts to revise outdated criminal justice procedures
③ expanding government roles in controlling the crime rate
④ changing the definition of humane treatment in modern criminal justice
⑤ humane treatment of suspects and the accused in the criminal justice system

정답 ⑤

형사 사법 제도에서 용의자와 피고인에 대한 인도적인 대우
humane treatment of suspects and the accused in the criminal justice system

본문은 형사 사법 절차에서 피의자와 피고인의 인권을 보호하는 것이 중요한 제약 요인으로 작용한다는 점을 강조하고 있다. 절차적 규칙과 증거법이 피고인의 인권을 보호하고 공정한 기회를 제공하며, 이들을 존중하는 방식으로 다뤄야 한다는 내용이 중심이다. 이는 "형사 사법 체계에서 피의자와 피고인의 인도적 처우"를 주제로 한 것으로 볼 수 있다.

① 범죄율과 사회 복지 간의 상관 관계
correlations between crime rates and social welfare
② 구식 형사 사법 절차를 개정하려는 노력
efforts to revise outdated criminal justice procedures
③ 범죄율 통제에서 정부의 역할 확대
expanding government roles in controlling the crime rate
④ 현대 형사 사법에서 인도적인 대우의 정의 변화
changing the definition of humane treatment in modern criminal justice

자신이 신뢰받지 못한다는 인식은 자기 반성을 위한 중요한 동기를 제공할 수 있다. 예를 들어, 직장에서 동료들에게 업무에 대한 공동 책임을 신뢰받지 못한다고 느끼는 직원은 자신이 다른 사람들을 실망시킨 부분이나 이전의 약속을 지키지 못한 부분을 되돌아볼 수 있다. 다른 사람들이 그녀를 신뢰하지 않는 것은 그녀가 자신의 의무를 다해 신뢰를 받을 자격을 얻도록 동기를 부여할 수 있다. 하지만 신뢰할 수 있고 의존할 수 있는 사람이 되려는 진심 어린 노력에도 불구하고 신뢰받지 못하면 혼란스러울 수 있고, 그로 인해 자신에 대한 의문을 가지며 자신을 불신하게 될 수 있다. 예를 들어, 밤에 외출할 때 부모가 의심스럽고 신뢰하지 않는다면, 규칙을 어기지 않고 계획을 솔직하게 말했음에도 불구하고, 부모의 지속적인 불신은 그녀의 도덕적인 정체성을 약화시킬 수 있다.

awareness 인식, 자각

distrust 불신, 의심

incentive 동기, 자극

self-reflection 자기 반성, 성찰

때로는 신임을 얻지 못한다는 인식이 자기 성찰에 필요한 동기를 제공할 수 있다.
Sometimes the awareness that one is distrusted can provide the necessary incentive for self-reflection.

employee 직원, 근로자

co-worker 동료

responsibility 책임, 의무

upon reflection 곰곰이 생각해 본 후

consistently 지속적으로, 일관되게

let down 실망시키다

follow through 끝까지 수행하다

commitment 약속, 책임

직장에서 자신의 동료들이 공유된 책무를 자신에게 믿고 맡기지 않고 있다는 사실을 깨달은 직원은 성찰을 통해 자신이 지속적으로 다른 사람들을 실망하게 했거나 이전의 약속 들을 이행하지 못했던 분야를 찾아낼 수 있다.
An employee who ① realizes she isn't being trusted by her co-workers with shared responsibilities at work might, upon reflection, identify areas where she has consistently let others down or failed to follow through on previous commitments.

forbid 금지하다, 막다

perform 수행하다, 실행하다

worthy 가치 있는, 자격이 있는

그러면 그녀에 대한 다른 사람들의 불신은, 그녀가 그들의 신임을 받을 만한 자격이 더 생기게 해주는 방식으로 그녀가 직무의 자기 몫을 수행하지 못하게 할(→하도록 동기를 부여할) 수 있다.
Others' distrust of her might then ② forbid (→motivate) her to perform her share of the duties in a way that makes her more worthy of their trust.

trustworthy 신뢰할 수 있는
dependable 신뢰할 만한, 믿을 수 있는
disorienting 디스오리엔팅 방향 감각을 잃게 하는, 혼란스럽게 하는
doubt 의심하다, 불확실하게 여기다
perception 인식, 지각

하지만 신뢰할 만하고 믿을 만한 사람이 되려는 노력을 성실하게 하는 사람에 대한 불신은 혼란스럽게 할 수 있고, 그녀로 하여금 자신의 인식을 의심하고 자신을 불신하게 할 수 있다.
But distrust of one who is ③ sincere in her efforts to be a trustworthy and dependable person can be disorienting and might cause her to doubt her own perceptions and to distrust herself.

suspicious 의심 많은, 수상쩍어하는
distrustful 불신하는, 의심하는

예를 들어 밤에 외출할 때 의심하고 믿지 않는 부모를 가진 십 대 소녀를 생각해 보라.
Consider, for instance, a teenager whose parents are ④ suspicious and distrustful when she goes out at night;

*forthright 폴쓰라이트 솔직한, 정직한
agreed-upon 합의된, 약속된
respectable 존경할 만한, 훌륭한
moral 도덕적인
undermine 약화시키다, 손상시키다
*pervasive 펄베이시브 만연한, 널리 퍼진
deceit 속임수, 기만
betrayal 배신, 배반

비록 그녀가 자신의 계획에 대해 솔직해 왔고 합의된 규칙은 어떤 것도 어기지 않았을지라도, 존경할 만한 도덕적 주체로서의 그녀의 정체성은 속임수와 배신을 예상하는 널리 스며 있는 부모의 태도에 의해 손상된다.
even if she has been forthright about her plans and is not ⑤ breaking any agreed-upon rules, her identity as a respectable moral subject is undermined by a pervasive parental attitude that expects deceit and betrayal.

30. 다음 글의 밑줄 친 부분 중, 문맥상 낱말의 쓰임이 적절하지 않은 것은?

Sometimes the awareness that one is distrusted can provide the necessary incentive for self-reflection. An employee who ① realizes she isn't being trusted by her co-workers with shared responsibilities at work might, upon reflection, identify areas where she has consistently let others down or failed to follow through on previous commitments. Others' distrust of her might then ② forbid her to perform her share of the duties in a way that makes her more worthy of their trust. But distrust of one who is ③ sincere in her efforts to be a trustworthy and dependable person can be disorienting and might cause her to doubt her own perceptions and to distrust herself. Consider, for instance, a teenager whose parents are ④ suspicious and distrustful when she goes out at night; even if she has been forthright about her plans and is not ⑤ breaking any agreed-upon rules, her identity as a respectable moral subject is undermined by a pervasive parental attitude that expects deceit and betrayal.

* forthright 솔직한, 거리낌 없는 * pervasive 널리 스며 있는

정답 ②

자신에 대한 타인의 불신은 자기 성찰로 이어져 타인의 신임을 받을 만한 자격이 더 생기도록 행동하게 한다고 했으므로, ②의 forbid를 motivate 로 바꾸어야 한다.

optimally 최적으로, 가장 적절하게

나무가 함께 자랄 때는 각 나무가 가능한 최고의 나무로 성장할 수 있도록 영양분과 물이 그것들 모두 사이에서 최적으로 분배된다.
When trees grow together, nutrients and water can be optimally divided among them all so that each tree can grow into the best tree it can be.

individual 개별적인, 개체
competition 경쟁, 경쟁자
*bereft 벌레프트 상실한, 빼앗긴

만약 여러분이 경쟁자로 여겨지는 나무를 제거하여 개별 나무를 '도와주면' 나머지 나무를 잃게 된다.
If you "help" individual trees by getting rid of their supposed competition, the remaining trees are bereft.

*stump 그루터기

그것들은 그루터기 외에는 무엇도 남아있지 않기 때문에 이웃 나무들에 메시지를 보내지만, 소용이 없다.
They send messages out to their neighbors unsuccessfully, because nothing remains but stumps.

productivity 생산성

이제 모든 나무가 그것 나름대로 자라 생산성에 큰 차이가 생긴다.
Every tree now grows on its own, giving rise to great differences in productivity.

*photosynthesize 광합성을 하다
positively 확실히, 분명히
trunk 나무 줄기

어떤 개체들은 당분이 줄기를 따라 확연히 흘러넘칠 때까지 미친 듯이 광합성을 한다.
(①) Some individuals photosynthesize like mad until sugar positively bubbles along their trunk.

그 결과, 그것들은 건강하고 더 잘 자라지만 특별히 오래 살지는 못한다.
(As a result, they are fit and grow better, but they aren't particularly long-lived.)

surround 둘러싸다, 에워싸다

이는 나무는 자신을 둘러싸고 있는 숲만큼만 강할 수 있기 때문이다.
(②) This is because a tree can be only as strong as the forest that surrounds it.

그리고 지금 숲에는 많은 패자가 있다.
(③) And there are now a lot of losers in the forest.

한때는 강한 구성원들의 지원을 받았을 약한 구성원들이 갑자기 뒤처진다.
(④) Weaker members, who would once have been supported by the stronger ones, suddenly fall behind.

decline 감소, 쇠퇴
passing sickness 일시적인 병
genetic makeup 유전적 구성
fall prey to ~의 희생이 되다
fungi 균류, 곰팡이

그것들의 쇠락 원인이 위치와 영양분 부족이든, 일시적인 질병이든, 혹은 유전적 구성이든, 이제 그것들은 곤충과 균류의 먹이가 된다.
(⑤) Whether the reason for their decline is their location and lack of nutrients, a passing sickness, or genetic makeup, they now fall prey to insects and fungi.

....

39. 글의 흐름으로 보아, 주어진 문장이 들어가기에 가장 적절한 곳을 고르시오.
As a result, they are fit and grow better, but they aren't particularly long-lived.

 When trees grow together, nutrients and water can be optimally divided among them all so that each tree can grow into the best tree it can be. If you "help" individual trees by getting rid of their supposed competition, the remaining trees are bereft. They send messages out to their neighbors unsuccessfully, because nothing remains but stumps. Every tree now grows on its own, giving rise to great differences in productivity. (①) Some individuals photosynthesize

like mad until sugar positively bubbles along their trunk. (②) This is because a tree can be only as strong as the forest that surrounds it. (③) And there are now a lot of losers in the forest. (④) Weaker members, who would once have been supported by the stronger ones, suddenly fall behind. (⑤) Whether the reason for their decline is their location and lack of nutrients, a passing sickness, or genetic makeup, they now fall prey to insects and fungi. [3점]
* bereft 잃은 * stump 그루터기 * photosynthesize 광합성하다

정답 ②

주어진 문장은 그것들이 건강하고 더 잘 자라지만 특별히 오래 살지는 못한다고 했으므로 건강하고 더 잘 자랄 수 있는 상황이 있는 문장 다음에, 그리고 특별히 오래 살지는 못하는 이유를 설명하는 문장 앞에 들어가야 한다. ② 앞에서 어떤 개체는 미친 듯이 광합성을 하여 당분이 줄기를 따라 확연히 흘러넘친다고 했고, ② 뒤에서는 나무들이 오래 살지 못하는 이유를 설명하고 있으므로, 주어진 문장이 들어가기에 가장 적절한 곳은 ②이다.

Farrington Wellness Center에 오신 것을 환영합니다.
Welcome to the Farrington Wellness Center.

저는 Hannah Dawson 박사입니다.
I'm Dr. Hannah Dawson.

아시다시피 잠은 많은 요인에 의해 영향을 받습니다.
As you know, sleep is affected by many factors.

research 연구, 조사

연구에 의하면, 그러한 요인 중 하나가 음식입니다. 어떤 음식은 수면에 좋습니다.
According to research, one such factor is food. Some foods are good for sleep.

loaded with ~이 풍부한
magnesium 마그네슘
promote 촉진하다, 증진하다

예를 들어 바나나에는 마그네슘이 많이 들어있는데, 이것은 근육의 긴장을 완화하는 데 도움을 줌으로써 수면을 촉진하는 미네랄입니다.
For example, bananas are loaded with magnesium, a mineral that promotes sleep by helping relax your muscles.

또 다른 좋은 식품은 우유입니다.
Another good food is milk.

dairy product 유제품
hormone 호르몬
regulate 조절하다, 조정하다

유제품은 신체가 수면을 조절하는 데 도움을 주는 호르몬을 만드는 것을 도와줍니다.
Dairy products help the body make a hormone that helps regulate sleep.

on the other hand 반면에
avoid 피하다, 삼가다

반면에, 특히 잠자리에 들기 전에 피해야 할 많은 음식이 있습니다.
On the other hand, there are many foods to avoid, especially before bed.

digest 소화하다

기름진 음식은 소화에 오랜 시간이 걸리고, 이는 수면의 질에 해를 끼치기 때문에 늦은 밤에 프렌치프라이는 주문하지 마시기 바랍니다.
Don't order French fries late at night because fatty foods take long to digest, which harms the quality of your sleep.

put away 치우다, 멀리하다

또한, 잠자리에 들기 전에는 사탕도 치워놓으시기 바랍니다.
Also, put away candies before bed.

sugary 설탕이 든, 단
blood sugar 혈당

단 음식은 혈당을 높이기 때문에 여러분이 깨어있게 할 수 있습니다.
Sugary foods can keep you awake because they increase your blood sugar.

따라서 잠자는 데 문제를 겪고 계시다면, 좋은 잠은 여러분이 무엇을 먹느냐에 달려 있으므로 여러분의 음식을 살펴보시기 바랍니다.
So if you're having problems sleeping, take a look at your diet because good sleep depends on what you eat.

conduct 수행하다, 실행하다
topic 주제, 화제

이제 이 주제에 관해 제가 실시한 연구에서 나온 일부 정보를 소개해 드리겠습니다.
Now, I'll present some information from studies I've conducted on this topic.

16. 여자가 하는 말의 주제로 가장 적절한 것은?

Welcome to the Farrington Wellness Center. I'm Dr. Hannah Dawson. As you know, sleep is affected by many factors. According to research, one such factor is food. Some foods are good for sleep. For example, bananas are loaded with magnesium, a mineral that promotes sleep by helping relax your muscles. Another good food is milk. Dairy products help the body make a hormone that helps regulate sleep. On the other hand, there are many foods to avoid, especially before bed. Don't order French fries late at night because fatty foods take long to digest, which harms the quality of your sleep. Also, put away candies before bed. Sugary foods can keep you awake because they increase your blood sugar. So if you're having problems sleeping, take a look at your diet because good sleep depends on what you eat. Now, I'll present some information from studies I've conducted on this topic.

① effects of food on sleep
② causes of eating disorders
③ ways to improve digestion
④ what not to eat to lose weight
⑤ importance of a balanced diet for health

정답 ①

잠을 잘 자게 하는 데 도움이 되는 음식과 그렇지 못한 음식을 소개하고 있는 내용이므로, 여자가 하는 말의 주제로 가장 적절한 것은 ① '음식이 수면에 미치는 영향' 이다.

② 식이 장애의 원인
causes of eating disorders
③ 소화를 개선하는 방법
ways to improve digestion
④ 체중을 줄이기 위해 먹지 말아야 할 것
what not to eat to lose weight
⑤ 건강을 위한 균형 잡힌 식사의 중요성
importance of a balanced diet for health

DAY 6

buddy 친구, 동료
Big Foot 빅풋 (전설 속의 거대한 유인원)

어느 날 밤 한 친구와 나는 그 Big Foot을 찾으러 가기로 결심했다.
One night a buddy and I decided we were going to go find that Big Foot.

set off 출발하다, 떠나다
head toward ~을 향해 가다

우리는 내 오래된 트럭을 타고 가장 높은 언덕을 향해 들판을 가로질러 출발했다.
We were in my old truck and we set off across the fields heading toward the tallest hill.

trail 작은 길, 오솔길

들판은 거칠었고, 따라갈 가장 좁은 길만이 있었다.
The fields were rough, with only the slightest trail to follow.

trench 도랑, 참호

길을 따라 들판에 파인 작은 구덩이들이 있었다.
Along the way there were small trenches dug in the fields.

나는 왜 그런지 전혀 알 수가 없었다.
I never figured out why.

우리가 언덕 꼭대기에 점점 가까워질수록,
As we got closer and closer to the top of the hill,

fearless 겁이 없는, 대담한

나는 실제로 겁이 나기 시작했고, 그것은 좀 드문 일이었는데, 왜냐하면 그 나이 때 나는 상당히 겁이 없었기 때문이었다.
I was actually becoming scared, which was kind of rare, because at that age I was pretty fearless.

thump 쿵 소리, 둔탁한 충격음

우리가 언덕 꼭대기에 도착했을 바로 그때, 크게 쿵 하는 소리가 났다!
As we got to the top of the hill, there was a loud thump!

sink down 가라앉다, 내려앉다
bed (트럭의) 짐칸

어떤 무거운 것이 (트럭 뒤편) 적재함에 뛰어든 것처럼 내 트럭이 내려앉았다.
My truck sunk down like something heavy had just jumped in the bed.

terrified 겁에 질린, 무서운

우리는 너무 무서워서 뒤를 볼 수가 없었다.
We were too terrified to look in the back.

panic 공황 상태에 빠지다, 당황하다
throw into reverse 후진 기어를 넣다
back down 후진하다, 물러나다

나는 공포에 사로잡혔고 트럭을 후진시켜 언덕 아래로 몰고 가기로 결심했다.
I panicked and decided to throw the truck into reverse and back down the hill.

roar 포효, 굉음

내가 그렇게 했을 때, 또 다른 쿵 하는 소리가 났고 그때 전에 전혀 들어본 적이 없는 엄청난 포효소리가 났다.
As I did so, there was another thump and a loud roar now came out like I'd never, ever heard before.

....

19. 다음 글에 나타난 'I'의 심경으로 가장 적절한 것은?
 One night a buddy and I decided we were going to go find that Big Foot. We were in my old truck and we set off across the fields heading toward the tallest hill. The fields were rough, with only the slightest trail to follow. Along the way there were small trenches dug in the fields. I never figured out why. As we got closer and closer to the top of the hill, I was

actually becoming scared, which was kind of rare, because at that age I was pretty fearless. As we got to the top of the hill, there was a loud thump! My truck sunk down like something heavy had just jumped in the bed. We were too terrified to look in the back. I panicked and decided to throw the truck into reverse and back down the hill. As I did so, there was another thump and a loud roar now came out like I'd never, ever heard before.

① relieved and relaxed
② pleased and delighted
③ bored and indifferent
④ alarmed and frightened
⑤ dissatisfied and angry

정답 ④

'I'는 친구와 함께 Big Foot을 찾으러 갔다가, 예상치 못한 소리와 충격을 경험하며 극도의 두려움을 느끼고 있다. 특히 "I was actually becoming scared", "We were too terrified to look in the back", "I panicked" 등의 표현에서 공포와 경악이 강조되고 있다. 따라서 'I'의 심경으로 가장 적절한 것은 "놀라고 두려운"이라는 의미의 ④ alarmed and frightened이다.

① 안도하고 편안한
relieved and relaxed
② 기쁘고 즐거운
pleased and delighted
③ 지루하고 무관심한
bored and indifferent
④ 놀라고 두려운
alarmed and frightened
⑤ 불만족하고 화난
dissatisfied and angry

sensory 감각의
specific 특정한, 구체적인
*satiety 포만감, 만족감
define 정의하다, 규정하다
appetite 식욕
subjective 주관적인
*hedonics 헤도닉스 쾌락성, 기호성

감각 특정적 포만이란 먹지 않은 음식이 주는 쾌락에는 변화가 거의 없는 가운데 식욕, 즉 먹고 있는 음식에 대한 주관적 애호가 감소하는 것으로 정의된다.
Sensory-specific satiety is defined as a decrease in appetite, or the subjective liking for the food that is consumed, with little change in the hedonics of uneaten food.

감각 특정적 포만의 결과로, 사람들은 다양한 종류의 음식을 먹을 때, 과식하는 경향이 있다.
As a result of sensory-specific satiety, when people consume a variety of foods, they tend to overeat.

더 다양한 종류의 음식은 사람들로 하여금 그렇지 않을 경우에 먹는 것보다 더 많이 먹게 한다.
A greater variety of food leads people to eat more than they would otherwise.

*sated 세이티드 충분히 만족한, 포만감을 느끼는
separate 별개의, 분리된

그러므로 배가 부르다는 것과 충분히 만족감을 느낀다는 것은 별개의 문제다.
So, being full and feeling sated are separate matters.

motivation 동기, 자극
apparent 분명한, 명백한

식욕, 즉 먹고자 하는 욕구가 회복된다는 것은, 많은 양의 식사를 하고 나서 배가 아주 불러서, 매일의 요구를 충족시킬 추가적인 에너지나 영양소가 필요하지는 않지만, 디저트 카트를 보고 나서 추가적인 칼로리를 더 섭취하기로 결심하는 사람이라면 누구에게나 분명하다.
The recovery of appetite or the motivation to eat is apparent to anyone who has consumed a large meal and is quite full, and does not require additional energy or nutrients to meet their daily needs, but decides to consume additional calories after seeing the dessert cart.

sensory property 감각적 특성

sufficient 충분한, 만족스러운

subject 실험 참가자, 피험자

음식의 감각적 특성의 작은 변화라 하더라도 음식의 섭취를 증가시키기 충분하다.

Small changes in the sensory properties of foods are sufficient to increase food intake.

presented with ~을 제공받은

relative to ~에 비해, 상대적으로

예컨대 서로 다른 모양의 파스타가 제공된 피실험자들은, 단 한 가지 형태의 파스타만을 먹는 피실험자들과 비교하여, 증가된 쾌락 평점과 증가된 에너지 섭취를 보였다.

For example, subjects who were presented with different shapes of pasta showed increased hedonic ratings and increased energy consumption relative to subjects eating only a single shape of pasta.

....

22. 다음 글의 주제로 가장 적절한 것은?

   Sensory-specific satiety is defined as a decrease in appetite, or the subjective liking for the food that is consumed, with little change in the hedonics of uneaten food. As a result of sensory-specific satiety, when people consume a variety of foods, they tend to overeat. A greater variety of food leads people to eat more than they would otherwise. So, being full and feeling sated are separate matters. The recovery of appetite or the motivation to eat is apparent to anyone who has consumed a large meal and is quite full, and does not require additional energy or nutrients to meet their daily needs, but decides to consume additional calories after seeing the dessert cart. Small changes in the sensory properties of foods are sufficient to increase food intake. For example, subjects who were presented with different shapes of pasta showed increased hedonic ratings and increased energy consumption relative to subjects eating only a single shape of pasta.

* satiety: 포만(감) * hedonics: 쾌락 * sated: 충분히 만족한

① necessity of consuming a varied diet in daily life

② reasons for people's rejection of unfamiliar foods

③ changes in people's preference for basic food items

④ impact of food variety on the amount of food people consume

⑤ importance of maintaining food diversity to prevent overeating

정답 ④

음식의 다양성이 사람들이 섭취하는 음식의 양에 미치는 영향
impact of food variety on the amount of food people consume

감각 특정적 포만을 설명한 다음에 그것의 결과로 다양한 음식을 먹게 되면 평소보다 더 많이 먹게 된다는 내용의 글이며, 이 내용은 둘째 문장 (As a result of sensory-specific satiety, when people consume a variety of foods, they tend to overeat.)에 분명히 드러나 있다. 따라서 정답은 ④ '음식의 다양성이 사람들이 섭취하는 음식의 양에 미치는 영향'이다.

① 일상생활에서 다양한 음식을 먹을 필요성
necessity of consuming a varied diet in daily life
② 사람들이 익숙하지 않은 음식을 거부하는 이유
reasons for people's rejection of unfamiliar foods
③ 기본적인 식품에 대한 사람들의 선호의 변화
changes in people's preference for basic food items
⑤ 과식을 막기 위해 음식의 다양성을 유지하는 것의 중요성
importance of maintaining food diversity to prevent overeating

ripening 숙성, 익음
bring about 초래하다, 유발하다
cell wall 세포벽

과일 숙성 과정은 세포벽의 연화, 감미, 색과 맛을 주는 화학 물질의 생산을 가져온다.
The fruit ripening process brings about the softening of cell walls, sweetening and the production of chemicals that give colour and flavour.

plant hormone 식물 호르몬
ethylene 에틸렌

그 과정은 에틸렌이라는 식물 호르몬의 생산에 의해 유도된다.
The process is induced by the production of a plant hormone called ethylene.

grower 재배자, 농부
retailer 소매업자
*deterioration 디테리오레이션 악화, 품질 저하
decay 부패, 썩음
worthless 가치 없는

(C) 재배자와 소매업자에게 문제는 숙성 이후에 때로는 아주 빠르게 품질 저하와 부패가 뒤따라서 제품이 가치 없게 된다는 것이다.
(C) The problem for growers and retailers is that ripening is followed sometimes quite rapidly by deterioration and decay and the product becomes worthless.

transport 운반하다, 수송하다
unripe 덜 익은, 미숙한

그러므로 토마토와 다른 과일은 일반적으로 익지 않았을 때 수확되어 운송된다.
Tomatoes and other fruits are, therefore, usually picked and transported when they are unripe.

(B) 일부 국가에서는 그런 다음 숙성을 유도하기 위해 소비자에게 판매하기 전에 에틸렌을 그것들에 살포한다.
(B) In some countries they are then sprayed with ethylene before sale to the consumer to induce ripening.

그러나 익기 전에 수확된 과일은 식물에서 익은 상태로 수확된 과일보다 맛이 덜하다.
However, fruit picked before it is ripe has less flavour than fruit picked ripe from the plant.

opportunity 기회
biotechnologist 생명공학자

따라서 생명공학자들은 과일의 숙성 및 연화 과정을 지연하는 데 있어서 기회를 엿보았다.
Biotechnologists therefore saw an opportunity in delaying the ripening and softening process in fruit.

interfere with ~을 방해하다, 간섭하다

(A) 에틸렌 생산을 방해하거나 에틸렌에 반응하는 과정을 방해함으로써 숙성을 늦출 수 있다면, 과일은 익어서 맛이 가득 찰 때까지 식물에 붙어 있을 수 있지만, 슈퍼마켓 선반에 도착했을 때에도 여전히 좋은 상태를 유지할 것이다.
(A) If ripening could be slowed down by interfering with ethylene production or with the processes that respond to ethylene, fruit could be left on the plant until it was ripe and full of flavour but would still be in good condition when it arrived at the supermarket shelf.

....

37. 주어진 글 다음에 이어질 글의 순서로 가장 적절한 것을 고르시오.
The fruit ripening process brings about the softening of cell walls, sweetening and the production of chemicals that give colour and flavour. The process is induced by the production of a plant hormone called ethylene.

(A) If ripening could be slowed down by interfering with ethylene production or with the processes that respond to ethylene, fruit could be left on the plant until it was ripe and full of flavour but would still be in good condition when it arrived at the supermarket shelf.
(B) In some countries they are then sprayed with ethylene before sale to the consumer to induce ripening. However, fruit picked before it is ripe has less flavour than fruit picked ripe from the plant. Biotechnologists therefore saw an opportunity in delaying the ripening and softening process in fruit.
(C) The problem for growers and retailers is that ripening is followed sometimes quite rapidly by deterioration and decay and the product becomes worthless. Tomatoes and other fruits are,

therefore, usually picked and transported when they are unripe. [3점]
* deterioration: (품질의) 저하

① (A) ─ (C) ─ (B) 　　② (B) ─ (A) ─ (C)
③ (B) ─ (C) ─ (A) 　　④ (C) ─ (A) ─ (B)
⑤ (C) ─ (B) ─ (A)

정답 ⑤

에틸렌이 과일 숙성 과정을 유도한다는 내용인 주어진 글 다음에 재배자와 소매업자가 과일 품질을 유지하는 데 있어서 겪는 어려움과 임시방편의 해결책을 소개하는 내 용인 (C)가 이어지고 그것이 근본적인 해결책이 될 수 없는 이유와 문제 해결을 위한 생명공학자들의 아이디어를 도입하는 내용인 (B)가 온 후 그 아이디어의 구체적인 내용과 가능성을 언급하는 내용인 (A)가 이어지는 것이 가장 적절한 글의 순서이므로, 정답은 ⑤ '(C)-(B)-(A)'이다.

Eurasia 유라시아
blessed 축복받은, 혜택을 받은
abundance 풍부함, 다량
very 바로 그
orientation 방향, 배치
promote 촉진하다, 장려하다
spread 퍼지다, 확산하다

유라시아는 우연히 생물학적 풍부함으로 축복받았을 뿐만 아니라 그 대륙의 바로 그 방향은 멀리 떨어진 지역 간의 농작물들의 확산을 크게 촉진시켰다.
Not only was Eurasia by chance blessed with biological abundance, but the very <u>orientation</u> of the continent greatly promoted the spread of crops between distant regions.

supercontinent 초대륙
*fragmented 분열된, 조각난
*rift 균열, 갈라진 틈
landmass 대륙 덩어리
stretch 뻗어 있다, 펼쳐지다
latitude 위도

초대륙 판게아가 조각났을 때, 그것은 유라시아를 동서 방향으로 가로지르는 넓은 땅덩어리로 그저 우연히 남겨두게 되었던 갈라진 틈을 따라 분열되었다. 그 전체 대륙은 세계를 둘러싼 거리의 3분의 1보다 더 많이, 하지만 대부분 상대적으로 좁은 위도의 범위 내에서 뻗어있다.
When the supercontinent Pangea fragmented, it was torn apart along rifts that just so happened to leave Eurasia as a broad landmass running in an east-west direction — the entire continent stretches more than a third of the way around the world, but mostly within a relatively narrow range of latitudes.

determine 결정하다, 좌우하다
growing season 성장기, 재배 기간
domesticate 재배하다, 길들이다
transplant 이식하다, 옮겨 심다
adaptation 적응, 조정

바로 그 지구의 위도가 기후와 성장 계절의 길이를 주로 결정하기 때문에, 유라시아의 한 지역에서 재배된 농작물들은 새로운 장소에의 적응에 대한 단지 최소한의 필요만 지닌 채 대륙을 가로질러 이식될 수 있다.
As it is the latitude on the Earth that largely determines the climate and length of the growing

season, crops domesticated in one part of Eurasia can be transplanted across the continent with only minimal need for adaptation to the new locale.

cultivation 경작, 재배
upland 고지대
Mesopotamia 메소포타미아

그러므로 예를 들어 밀 재배는 터키의 고지대로부터 메소포타미아 전역, 유럽으로, 그리고 인도에 이르기까지 손쉽게 퍼져나갔다.
Thus wheat cultivation spread readily from the uplands of Turkey throughout Mesopotamia, to Europe, and all the way round to India, for example.

north-south 남북 방향의
lead to 초래하다, 이끌다

대조적으로 아메리카의 한 쌍의 대륙은 북남 방향으로 놓여 있다.
The twin continents of the Americas, by contrast, lie in a north-south direction.

re-adapt 다시 적응하다

이곳에서는 한 지역에서 본래 재배된 농작물들이 또 다른 지역으로 퍼지는 것은 식물종을 다른 성장 환경에 재적응시키는 훨씬 더 어려운 과정을 야기했다.
Here, the spreading of crops originally domesticated in one region to another led to a much harder process of re-adapting the plant species to different growing conditions.

....

31. 다음 빈칸에 들어갈 말로 가장 적절한 것을 고르시오.
 Not only was Eurasia by chance blessed with biological abundance, but the very _____ of the continent greatly promoted the spread of crops between distant regions. When the supercontinent Pangea fragmented, it was torn apart along rifts that just so happened to leave Eurasia as a broad landmass running in an east-west direction — the entire continent stretches more than a third of the way around the world, but mostly within a relatively narrow range of latitudes. As it is the latitude on the Earth that largely determines the climate and length of the growing season, crops domesticated in one part of Eurasia can be transplanted across the continent with only minimal need for adaptation to the new locale. Thus wheat cultivation

spread readily from the uplands of Turkey throughout Mesopotamia, to Europe, and all the way round to India, for example. The twin continents of the Americas, by contrast, lie in a north-south direction. Here, the spreading of crops originally domesticated in one region to another led to a much harder process of re-adapting the plant species to different growing conditions. [3점]

* fragment: 조각나다 * rift: 갈라진 틈

① isolation   ② orientation
③ diversity   ④ conservation
⑤ instability

정답 ②

유라시아 대륙이 농업 확산에 유리했던 이유로 지리적 특징이 강조되고 있다. 특히 유라시아가 동서 방향으로 넓게 뻗어 있어 기후와 성장기가 유사한 지역이 많아 작물 재배가 용이했다고 설명하고 있다. 이에 반해 아메리카 대륙은 남북 방향으로 뻗어 있어 작물의 적응이 어려웠다고 대비하고 있다.

따라서 빈칸에는 "방향"을 의미하는 ② orientation 이 들어가는 것이 가장 적절하다.

① 고립 isolation
③ 다양성 diversity
④ 보존 conservation
⑤ 불안정성 instability

ethical 윤리적인, 도덕적인
issue 문제, 쟁점

윤리적 문제를 인식하는 것은 비즈니스 윤리를 이해하는 데 가장 중요한 단계이다.
Recognizing ethical issues is the most important step in understanding business ethics.

identifiable 식별 가능한
evaluate 평가하다
unethical 비윤리적인

윤리적 문제는 옳거나 그르다고, 윤리적 또는 비윤리적이라고 평가될 수 있는 여러 가지 행동들 가운데에서 한 사람이 선택하기를 요구하는 식별 가능한 문제, 상황 또는 기회이다.
An ethical issue is an identifiable problem, situation, or opportunity that requires a person to choose from among several actions that may ① be evaluated as right or wrong, ethical or unethical.

alternative 대안, 선택지
decision 결정, 판단
personal value 개인적 가치
competence 능력, 역량
business area 사업 분야
concern 관심사, 문제

대안 중에서 선택하고 결정을 내리는 방법을 배우는 것은 훌륭한 개인적 가치관뿐만 아니라 관계가 있는 비즈니스 분야에 대한 지식 역량도 필요로 한다.
② Learn (→Learning) how to choose from alternatives and make a decision requires not only good personal values, but also knowledge competence in the business area of concern.

employee 직원, 근로자
rely on ~에 의존하다
code of ethics 윤리 강령
discussion 토론, 논의
co-worker 동료
appropriate 적절한, 알맞은
conduct 행동, 행위

또한 직원들은 언제 자신이 속한 조직의 정책과 윤리 강령에 의존할지 혹은 언제 동료 또는 관리자와 적절한 행동
에 대해 논의해야 할지를 알아야 한다.
Employees also need to know when to rely on their organizations' policies and codes of ethics
or ③ <u>have</u> discussions with co-workers or managers on appropriate conduct.

gray area 애매한 부분, 중간 영역
dilemma 딜레마, 난제
no matter how ~가 어떻게 하든 간에

윤리적 의사결정이 항상 쉬운 것은 아닌데, 왜냐하면 결정이 어떻게 내려지든 딜레마를 만드는 회색 영역이 늘 있
기 때문이다.
Ethical decision making is not always easy because there are always gray areas ④ <u>that</u> create
dilemmas, no matter how decisions are made.

engage in ~에 참여하다, 관여하다
time theft 근무 시간 도둑질

예를 들어, 직원은 시간 훔치기를 하는 동료에 대해 보고해야 하는가?
For instance, should an employee report on a co-worker engaging in time theft?

salesperson 판매원, 영업 사원
leave out 생략하다, 제외하다
poor safety record 낮은 안전 기록
presentation 발표, 설명

판매원은 고객에게 프레젠테이션을 할 때 어떤 제품의 안전 상태가 좋지 않다는 기록에 대한 사실을 생략해야 하
는가?
Should a salesperson leave out facts about a product's poor safety record in his presentation
to a customer?

decision maker 의사 결정자
guidance 지도, 조언

그러한 질문은 의사결정자가 자신이 선택한 윤리를 평가하여 지침을 요청할 것인지 말지의 여부를 결정할 것을 요
구한다.
Such questions require the decision maker to evaluate the ethics of his or her choice and
decide ⑤ <u>whether</u> to ask for guidance.

29. 다음 글의 밑줄 친 부분 중, 어법상 틀린 것은?

 Recognizing ethical issues is the most important step in understanding business ethics. An ethical issue is an identifiable problem, situation, or opportunity that requires a person to choose from among several actions that may ① be evaluated as right or wrong, ethical or unethical. ② Learn how to choose from alternatives and make a decision requires not only good personal values, but also knowledge competence in the business area of concern. Employees also need to know when to rely on their organizations' policies and codes of ethics or ③ have discussions with co-workers or managers on appropriate conduct. Ethical decision making is not always easy because there are always gray areas ④ that create dilemmas, no matter how decisions are made. For instance, should an employee report on a co-worker engaging in time theft? Should a salesperson leave out facts about a product's poor safety record in his presentation to a customer? Such questions require the decision maker to evaluate the ethics of his or her choice and decide ⑤ whether to ask for guidance.

정답 ②

Learn은 술어 동사 requires의 주어 역할을 할 수 없으므로 주어 역할을 할 수 있는 동명사 Learning 등으로 고쳐야 한다.

① 선행사인 several actions는 evaluate라는 행위의 대상이므로 수동태인 be evaluated는 어법상 적절하다.
③ rely on과 or로 연결되어 to에 이어지는 구조이므로 어법상 적절하다.
④ create의 주어 역할을 하면서 gray areas를 수식하는 관계절을 이끄는 주격 관계 대명사 that은 어법상 적절하다.
⑤ 'whether + to 부정사'는 '~할 것인지'라는 뜻으로 decide의 목적어 역할을 하므로 어법상 적절하다.

land use change 토지 이용 변화

토지 이용 변화는 기후에 대해 좋을 수도 나쁠 수도 있다.
Land use change can be good or bad for the climate.

photosynthesis 광합성
convert 변환하다, 바꾸다
carbon dioxide 이산화탄소
carbohydrate 탄수화물

식물은 광합성을 사용하여 공기로부터의 이산화탄소와 물을 탄수화물로 전환한다.
Plants use photosynthesis to convert carbon dioxide from the air and water to carbohydrates.

building block 구성 요소, 기초
plant growth 식물 성장

(C) 그러한 탄수화물은 동물과 미생물들을 위한 식량뿐만 아니라 식물이 살아가기 위해 필요한 에너지와 식물 성장을 위한 기본 구성요소를 제공한다.
(C) Those carbohydrates provide the energy plants need to live, and the building blocks for plant growth, as well as food for animals and microorganisms.

healthy ecosystem 건강한 생태계
pull out 끌어내다, 제거하다

건강한 생태계에서 식물들은 그것들이, 그리고 그것들을 소비하는 동물들과 미생물들이 필요로 하는 것보다 더 많은 탄소를 대기로부터 끌어온다.
In healthy ecosystems the plants pull more carbon out of the atmosphere than they, and the animals and microorganisms that consume them, need.

biomass 생물량, 생물체
tree trunk 나무 줄기
fungi 균류, 곰팡이
carbon compound 탄소 화합물

(B) 그 남는 탄소는 나무 몸통, 토양 박테리아, 균류와 같은 살아있는 바이오매스 안에, 그리고 탄소 화합물로서

토양 안에 저장된다.
(B) That extra carbon is stored in living biomass like tree trunks and soil bacteria and fungi, and as carbon compounds in the soil.

deforestation 삼림 벌채
plowing 경작, 쟁기질
severely 심하게, 심각하게
disturb 방해하다, 교란하다
plant community 식물 군락
photosynthesize 광합성을 하다
depend on 의존하다

그러나 산림파괴나 경작과 같은 행동들이 식물 군집을 심각하게 교란할 때, 남아있는 식물들은 자신들과, 그에 더해서 그들에게 의존하는 모든 동물들과 미생물들을 먹일 만큼 충분히 광합성을 할 수 없게 된다.
But when actions like deforestation or plowing severely disturb a plant community, the remaining plants cannot photosynthesize enough to feed themselves, plus all the animals and microorganisms that depend on them.

microorganism 미생물
respire 호흡하다
atmosphere 대기

(A) 그러한 상황에서 미생물들은 흙과 식물들과 동물들에 저장된 탄소를 소비하고, 그 저장된 탄소를 다시 대기로 이산화탄소로서 내뿜는다.
(A) In those conditions microorganisms consume carbon that has been stored in the soil and in plants and animals, and respire that stored carbon back to atmosphere as CO2.

만약에 원래 생태계가 숲이었다면, 나무에 저장된 탄소의 많은 부분은 또한 화재를 통해 이산화탄소로 전환될지 모른다.
If the original ecosystem was a forest, much of the carbon stored in the trees may also be converted to CO2 through burning.

37. 주어진 글 다음에 이어질 글의 순서로 가장 적절한 것을 고르시오.

Land use change can be good or bad for the climate. Plants use photosynthesis to convert carbon dioxide from the air and water to carbohydrates.

(A) In those conditions microorganisms consume carbon that has been stored in the soil and in plants and animals, and respire that stored carbon back to atmosphere as CO2. If the original ecosystem was a forest, much of the carbon stored in the trees may also be converted to CO2 through burning.

(B) That extra carbon is stored in living biomass like tree trunks and soil bacteria and fungi, and as carbon compounds in the soil. But when actions like deforestation or plowing severely disturb a plant community, the remaining plants cannot photosynthesize enough to feed themselves, plus all the animals and microorganisms that depend on them.

(C) Those carbohydrates provide the energy plants need to live, and the building blocks for plant growth, as well as food for animals and microorganisms. In healthy ecosystems the plants pull more carbon out of the atmosphere than they, and the animals and microorganisms that consume them, need.

① (A) – (C) – (B)　　　　　② (B) – (A) – (C)
③ (B) – (C) – (A)　　　　　④ (C) – (A) – (B)
⑤ (C) – (B) – (A)

정답 ⑤ (C) – (B) – (A)

주어진 문장은 "토지 이용 변화가 기후에 좋은 영향을 미칠 수도 있고 나쁜 영향을 미칠 수도 있다. 식물은 광합성을 이용해 공기 중의 이산화탄소와 물을 탄수화물로 전환한다."라는 내용이다. 이어질 글의 순서를 분석해보면 다음과 같다.

(C)는 "이러한 탄수화물은 식물이 살아가는 데 필요한 에너지를 제공하며, 식물 성장의 기본 요소이자 동물과 미생물의 먹이가 된다. 건강한 생태계에서는 식물이 대기 중에서 뽑아내는 탄소의 양이 그들 자신과 그들을 소비하는 동물 및 미생물들이 필요로 하는 양보다 많다."라는 내용으로, 광합성 과정과 탄소 저장이 이루어지는 건강한 생태계를 설명하고 있다.

(B)는 "추가적인 탄소는 나무줄기나 토양 박테리아 및 균류 같은 살아 있는 생물체와 토양 내 탄소 화합물에 저장된다. 하지만 삼림 벌채나 경작과 같은 행위가 식물 군집을 심각하게 교란하면 남아 있는 식물들은 자신과 그것에 의존하는 동물과 미생물들을 위한 충분한 광합성을 할 수 없게 된다."라고 설명하며, 토지 이용 변화가 탄소 저장에 미치는 영향을 구체화한다.

(A)는 "이러한 환경에서 미생물들은 토양과 식물 및 동물에 저장된 탄소를 소비하고, 저장된 탄소를 CO2로 다시 대기 중으로 방출한다. 원래의 생태계가 숲이었다면, 나무에 저장된 많은 탄소가 연소를 통해 CO2로 변할 수도 있다."라고 설명하며, 탄소 방출 과정과 부정적 영향을 마무리 짓는다.

millennium 밀레니엄, 시대, 천년
descendant 후손, 자손
head off 출발하다, 향하다
star system 항성계

다음 시대의 후반부 언젠가, 우리의 후손들은 다른 항성계로 떠날 수도 있다.
Sometime late in the next millennium, our descendants may head off to other star systems.

*comet 혜성
stepping-stone 디딤돌, 발판
loosely 헐겁게, 느슨하게
bound 묶인, 연결된

그들은, 그중 일부가 우리의 태양에 그저 느슨하게 묶여 있는 혜성들을 (그들이) 디딤돌로 사용할 수도 있는데, 왜냐하면 그것들은 가장 가까운 항성계, Alpha Centauri에 거의 (거리상으로) 중간에 이르기 때문이다.
They may use comets as stepping-stones, some of which are only ① <u>loosely</u> bound to our sun because they reach almost halfway to the nearest star system, Alpha Centauri.

remote 먼, 멀리 떨어진
colonize 식민지화하다, 개척하다
galaxy 은하
living organism 생물, 살아있는 유기체

우리의 먼 후손들은 지구에 첫 살아 있는 유기체들이 한때 지구의 초기 바다를 점령했던 것과 같이 우리 은하계의 대부분을 결국 점령할 수도 있다.
Our remote descendants may eventually colonize much of our galaxy just as the first living organisms on Earth once colonized Earth's young oceans.

interstellar 항성 간의, 성간의
migration 이동, 이주
depend on ~에 달려 있다, 의존하다
unimagined 상상하지 못한
sustainable 지속 가능한
*hibernation 하이버네이션 동면, 겨울잠

성간(星間) 이동은 우주선을 추진하기 위한, 지속 가능한 환경을 유지하기 위한, 인간을 수세기 동안 지속되는 동면에 들어가게 하기 위한, 아직 상상이 되지 않는 기술에 의존할 것이다.
Interstellar migrations will depend on as yet unimagined technologies for driving ships, for maintaining sustainable environments, and for putting humans into hibernations ② last (→ lasting) for centuries.

voyage 항해, 여행
hope of returning 돌아올 희망

또한 성간(星間) 이동은 돌아올 희망이 거의 없거나 전혀 없는 길고 위험한 여정의 위험을 무릅쓸 의지가 있는 집단들의 존재에 달려 있을 것이다.
Interstellar journeys will also depend on the existence of groups willing ③ to risk long and dangerous voyages with little or no hope of returning.

빛의 속도의 1%로 이동하는 우주선이 Alpha Centauri(항성)계에 도달하는 데에는 400년 이상이 걸릴 것이다.
It would take spaceships ④ <u>traveling</u> at 1 percent of the speed of light more than four hundred years to reach the Alpha Centauri system.

settle 정착하다
throughout ~전역에, 전체에 걸쳐
Milky Way 은하수
span 기간, 범위
rule 지배하다, 다스리다

그러나 그들이 그곳에서부터 비슷한 속도로 퍼져 나간다면, 그들은 1억 년 이내에 은하계 도처의 항성계를 정착시킬 수 있을 것이고, 이는 공룡이 우리 지구를 지배했던 이후의 (시간의) 기간보다 아주 조금 더 길다.
But if they spread out from there at a similar rate, they could settle star systems throughout the Milky Way within one hundred million years, ⑤ <u>which</u> is just a bit longer than the span of time since dinosaurs ruled our Earth.

....

29. 다음 글의 밑줄 친 부분 중, 어법상 틀린 것은? [3점]
   Sometime late in the next millennium, our descendants may head off to other star systems. They may use comets as stepping-stones, some of which are only ① <u>loosely</u> bound to our sun because they reach almost halfway to the nearest star system, Alpha Centauri. Our remote descendants may eventually colonize much of our galaxy just as the first living organisms on

Earth once colonized Earth's young oceans. Interstellar migrations will depend on as yet unimagined technologies for driving ships, for maintaining sustainable environments, and for putting humans into hibernations ② <u>last</u> for centuries. Interstellar journeys will also depend on the existence of groups willing ③ <u>to risk</u> long and dangerous voyages with little or no hope of returning. It would take spaceships ④ <u>traveling</u> at 1 percent of the speed of light more than four hundred years to reach the Alpha Centauri system. But if they spread out from there at a similar rate, they could settle star systems throughout the Milky Way within one hundred million years, ⑤ <u>which</u> is just a bit longer than the span of time since dinosaurs ruled our Earth.

* comet 혜성 * hibernation 동면

정답 ②

for putting humans into hibernations ② last(→lasting) for centuries.

원래 문장 "for putting humans into hibernations last for centuries."에서 last for centuries는 동사구인데, 문맥상 동사가 들어갈 자리가 아니다. 문장을 올바르게 해석하면 "사람들을 수세기 동안 지속되는 동면 상태로 두는 것"이라는 의미가 되어야 한다.

하지만 현재 문장에서 "hibernations last for centuries"는 마치 독립적인 절처럼 보이는데, 사실 이는 hibernation을 수식해야 하는 역할을 한다. 이런 경우, 동사 last를 그대로 쓰는 것이 아니라 현재분사 lasting을 사용해야 한다.

lasting for centuries → 현재분사구가 앞의 명사 hibernation을 직접 수식하는 형태로, "수세기 동안 지속되는 동면"이라는 의미를 자연스럽게 전달한다. 따라서 올바른 문장은 "for putting humans into hibernation lasting for centuries."

① loosely bound
"They may use comets as stepping-stones, some of which are only loosely bound to our sun because they reach almost halfway to the nearest star system, Alpha Centauri."
loosely는 부사로, bound(과거분사)을 수식하고 있다.
"be bound to"는 "~에 묶여 있다, 결합되어 있다"라는 의미로, 여기서는 "only loosely bound to our sun"(태양에 약하게 결합되어 있는)이라는 의미가 되어 문맥상 적절하다.

③ to risk
"Interstellar journeys will also depend on the existence of groups willing to risk long and dangerous voyages with little or no hope of returning."
willing은 형용사로, "~할 의향이 있는"이라는 뜻이며, "willing to + 동사원형" 형태로 사용된다.

따라서 "willing to risk"는 "위험을 감수할 의향이 있는"이라는 의미로 문맥상 적절하다.

④ traveling
"It would take spaceships traveling at 1 percent of the speed of light more than four hundred years to reach the Alpha Centauri system."
spaceships를 수식하는 분사구문으로, 현재분사 "traveling"이 사용되었다.
분사구문은 명사를 꾸밀 때 "명사 + 현재분사 (~ing)" 형태로 사용되며, 여기서 "spaceships traveling at 1 percent of the speed of light"는 "빛의 속도의 1%로 이동하는 우주선"이라는 의미로 문맥상 적절하다.

⑤ which
"But if they spread out from there at a similar rate, they could settle star systems throughout the Milky Way within one hundred million years, which is just a bit longer than the span of time since dinosaurs ruled our Earth."
관계대명사 "which"는 앞의 "one hundred million years"를 선행사로 받으며, "which is just a bit longer than the span of time~"이라는 주격 관계대명사절을 이끌고 있다.
즉, "그것(one hundred million years)은 공룡이 지구를 지배했던 이후의 시간보다 약간 더 길다"라는 의미로 문맥상 적절하다.

quite some time 상당한 시간, 오랫동안
hands-on 직접 해보는, 실습 중심의
participation 참여, 참가

상당 기간 동안, 과학 교육자들은 '직접 해보는' 활동이 아이들이 과학 관련 활동에 참여하는 것을 통해 이해하게 하는 데 대한 해답이라고 믿었다.
For quite some time, science educators believed that "hands-on" activities were the answer to children's understanding through their participation in science-related activities.

merely 단순히, 그저
engage in ~에 참여하다, 종사하다
manipulate 조작하다, 다루다
organize 조직하다, 정리하다
comprehension 이해, 파악

많은 교사들은 학생들이 딘지 활동에 참여하고 사물을 조작하는 것만으로 얻게 되는 정보와 이해하게 되는 지식을 개념 이해로 체계화할 것이라고 믿었다.
Many teachers believed that students merely engaging in activities and (a) manipulating objects would organize the information to be gained and the knowledge to be understood into concept comprehension.

*pendulum 추, 진자
component 요소, 구성 요소
inquiry 인쿼리 탐구, 조사
inherent 내재된, 본질적인
material 재료, 자료
*metacognition 메타코그니션 메타인지, 사고에 대한 인식

교육자들은 지식이 자료 자체에 내재되어 있는 것이 아니라 학생들이 그 활동에서 한 것에 대한 생각과 초(超)인지에 있다는 것을 깨달으면서 '직접 해보는' 탐구의 요소 쪽으로 추가 너무 많이 기울었다는 것을 알아차리기 시작했다.
Educators began to notice that the pendulum had swung too far to the "hands-on" component of inquiry as they realized that the knowledge was not (b) inherent in the materials themselves, but in the thought and metacognition about what students had done in the activity.

이제 우리는 과학을 배우는 것에 대해 말할 때에 '직접 해보는'이 위험한 문구라는 것을 알게 되었다.

We now know that "hands-on" is a dangerous phrase when speaking about learning science.

ingredient 요소, 부분
minds-on 사고 중심의, 사고를 요구하는
instructional 교육적인, 교수의

누락된 요소는 교육 경험의 '사고를 요구하는' 부분이다.
The (c) missing ingredient is the "minds-on" part of the instructional experience.

uncertainty 불확실성
re-creation 재창조, 재구성
evaluate 평가하다
preconception 선입견, 기존 개념
thoughtful 사려 깊은, 신중한
bring about 초래하다, 발생시키다

어떤 활동에서든 의도된 지식에 대한 불확실성(→ 명료성)은 각 학생의 개념 재창조에서 비롯되는데, 그 활동을 한 뒤에, 사려 깊은 선생님의 지도하에 자신의 선입견에 대해 토론하고, 사고하고, 논쟁하고, 듣고, 평가하는 것을 통해서 이것을 가져올 수 있다.
(d) Uncertainty (→Clarity) about the knowledge intended in any activity comes from each student's re-creation of concepts — and discussing, thinking, arguing, listening, and evaluating one's own preconceptions after the activities, under the leadership of a thoughtful teacher, can bring this about.

*aerodynamics 공기 역학

결국, 음식물 던지기 장난은 직접 해보는 활동이지만, 여러분이 배워야 했던 것은 으깬 감자를 날리는 공기 역학에 관한 것이었다!
After all, a food fight is a hands-on activity, but about all you would learn was something about the aerodynamics of flying mashed potatoes!

extend 확장하다, 확대하다
far beyond 훨씬 넘어서

자연 세계에 대한 지식과 이론을 구축하기 위해 학생들이 필요로 하는 것에 대한 우리의 견해는 '직접 해보는 활동'을 훨씬 넘어서는 것이다.
Our view of what students need to build their knowledge and theories about the natural world

(e) extends far beyond a "hands-on activity."

interact with ~와 상호 작용하다
sense-making 의미 구성, 이해 과정

과학 수업에서 학생들이 재료를 사용하고 상호 작용하는 것이 중요하기는 하지만, 학습은 '직접 해보는' 학생들의 경험에 대해 의미를 부여하는 것으로부터 나온다.
While it is important for students to use and interact with materials in science class, the learning comes from the sense-making of students' "hands-on" experiences.

[41 ~ 42] 다음 글을 읽고, 물음에 답하시오.

 For quite some time, science educators believed that "hands-on" activities were the answer to children's understanding through their participation in science-related activities. Many teachers believed that students merely engaging in activities and (a) <u>manipulating</u> objects would organize the information to be gained and the knowledge to be understood into concept comprehension. Educators began to notice that the pendulum had swung too far to the "hands-on" component of inquiry as they realized that the knowledge was not (b) <u>inherent</u> in the materials themselves, but in the thought and metacognition about what students had done in the activity. We now know that "hands-on" is a dangerous phrase when speaking about learning science. The (c) <u>missing</u> ingredient is the "minds-on" part of the instructional experience. (d) <u>Uncertainty</u> about the knowledge intended in any activity comes from each student's re-creation of concepts — and discussing, thinking, arguing, listening, and evaluating one's own preconceptions after the activities, under the leadership of a thoughtful teacher, can bring this about. After all, a food fight is a hands-on activity, but about all you would learn was something about the aerodynamics of flying mashed potatoes! Our view of what students need to build their knowledge and theories about the natural world (e) <u>extends</u> far beyond a "hands-on activity." While it is important for students to use and interact with materials in science class, the learning comes from the sense-making of students' "hands-on" experiences.
* pendulum 추(錘) * metacognition 초(超)인지 * aerodynamics 공기 역학

41.
윗글의 제목으로 가장 적절한 것은?
① "Hands-on" Activities as a Source of Creativity
② Activity-oriented Learning Enters Science Education!
③ Figure Out What Students Like Most in Science Class

④ Joy and Learning: More Effective When Separated
⑤ Turn "Minds-on" Learning On in Science Class

정답 ⑤

과학 수업에서 "마음으로 하는" 학습을 활성화하다
Turn "Minds-on" Learning On in Science Class

종래의 과학 교육에서는 '직접 해보는 (hands-on)' 활동을 강조했으나, 요즘에는 그 경험에서 '사고를 요구하여 (minds-on)' 어떤 의미를 이끌어내는 교육이 중요시되고 있다는 내용의 글이므로, ⑤ '과학 수업에서 '사고를 요구하는' 학습을 켜라'가 글의 제목으로 가장 적절하다.

① 창의성의 원천으로서의 "실습" 활동
"Hands-on" Activities as a Source of Creativity
② 활동 중심 학습이 과학 교육에 등장하다
Activity-oriented Learning Enters Science Education!
③ 학생들이 과학 수업에서 가장 좋아하는 것을 알아내다
Figure Out What Students Like Most in Science Class
④ 기쁨과 학습: 분리될 때 더 효과적
Joy and Learning: More Effective When Separated

42.
밑줄 친 (a) ~ (e) 중에서 문맥상 낱말의 쓰임이 적절하지 않은 것은? [3점]
① (a)　　② (b)　　③ (c)　　④ (d)　　⑤ (e)

정답 ④

과학 활동에서 학생들이 자신의 경험으로부터 어떤 개념을 이끌어 내어 그것에 어떤 의미를 부여할 수 있어야 그것에 대해 명확하게 이해할 수 있게 된다는 글의 흐름이 되어야 하므로, 밑줄 친 (d)의 Uncertainty(불명확성)는 Clarity(명료성) 로 바꿔 써야 한다.

immaturity 이매츄어리티 미성숙, 미발달

인간은 이미 다른 어떤 종보다 더 긴 기간의 보호받는 미성숙 상태, 즉 더 긴 어린 시절을 갖는다.
Humans already have a longer period of protected immaturity — a longer childhood — than any other species.

correlate with ~와 상관관계가 있다
evolutionary 진화의, 발전적인
strategy 전략, 방안
depend on ~에 의존하다, 달려 있다
flexibility 유연성, 융통성

종 전체에서, 긴 어린 시절은 유연성, 지능, 그리고 학습에 의존하는 진화 전략과 상호 관련이 있다.
Across species, a long childhood is correlated with an evolutionary strategy that depends on flexibility, intelligence, and learning.

developmental 발달의, 성장의
division of labor 역할 분담, 노동 분업

거기에는 발달상의 분업이 있다.
There is a developmental division of labor.

caregiver 보호자, 양육자

보호자가 그것(아이들의 생존)을 책임지기 때문에, 아이들은 자신의 생존에 대해 걱정하지 않고 자신의 특정 환경에 대해 자유롭게 배우게 된다.
Children get to learn freely about their particular environment without worrying about their own survival — caregivers look after that.

어른들은 그 환경에서 짝을 맺고, 사냥을 하고, 어른으로서 일반적으로 잘 해내기 위해 자신이 어렸을 때 배운 것을 사용한다.
Adults use what they learned as children to mate, hunt, and generally succeed as grown-ups in that environment.

R&D (research and development) 연구 개발

아이들은 인류의 R&D(연구개발) 부서이다.
Children are the R&D (research and development) department of the human species.

우리 어른들은 생산과 마케팅(부서)이다.
We grown-ups are production and marketing.

start out 시작하다, 출발하다
brilliantly 훌륭하게, 뛰어나게
helpless 무력한, 의지할 곳 없는
dependent 의존적인, 기대는
terrible at ~을 못하는

우리는 모든 것을 배우는 데는 훌륭하지만 거의 어떤 것이든 하는 데에는 엉망인, 놀랍도록 유연하지만 무력하고 의존적인 아기로 시작한다.
We start out as brilliantly flexible but helpless and dependent babies, great at learning everything but terrible at doing just about anything.

우리는 결국 학습에는 그다지 능숙하지 않지만 계획과 실행은 매우 잘하는, 훨씬 덜 유연하지만 훨씬 더 효율적이고 효과적인 어른이 된다.
We end up as much less flexible but much more efficient and effective adults, not so good at learning but terrific at planning and acting.

....

21. 밑줄 친 production and marketing이 다음 글에서 의미하는 바로 가장 적절한 것은?
 Humans already have a longer period of protected immaturity — a longer childhood — than any other species. Across species, a long childhood is correlated with an evolutionary strategy that depends on flexibility, intelligence, and learning. There is a developmental division of labor. Children get to learn freely about their particular environment without worrying about their own survival — caregivers look after that. Adults use what they learned as children to mate, hunt, and generally succeed as grown-ups in that environment. Children are the R&D (research and development) department of the human species. We grown-ups are production and marketing. We start out as brilliantly flexible but helpless and dependent babies, great at learning everything but terrible at doing just about anything. We end up as much less flexible but much more efficient and effective adults, not so good at learning but terrific at planning and acting.

① agents who conduct the tasks of living with what they learned
② executives who assign roles according to one's characteristics
③ actors who realize their dreams by building better relations
④ traders who contribute to economic development
⑤ leaders who express their thoughts to others

정답 ①

자신이 배운 것을 바탕으로 삶의 과제를 수행하는 사람들
agents who conduct the tasks of living with what they learned

문장에서 "Children are the R&D (research and development) department of the human species. We grown-ups are production and marketing."라는 부분을 보면, 어린이는 연구·개발(R&D) 단계로서 자유롭게 배울 기회를 가지며, 성인은 배운 것을 활용하여 살아가는 역할을 한다고 설명하고 있다.

즉, "production and marketing"은 어린 시절에 배운 것을 바탕으로 성인이 되어 실제 생활을 영위하는 역살을 의미한다. 따라서 "배운 것을 바탕으로 생활 과업을 수행하는 사람들"이라는 의미가 가장 적절하며, 정답은 ① agents who conduct the tasks of living with what they learned이다.

② 자신의 특성에 맞게 역할을 배정하는 경영자들
executives who assign roles according to one's characteristics
③ 더 나은 관계를 구축하여 꿈을 실현하는 배우들
actors who realize their dreams by building better relations
④ 경제 발전에 기여하는 상인들
traders who contribute to economic development
⑤ 자신의 생각을 다른 사람들에게 표현하는 리더들
leaders who express their thoughts to others

approve 승인하다, 허가하다
request 요청, 신청
tuition 학비, 수업료

회사에서 제 대학 등록금을 지불해 달라는 제 요청을 승인해 주셔서 귀하께 감사드리고 싶습니다.
I would like to thank you for approving my request that the company pay for my college tuition.

*Human Resources 인사부
inform 알리다, 통보하다

귀하께서 (등록금) 지불에 대한 제 요청에 서명해 주셨다고 인사 부서에서 저에게 오늘 알려 주었습니다.
Today, Human Resources informed me that you had signed my request for payment.

financial 재정적인, 경제적인
relief 완화, 도움
make a difference 변화를 가져오다, 영향을 주다

이 재정상의 (부담) 완화가 제 인생에서 커다란 차이를 만들어 줄 것이라고 귀하께 말씀드리고 싶습니다.
I want to tell you that this financial relief will make a great difference in my life.

이제 저는 제 일에 더 집중할 수 있습니다.
Now, I can focus more on my job.

contribute 기여하다, 공헌하다

이렇게 함으로써 저는 제 일을 더 잘할 수 있고, 회사에 더 많이 기여할 수 있을 것입니다.
This will enable me to perform better at my work and contribute more to the company.

faith 신뢰, 믿음

제 등록금에 대한 귀하의 지원과 저에 대한 귀하의 신뢰에 다시 한 번 감사드립니다.
Once again, I appreciate your support of my tuition and your faith in me.

18. 다음 글의 목적으로 가장 적절한 것은?

Dear Mr. Johnson,
I would like to thank you for approving my request that the company pay for my college tuition. Today, Human Resources informed me that you had signed my request for payment. I want to tell you that this financial relief will make a great difference in my life. Now, I can focus more on my job. This will enable me to perform better at my work and contribute more to the company. Once again, I appreciate your support of my tuition and your faith in me.
Sincerely,
Warwick Smith
* Human Resources: 인사 부서
① 학비 지원 승인에 감사하려고
② 대학 입학 추천서를 부탁하려고
③ 장학금 신청 자격을 문의하려고
④ 급여 인상 계획 승인을 요청하려고
⑤ 업무 효율성 향상 방안을 제안하려고

정답 ①

첫 문장인 I would like to thank you for approving my request that the company pay for my college tuition에 이 글을 쓴 목적이 잘 드러나 있다. 따라서 ①이 글의 목적으로 가장 적절하다.

DAY 7

*hallmark 특징, 특성
evaluate 평가하다, 판단하다
assess 평가하다, 검토하다
tightly 단단하게, 빽빽하게

홍차의 품질을 평가하는 특징 가운데 하나는 얼마나 단단히 잎이 말려 있는지를 평가하는 것이다.
One of the hallmarks of evaluating the quality of a black tea is by assessing how tightly the leaves are rolled.

uniformly 균일하게, 일정하게

일반적으로 더 높은 등급의 차는 잎이 단단히 그리고 균일하게 말린 차이다.
Generally, higher-graded teas are teas with leaves that are tightly and uniformly rolled.

loosely 느슨하게
inconsistently 불규칙하게, 일관되지 않게

반면에, 더 낮은 등급의 차는 잎이 느슨하고 일관성 없이 말린 차이다.
① Lower-graded teas, on the other hand, are teas with leaves that are loosely and inconsistently rolled.

steep 적시다, (차를) 우리다
*steepability 우려낼 수 있는 능력

그렇다고는 하지만, 말림의 단단함은 차의 맛과 관련 있는 것보다 잎이 우려지는 정도와 더 많은 관련이 있다.
② With that said, the tightness of the roll has more to do with the steepability of a leaf than it does with the taste of a tea.

evaluate 평가하다, 판단하다
merely 단순히, 단지

따라서, 단지 찻잎이 단단히 말려 있지 않다는 이유로 그 차의 음용 가능성과 맛을 평가해서는 안 된다.
④ Therefore, one should not evaluate the tea's drinkability or taste merely because its leaves are not tightly rolled.

사람들이 단단하게 말린 더 비싸거나 더 높은 등급의 홍차보다 더 느슨하게 말린 홍차의 맛을 선호하는 것을 발견하는 것은 흔하다.
⑤ It is common to find that people prefer the taste of looser rolled black teas over more expensive or more highly graded black teas that have been tightly rolled.

....

35. 다음 글에서 전체 흐름과 관계 없는 문장은?

　One of the hallmarks of evaluating the quality of a black tea is by assessing how tightly the leaves are rolled. Generally, higher-graded teas are teas with leaves that are tightly and uniformly rolled. ① Lower-graded teas, on the other hand, are teas with leaves that are loosely and inconsistently rolled. ② With that said, the tightness of the roll has more to do with the steepability of a leaf than it does with the taste of a tea. ③ The rolling of leaves is done by machine or, sometimes, by hand to break the cell walls of the leaves and release essential oils. ④ Therefore, one should not evaluate the tea's drinkability or taste merely because its leaves are not tightly rolled. ⑤ It is common to find that people prefer the taste of looser rolled black teas over more expensive or more highly graded black teas that have been tightly rolled.
* hallmark: 특징, 특질 * steepability: (차를) 우려낼 수 있음

정답 ③

rolling 말기, 비비기
cell wall 세포벽
release 방출하다, 내보내다

잎을 마는 것은 잎의 세포벽을 깨뜨려 정유(精油)를 방출하기 위해 기계에 의해, 혹은 때로는 손에 의해 이루어진다.
③ The rolling of leaves is done by machine or, sometimes, by hand to break the cell walls of the leaves and release essential oils.

홍차의 품질을 평가하는 특징 가운데 하나가 얼마나 잎이 단단히 말려있는지를 평가 하는 것이긴 하지만 말림의 정도와 맛과는 큰 관련이 없다는 내용의 글인데, ③은 차의 잎을 마는 방식에 관해 기술하고 있으므로 전체 흐름과 관계가 없다.

detect 탐지하다, 찾아내다
*contraband 밀수품
discriminate 구별하다, 식별하다

개가 마약, 폭발물, 밀수품, 혹은 다른 품목들을 탐지하도록 훈련받을 때, 조련사는 사실 개에게 냄새 맡는 법을 가르치지 않는데, 개는 이미 한 냄새를 다른 냄새와 구별하는 법을 알고 있기 때문이다.
When a dog is trained to detect drugs, explosives, contraband, or other items, the trainer doesn't actually teach the dog how to smell; the dog already knows how to discriminate one scent from another.

versus ~에 비해, ~와 대조적으로

오히려 개는 다른 냄새와 대조하여 한 냄새에 의해 감정적으로 자극을 받도록 훈련된다.
Rather, the dog is trained to become emotionally aroused by one smell versus another.

emotional charge 감정적 반응, 감정의 부여
drawn to ~에 끌리다, 관심을 가지다

단계적 훈련 과정에서, 조련사는 어느 특정한 냄새에 '정서적 감흥'을 부여하며, 그래서 개는 다른 모든 냄새에 우선하여 그 냄새에 이끌린다.
① In the step-by-step training process, the trainer attaches an "emotional charge" to a particular scent so that the dog is drawn to it above all others.

cue 신호, 암시

그런 다음, 그 개는 조련사가 개의 행동을 통제하거나 발산시킬 수 있도록 신호에 따라 바라는 품목을 찾아내도록 훈련된다.
② And then the dog is trained to search out the desired item on cue, so that the trainer can control or release the behavior.

arousal 어라우절 각성, 흥분
training regime 트레이닝 레짐 훈련 방식, 교육 체계
food treat 음식 보상, 간식

이러한 정서적 자극은 또한 개와 당기기 놀이를 하는 것이 단지 개에게 맛있는 특별한 먹이를 주는 것보다 훈련 체계에서 더욱 강력한 정서적 보상이 되는 이유이기도 한데, 왜냐하면 조련사가 당기기 게임에 더 많은 감정을 투

입하기 때문이다.
③ This emotional arousal is also why playing tug with a dog is a more powerful emotional reward in a training regime than just giving a dog a food treat, since the trainer invests more emotion into a game of tug.

***tug 잡아당김**
compelling 매력적인, 흥미로운

개의 관점에서 그 당기기 장난감은 조련사가 그 장난감에 의해 '흥분하기' 때문에 흥미진진하다.
⑤ From a dog's point of view, the tug toy is compelling because the trainer is "upset" by the toy.

....

35. 다음 글에서 전체 흐름과 관계 없는 문장은?
When a dog is trained to detect drugs, explosives, contraband, or other items, the trainer doesn't actually teach the dog how to smell; the dog already knows how to discriminate one scent from another. Rather, the dog is trained to become emotionally aroused by one smell versus another. ① In the step-by-step training process, the trainer attaches an "emotional charge" to a particular scent so that the dog is drawn to it above all others. ② And then the dog is trained to search out the desired item on cue, so that the trainer can control or release the behavior. ③ This emotional arousal is also why playing tug with a dog is a more powerful emotional reward in a training regime than just giving a dog a food treat, since the trainer invests more emotion into a game of tug. ④ As long as the trainer gives the dog a food reward regularly, the dog can understand its "good" behavior results in rewards. ⑤ From a dog's point of view, the tug toy is compelling because the trainer is "upset" by the toy.
* contraband: 밀수품 * tug: 잡아당김

정답 ④

조련사가 정기적으로 개에게 먹이를 주는 한, 개는 자신의 '좋은' 행동이 보상을 초래한다는 것을 이해할 수 있다.
④ As long as the trainer gives the dog a food reward regularly, the dog can understand its "good" behavior results in rewards.

특정한 냄새에 대해 정서적 흥분을 하게 하고 당기기 놀이를 통해서 특정한 품목이나 냄새에 대해 정서적 자극을 갖게 하는 것이 특별한 먹이로 보상해 주는 것보다 더 효 과적이라는 내용이 글의 흐름이다. 먹이를 주는 것을 통해 개가 좋은 보상에 대해 이해 할 수 있게 해줄 수 있다는 내용의 ④는 글의 흐름과 관계가 없다.

*avian 에이비안 조류의
stage 단계, 과정

조류의 노래 학습은 두 단계로 이루어지는데,
Avian song learning occurs in two stages:

첫째로는 노래를 암기해야 하고 둘째로는 노래를 연습해야 한다.
first, songs must be memorized and, second, they must be practiced.

overlap 겹치다, 중복되다
impressive 인상적인, 놀라운
long-term memory 장기 기억
storage 저장, 보관

일부 종에서는 이 두 가지 일이 겹치기도 하지만, 다른 종에서는 연습 전 몇 달 동안 암기가 이루어질 수 있는데, 이는 장기 기억 저장의 인상적인 예를 제공한다.
In some species these two events overlap, but in others memorization can occur before practice by several months, providing an impressive example of long-term memory storage.

initial 처음의, 초기의
reproduce 재현하다, 복제하다

어린 새가 암기한 노래를 재현하려는 초기의 노력은 대체로 성공적이지 못하다.
① The young bird's initial efforts to reproduce the memorized song are usually not successful.

uneven 고르지 않은, 불규칙한
pitch 음의 높낮이, 음조
irregular 불규칙한
out of order 순서가 어긋난

이러한 초기의 노래에는 고르지 않은 음정과 불규칙한 박자, 그리고 순서가 맞지 않거나 제대로 재현되지 않은 음이 있을 수도 있다.
② These early songs may have uneven pitch, irregular tempo, and notes that are out of order or poorly reproduced.

reveal 드러내다, 보여주다
practice period 연습 기간
fine-tune 미세하게 조정하다
template 기준, 틀

하지만 몇 주 또는 몇 달에 걸쳐 녹음된 노래의 음향 그래프를 보면, 이 연습 기간 동안 새가 암기된 본보기를 정확하게 모방할 때까지 미세 조정의 노력을 기울인다는 것을 알 수 있다.
③ However, sound graphs of songs recorded over several weeks or months reveal that during this practice period the bird fine-tunes his efforts until he produces an accurate copy of the memorized template.

이 과정에서는 자신이 노래하는 것을 들어야 하는데,
⑤ This process requires hearing oneself sing;

deafened 청각을 잃은, 귀가 먼

만약 새들이 암기한 후이지만 연습 기간 전에 귀가 먹으면 암기된 노래를 재현할 수 없다.
birds are unable to reproduce memorized songs if they are deafened after memorization but before the practice period.

....

35. 다음 글에서 전체 흐름과 관계 없는 문장은?

 Avian song learning occurs in two stages: first, songs must be memorized and, second, they must be practiced. In some species these two events overlap, but in others memorization can occur before practice by several months, providing an impressive example of long-term memory storage. ① The young bird's initial efforts to reproduce the memorized song are usually not successful. ② These early songs may have uneven pitch, irregular tempo, and notes that are out of order or poorly reproduced. ③ However, sound graphs of songs recorded over several weeks or months reveal that during this practice period the bird fine-tunes his efforts until he produces an accurate copy of the memorized template. ④ An important idea to emerge from the study of birdsong is that song learning is shaped by preferences and limitations. ⑤ This process requires hearing oneself sing; birds are unable to reproduce memorized songs if they are deafened after memorization but before the practice period.
* avian: 조류의

정답 ④

emerge 나타나다, 떠오르다

새소리 연구를 통해 드러날 수 있는 중요한 아이디어는 노래 학습은 선호하는 것과 한계점에 의해 형성된다는 것이다.
④ An important idea to emerge from the study of birdsong is that song learning is shaped by preferences and limitations.

새의 노래 학습을 두 단계로 나누어 노래 암기 및 연습 과정에서 나타나는 여러 특징 을 나열하는 내용의 글이므로, 새소리 연구를 통해 드러나는 노래 학습 형성 요인에 대한 내용인 ④는 글의 전체 흐름과 관계가 없다.

cultural significance 문화적 중요성
attempt 시도, 노력

색들이 사회 내에서 의미와 문화적인 의의를 갖게 됨에 따라 그것들의 사용을 제한하는 시도들이 이루어졌다.
As colors came to take on meanings and cultural significance within societies, attempts were made to (restrict) their use.

phenomenon 현상
sumptuary law 썸츄어리-로 사치 금지법

이 현상의 가장 극단적인 예시는 사치 금지법이었다.
The most extreme example of this phenomenon was the sumptuary laws.

pass (법을) 제정하다
modern period 근대

이것은 고대 그리스와 로마에서 통과되었고 실례들이 고대 중국과 일본에서 발견될 수 있지만, 그것은 초기 근대에 서서히 사라지기 전에 12세기 중반부터 유럽에서 가장 완전하게 표출되었다.
While these were passed in ancient Greece and Rome, and examples can be found in ancient China and Japan, they found their fullest expressions in Europe from the mid-twelfth century, before slowly disappearing in the early modern period.

touch on ~에 영향을 미치다, 언급하다
furnishing 가구, 장식
enforce 강제하다, 시행하다
social boundary 사회적 경계
encode 부호화하다, 규정하다

그러한 법들은 식단에서 의복과 가구까지 어떤 것에도 관여할 수 있었고 사회적인 계층을 분명한 시각적 체계로 부호화함으로써 사회적인 경계선을 강요하는 것을 추구했다.
Such laws could touch on anything from diet to dress and furnishings, and sought to enforce social boundaries by encoding the social classes into a clear visual system:

peasant 농민, 소작농
craftsman 장인, 기능공

즉, 다시 말해서 농부는 농부처럼 먹고 입어야 하고 기술자는 기술자처럼 먹고 입어야 한다.
the peasants, in other words, should eat and dress like peasants; craftsmen should eat and dress like craftsmen.

vital 중요한, 필수적인
signifier 상징, 표시
dull 흐릿한, 칙칙한
earthy 흙빛의, 소박한
russet 적갈색
explicitly 명확하게, 분명히
confine 제한하다, 가두다
rural 시골의, 농촌의
preserve 특정 집단의 전유물

색은 이 사회적 언어에서 중대한 기표였는데, 황갈색과 같은 칙칙한 흙색은 가장 가난한 시골 농부들에게 명시적으로 국한된 반면 진홍색과 같은 밝은색들은 선택된 소수의 전유물이었다.
Color was a vital signifier in this social language — dull, earthy colors like russet were explicitly confined to the poorest rural peasants, while bright ones like scarlet were the preserve of a select few.

....

31. 다음 빈칸에 들어갈 말로 가장 적절한 것을 고르시오.
 As colors came to take on meanings and cultural significance within societies, attempts were made to ______ their use. The most extreme example of this phenomenon was the sumptuary laws. While these were passed in ancient Greece and Rome, and examples can be found in ancient China and Japan, they found their fullest expressions in Europe from the mid-twelfth century, before slowly disappearing in the early modern period. Such laws could touch on anything from diet to dress and furnishings, and sought to enforce social boundaries by encoding the social classes into a clear visual system: the peasants, in other words, should eat and dress like peasants; craftsmen should eat and dress like craftsmen. Color was a vital signifier in this social language — dull, earthy colors like russet were explicitly confined to the poorest rural peasants, while bright ones like scarlet were the preserve of a select few.

① export   ② restrict   ③ conceal
④ liberate   ⑤ tolerate

정답 ② restrict 제한하다

본문에서는 색상이 사회에서 의미와 문화적 중요성을 갖게 되면서 그 사용에 대해 규제하려는 시도가 있었음을 설명하고 있다. 이러한 규제는 특히 신분을 시각적으로 구분하기 위한 법률인 사치법(sumptuary laws)에 의해 극명하게 나타나 있다. 사치법은 색채 사용을 제한하여 특정 계층만이 특정 색을 사용할 수 있도록 하였음을 알 수 있다. 예를 들어, 흙빛의 색상은 가장 가난한 농민에게 국한되었고, 밝은 색상은 소수의 특권층에게만 허용되었음을 볼 수 있다. 따라서 빈칸에 들어갈 단어로는 색채 사용을 제한한다는 의미의 restrict 가 가장 적절하다.

① export 수출하다
③ conceal 숨기다
④ liberate 해방시키다
⑤ tolerate 참다

blushing 얼굴이 붉어짐, 홍조
uniquely 유일하게, 독특하게
represent 나타내다, 상징하다
involuntary 무의식적인, 자발적이지 않은
physical reaction 신체 반응
embarrassment 당혹감, 난처함
self-consciousness 셀프 컨셔스니스 자의식
social environment 사회적 환경

다윈은 얼굴이 붉어지는 것을 특별나게 인간적인 것으로, 사회적 환경에서 당혹감과 자의식에 의한 무의식적인 신체 반응을 나타내는 것으로 여겼다.
Darwin saw blushing as uniquely human, representing an involuntary physical reaction caused by embarrassment and self-consciousness in a social environment.

(B) 우리가 혼자 있을 때는 어색하거나 부끄럽거나 창피하다고 느끼더라도 얼굴이 붉어지지 않는데,
(B) If we feel awkward, embarrassed or ashamed when we are alone, we don't blush;

얼굴이 붉어지는 것은 우리가 다른 사람들이 우리를 어떻게 생각할지에 대해 염려하기 때문인 것으로 보인다.
it seems to be caused by our concern about what others are thinking of us.

bring on 유발하다, 초래하다

연구에 따르면 단지 얼굴이 붉어진다는 말을 듣는 것만으로도 얼굴이 붉어진다는 것이 확인되었다.
Studies have confirmed that simply being told you are blushing brings it on.

see through 꿰뚫어 보다, 간파하다

우리는 다른 사람들이 우리의 피부를 꿰뚫어 우리의 마음을 들여다볼 수 있는 것처럼 느낀다.
We feel as though others can see through our skin and into our mind.

disappear 사라지다, 없어지다
psychologist 심리학자
argue 주장하다, 논의하다
serve a purpose 목적을 수행하다

(C) 그러나 우리가 때로 자신도 모르는 사이에 얼굴이 새빨개질 때 사라지고 싶어 하지만, 심리학자들은 얼굴이 붉어지는 것이 실제로는 긍정적인 사회적 목적에 부합한다고 주장한다.
(C) However, while we sometimes want to disappear when we involuntarily go bright red, psychologists argue that blushing actually serves a positive social purpose.

social norm 사회적 규범

얼굴이 붉어질 때, 그것은 사회적 규범을 어겼다는 것을 우리가 인정한다는 것을 다른 사람에게 알리는 신호이자
When we blush, it's a signal to others that we recognize that a social norm has been broken;

*faux pas 퍼우-파 실수, 잘못된 행동

실수에 대한 사과이다.
it is an apology for a faux pas.

brief 짧은, 순간적인
loss of face 체면 손상, 망신
cohesion 결속력, 응집력

(A) 아마도 우리가 잠시 체면을 잃는 것이 집단의 장기적인 결속에 도움이 될 수 있을 것이다.
(A) Maybe our brief loss of face benefits the long-term cohesion of the group.

favourable light 호의적인 시각

흥미롭게도 누군가가 사회적 실수를 저지른 후 얼굴을 붉히면, 우리는 그 사람을 얼굴을 붉히지 않는 사람보다 더 호의적인 시각으로 바라보게 된다.
Interestingly, if someone blushes after making a social mistake, they are viewed in a more favourable light than those who don't blush.

....

37. 주어진 글 다음에 이어질 글의 순서로 가장 적절한 것을 고르시오.
 Darwin saw blushing as uniquely human, representing an involuntary physical reaction caused by embarrassment and self-consciousness in a social environment.

(A) Maybe our brief loss of face benefits the long-term cohesion of the group. Interestingly, if someone blushes after making a social mistake, they are viewed in a more favourable light than those who don't blush.

(B) If we feel awkward, embarrassed or ashamed when we are alone, we don't blush; it seems to be caused by our concern about what others are thinking of us. Studies have confirmed that simply being told you are blushing brings it on. We feel as though others can see through our skin and into our mind.

(C) However, while we sometimes want to disappear when we involuntarily go bright red, psychologists argue that blushing actually serves a positive social purpose. When we blush, it's a signal to others that we recognize that a social norm has been broken; it is an apology for a faux pas. [3점]
* faux pas: 실수

① (A) ― (C) ― (B)　　　　② (B) ― (A) ― (C)
③ (B) ― (C) ― (A)　　　　④ (C) ― (A) ― (B)
⑤ (C) ― (B) ― (A)

정답 ③

다윈이 얼굴이 붉어지는 것을 특별나게 인간적인 것으로 여겼다는 내용의 주어진 글 다음에는 앞서 언급한 사회적 환경과 관련하여 얼굴이 붉어지는 것은 다른 사람들이 자신을 어떻게 생각할지에 대해 염려하기 때문이라고 설명하는 (B)가 먼저 온다. 그 다음에는 이렇게 얼굴이 붉어지는 것이 당혹감을 주지만 실제로는 그것이 긍정적인 사회적 목적에 부합한다는 내용을 However로 시작하여 제시하는 (C)가 오고, 앞서 언급한 사회적 목적과 관련하여 얼굴이 붉어지는 것이 실수에 대한 사과의 표시여서 아마도 집단의 장기적인 결속에 도움이 될 수도 있다는 내용의 (A)가 이어져야 한다. 따라서 주어진 글 다음에 이어질 글의 순서로 가장 적절한 것은 ③이다.

average talent 평균적인 재능
notable 주목할 만한, 뛰어난
various 다양한, 여러 가지의
embrace 받아들이다, 포괄하다

평균적인 재능을 가진 사람이라도 다양한 과학 분야에서 주목할 만한 성과를 낼 수 있는데, 한 번에 그것들 모두를 수용하려고 하지 않는 한 그렇다.
Even those with average talent can produce notable work in the various sciences, so long as they do not try to embrace all of them at once.

concentrate 집중하다, 전념하다
period 기간, 시기
attainment 성취, 달성
sphere 스피어 영역, 분야

대신에 그들은 한 주제 다음에 다른 주제로(즉, 다른 기간에) 집중해야 하는데, 비록 나중의 작업은 다른 영역에서의 더 이전의 성취를 약화시킬 수 있지만 말이다.
Instead, they should concentrate attention on one subject after another (that is, in different periods of time), although later work will weaken earlier attainments in the other spheres.

amount to 결국 ~이 되다
universal science 보편적 과학

이것은 뇌가 보편적인 과학에 '시간' 속에서 적응하는 것이지 '공간' 속에서 적응하는 것이 아니라고 말하는 것과 마찬가지이다.
This amounts to saying that the brain adapts to universal science in time but not in space.

proceed 진행하다, 나아가다

사실, 뛰어난 능력을 가진 사람들도 이런 식으로 나아간다.
In fact, even those with great abilities proceed in this way.

astonished 놀란, 경이로운
publication 출판, 논문

따라서 우리가 서로 다른 과학 분야에 출판물을 가진 사람에게 놀랄 때, 각 주제가 특정 기간 동안 탐구되었다는 것을 인식하라.

Thus, when we are astonished by someone with publications in different scientific fields, realize that each topic was explored during a specific period of time.

condense 응축하다, 압축하다
formula 공식, 방식
abbreviated 어브리비에이티드 단축된, 축약된

더 이전에 얻은 지식은 확실히 저자의 마음에서 사라지지 않았을 것이지만 그것은 공식이나 크게 축약된 기호로 응축되어 단순화되었을 것이다.

Knowledge gained earlier certainly will not have disappeared from the mind of the author, but it will have become simplified by condensing into formulas or greatly abbreviated symbols.

sufficient 충분한, 만족할 만한
perception 인식, 지각
*cerebral 대뇌의, 뇌의
retain 유지하다, 보존하다

따라서 대뇌 칠판에 새로운 이미지를 인식하고 학습할 수 있는 충분한 공간이 남아 있다.

Thus, sufficient space remains for the perception and learning of new images on the cerebral blackboard.

→ 하나의 과학 주제를 탐구한 다음에 다른 주제를 탐구하는 것은 과학 전반에 걸친 주목할 만한 작업을 가능하게 하는데, 이전에 습득된 지식은 뇌 안에서 단순화된 형태로 유지되며 이는 새로운 학습을 위한 공간을 남겨두기 때문이다.

Exploring one scientific subject after another (A) <u>enables</u> remarkable work across the sciences, as the previously gained knowledge is retained in simplified forms within the brain, which (B) <u>leaves</u> room for new learning.

40. 다음 글의 내용을 한 문장으로 요약하고자 한다. 빈칸 (A), (B)에 들어갈 말로 가장 적절한 것은?

 Even those with average talent can produce notable work in the   various sciences, so long as they do not try to embrace all of them at once. Instead, they should concentrate attention on one subject after another (that is, in different periods of time), although later work will weaken earlier attainments in the other spheres. This amounts to saying that the brain adapts to universal science in time but not in space. In fact, even those with great abilities proceed in this way. Thus, when we are astonished by someone with publications in different scientific fields, realize that each topic was explored during a specific period of time. Knowledge gained earlier certainly will not have disappeared from the mind of the author, but it will have become simplified by condensing into formulas or greatly abbreviated symbols. Thus, sufficient space remains for the perception and learning of new images on the cerebral blackboard.
* condense: 응축하다 ** cerebral: 대뇌의

→ Exploring one scientific subject after another (A) remarkable work across the sciences, as the previously gained knowledge is retained in simplified forms within the brain, which (B) room for new learning.

	(A)	(B)		(A)	(B)
①	enables	leaves	②	challenges	spares
③	delays	creates	④	requires	removes
⑤	invites	diminishes			

정답 ①

과학 주제를 차례로 탐구하게 되면 이전에 습득한 지식은 저자의 마음에서 사라지지 않고 공식이나 크게 축약된 기호로 응축되어 단순화되어 새로운 이미지를 인식하고 학습할 수 있는 공간이 충분히 남아 있어 과학 전반에 걸쳐 주목할 만한 연구를 할 수 있다는 내용의 글이다. 따라서 요약문의 빈칸 (A), (B)에 들어갈 말로 가장 적절한 것은 ① '가능하게 하다 – 남겨두다'이다.

② 어렵게 하다 - 남겨놓다
③ 지연시키다 – 만들다
④ 필요로 하다 - 없애다
⑤ 가져오다 – 감소시키다

empathy 공감, 감정 이입
antimatter 반물질

분노와 공감은 물질과 반물질처럼 같은 시간 같은 장소에 존재할 수 없다.
Anger and empathy — like matter and antimatter — can't exist in the same place at the same time.

하나를 들여보내면 다른 하나는 내보내야 한다.
Let one in, and you have to let the other one go.

blamer 비난하는 사람
*ranting 고함, 폭언
dead in its tracks 즉각적으로, 완전히

따라서 비난자를 공감 속으로 이동시킬 때, 여러분은 그 사람의 분노에 찬 폭언을 즉시 멈추게 한다.
So when you shift a blamer into empathy, you stop the person's angry ranting dead in its tracks.

on the defensive 방어적인 태도를 취하는

(C) 그렇다면 방어하는 쪽에 있는 사람은 어떤가?
(C) And what about the person who's on the defensive?

outward 외부로, 표면적으로
ignorant 무지한, 알지 못하는
blind to ~을 보지 못하는, 무관심한

처음에 이 인간 펀칭백은 자신이 그 무엇을 밖으로 잘 보여주려 애써도 그 무지한 비난자가 그것을 보지 못하므로 좌절한다.
Initially, this human punching bag is frustrated because no matter what he or she is trying to mirror outward the ignorant blamer is blind to it.

barely 간신히, 거의 ~않게

그 결과 공격당하는 사람은 대체로 조용한, 간신히 통제되고 있는 분노 상태에 있게 된다.

As a result, the person who's under attack is usually in a state of quiet, barely controlled rage.

defender 방어하는 사람, 변호자
*spontaneously 자발적으로, 자연스럽게
ally 동맹, 협력자

(B) 그러나 갑자기 뜻밖에도 그 비난자는 방어자가 정말 얼마나 슬픈지, 얼마나 화가 나 있는지, 얼마나 겁먹었는지, 또는 얼마나 외로운지를 알게 되고, 자연스럽게 동맹자로 바뀐다.
(B) Suddenly and unexpectedly, however, the blamer knows just how sad, angry, scared, or lonely the defender feels and spontaneously turns into an ally.

방어자가 자신이 비난자에 의해 이해받고 있으며 서로가 같은 편이라고 느낄 때, 방어할 것은 아무것도 없다.
When the defender feels understood by the blamer and that they are on the same side, there's nothing to defend against.

unspoken 말하지 않은, 암묵적인
frustration 좌절, 불만

방어자의 벽이, 그리고 그 벽과 함께 입 밖에 내지 못한 그의 분노와 좌절이 사라진다.
The defender's wall, and with it his unspoken rage and frustration, disappears.

hatred 증오, 미움
trigger 유발하다, 촉발하다
tremendous 엄청난, 거대한
miraculously 미라큘러슬리 기적적으로
rage 분노
forgiveness 용서
willingness 기꺼이 하려는 마음

(A) 비난자에 대해 더는 '두려움이나 증오'를 느끼지 않게 됨으로써 오는 안도감으로 인해 엄청난 고마움이 물밀듯이 자연스럽게 밀려오고, 기적적으로 그 사람의 조용한 분노는 용서로 그리고 그것을 넘어 해결을 향해 기꺼이 일하고자 하는 의지로 바뀐다.
(A) The relief from no longer feeling "fear or hatred" toward the blamer spontaneously triggers a tremendous rush of gratitude and — miraculously — the person's quiet rage turns into forgiveness and, beyond that, a willingness to work toward solutions.

36. 주어진 글 다음에 이어질 글의 순서로 가장 적절한 것을 고르시오.

 Anger and empathy — like matter and antimatter — can't exist in the same place at the same time. Let one in, and you have to let the other one go. So when you shift a blamer into empathy, you stop the person's angry ranting dead in its tracks.

(A) The relief from no longer feeling "fear or hatred" toward the blamer spontaneously triggers a tremendous rush of gratitude and — miraculously — the person's quiet rage turns into forgiveness and, beyond that, a willingness to work toward solutions.

(B) Suddenly and unexpectedly, however, the blamer knows just how sad, angry, scared, or lonely the defender feels and spontaneously turns into an ally. When the defender feels understood by the blamer and that they are on the same side, there's nothing to defend against. The defender's wall, and with it his unspoken rage and frustration, disappears.

(C) And what about the person who's on the defensive? Initially, this human punching bag is frustrated because no matter what he or she is trying to mirror outward the ignorant blamer is blind to it. As a result, the person who's under attack is usually in a state of quiet, barely controlled rage. * rant: 폭언하다 * spontaneously: 자연스럽게

① (A) - (C) - (B)　　　　② (B) - (A) - (C)
③ (B) - (C) - (A)　　　　④ (C) - (A) - (B)
⑤ (C) - (B) - (A)

정답 ⑤

주어진 문장은 분노와 공감은 동시에 존재할 수 없으며, 공감을 유도하면 분노를 멈추게 할 수 있다는 내용을 설명하고 있다. 이어질 글의 논리적 흐름을 분석하면 다음과 같다.

(C) 방어적인 입장에 있는 사람의 심리 상태 설명
방어적인 사람은 상대가 자신의 감정을 이해하지 못하기 때문에 좌절감을 느끼며, 조용하지만 억제된 분노를 품고 있다.
(B) 공감이 발생하는 순간의 변화
갑자기, 공격하던 사람이 방어하는 사람의 감정을 이해하게 되면서 적대감이 사라지고 동료 의식이 생긴다. 방어하는 사람도 이해받는 느낌을 받아 더 이상 방어할 필요가 없어지며, 감정적 벽이 허물어진다.
(A) 공감의 결과와 해결책으로의 발전
분노와 두려움이 사라진 순간, 자연스럽게 감사의 감정이 생겨나며, 분노는 용서로 바뀌고 더 나아가 해결책을 찾으려는 의지가 생긴다.

따라서 가장 적절한 순서는 (C) → (B) → (A)이며, 정답은 ⑤이다.

*hectic 정신없이 바쁜, 빡빡한

삶은 매우 바쁘게 돌아갑니다.
Life is hectic.

우리의 하루는 너무 많은 '해야 하는 것들'로 가득 차서 우리는 '하고 싶어 하는 것들'을 할 시간이 없다고 느낍니다.
Our days are filled with so many of the "have tos" that we feel there's no time left for the "want tos."

게다가, 다른 사람들과 함께 우리의 모든 시간을 보내는 것은 우리에게 리셋 버튼을 누르고 쉴 수 있는 능력을 주지 않습니다.
Further, spending all our time with others doesn't give us the ability to hit the reset button and relax.

unmanaged 관리되지 않은
fatigue 피로, 피곤함
resentment 분노, 억울함

우리 자신이나 우리에게 중요한 것들을 위해 시간을 거의 또는 전혀 남겨놓지 않는 것은 관리되지 않는 스트레스, 좌절감, 피로, 분노, 또는 더 나쁜 것은 건강 문제로 이어질 수 있습니다.
Leaving little to no time for ourselves or for the things that are important to us can lead to unmanaged stress, frustration, fatigue, resentment, or worse, health issues.

build in 포함하다, 구성하다
manageable 감당할 수 있는, 관리할 수 있는

그러나 규칙적인 '여러분의 시간'을 구축하는 것은 많은 이득을 제공할 수 있는데, 이 모든 것들이 삶을 좀 더 달콤하고 좀 더 관리하기 쉽게 하는 데 도움을 줍니다.
Building in regular "you time," however, can provide numerous benefits, all of which help to make life a little bit sweeter and a little bit more manageable.

struggle 애쓰다, 고군분투하다
inability 무능력, 불가능
prioritize 프라이어리타이즈 우선순위를 정하다

안타깝게도, 많은 사람은 자신만의 필요한 사항에 우선순위를 매기지 못해 목표에 도달하는 일로 고심하고 있습니다.
Unfortunately, many individuals struggle with reaching goals due to an inability to prioritize their own needs.

requirement 요구사항, 필요조건
dedicate 바치다, 헌신하다

하지만 혼자만의 시간은 여러분이 자신만의 목표를 향해 나아가고, 자신만의 개인적인 필요사항들을 충족시키며, 더 나아가 자신의 개인적인 꿈을 탐험하기 위해 시간을 바칠 수 있도록 일상적인 책임과 다른 사람들의 요구 사항으로부터 강제로라도 잠시 휴식을 취할 수 있게 합니다.
Alone time, however, forces you to take a break from everyday responsibilities and the requirements of others so you can dedicate time to move forward with your own goals, meet your own personal needs, and further explore your personal dreams.

....

20. 다음 글에서 필자가 주장하는 바로 가장 적절한 것은?
 Life is hectic. Our days are filled with so many of the "have tos" that we feel there's no time left for the "want tos." Further, spending all our time with others doesn't give us the ability to hit the reset button and relax. Leaving little to no time for ourselves or for the things that are important to us can lead to unmanaged stress, frustration, fatigue, resentment, or worse, health issues. Building in regular "you time," however, can provide numerous benefits, all of which help to make life a little bit sweeter and a little bit more manageable. Unfortunately, many individuals struggle with reaching goals due to an inability to prioritize their own needs. Alone time, however, forces you to take a break from everyday responsibilities and the requirements of others so you can dedicate time to move forward with your own goals, meet your own personal needs, and further explore your personal dreams.
* hectic: 매우 바쁜

① 자신을 위한 시간을 확보하여 원하는 바를 추구할 필요가 있다.
② 타인과의 정기적인 교류를 통해 스트레스를 해소해야 한다.
③ 자신의 분야에서 성공하려면 체계적인 시간 관리가 중요하다.
④ 개인의 이익과 공공의 이익 간의 조화를 이루어야 한다.
⑤ 업무의 우선순위는 동료와 협의하여 정해야 한다.

정답 ①

관광은 그저 휴가를 보내는 것 이상을 위해 중요하다.
Tourism is important for more than just vacationing.

host community 주최 지역, 현지 공동체

관광은 다른 장소와 문화로부터 온 사람들이 함께 모일 수 있도록 해 주고, 그리하여 관광객과 관광지의 지역사회가 서로의 차이점과 유사점에 대해 배운다.
Tourism allows people from different places and cultures to come together, and then tourists and host communities learn about each other's differences and similarities.

그들은 또한 새로운 취향과 사고방식을 배우는데, 그것이 관광지에 사는 사람들과 관광객들 사이의 보다 나은 이해로 이어질 수 있다.
They also learn new tastes and ways of thinking, which may lead to a better understanding between hosts and tourists.

관광의 또 다른 긍정적인 효과는 그것이 한 사회의 문화, 특히 그 문화의 예술 형태의 생존을 위해 제공하는 도움이다.
Another positive effect of tourism is the aid it provides for the survival of a society's culture, especially the culture's art forms.

folk dance 민속 무용

관광객들에게 고유의 미술품을 팔거나 그들을 위해 민속춤을 공연할 기회는 지역 예술가들에게 전통적인 예술 형태를 보존하도록 용기를 북돋아 줄 수 있다.
The opportunity to sell native artworks to tourists or perform folk dances for them may encourage local artists to preserve traditional art forms.

Fijian 피지 사람, 피지의
palm mat 야자수 깔개
profitable 수익성이 있는

예를 들어, 피지 제도에 사는 사람들은 그들의 야자수 깔개와 조개껍질로 만든 장신구를 돈벌이가 되는 관광 사업으로 발전시켰다.
For example, Fijians have developed their palm mat and shell jewelry crafts into profitable

tourist businesses.

그들은 또한 민속춤과 불 속 걷기 공연을 함으로써 추가적인 소득을 얻고 있다.
They also earn additional income by performing folk dances and fire walking.

....

23. 다음 글의 주제로 가장 적절한 것은?
Tourism is important for more than just vacationing. Tourism allows people from different places and cultures to come together, and then tourists and host communities learn about each other's differences and similarities. They also learn new tastes and ways of thinking, which may lead to a better understanding between hosts and tourists. Another positive effect of tourism is the aid it provides for the survival of a society's culture, especially the culture's art forms. The opportunity to sell native artworks to tourists or perform folk dances for them may encourage local artists to preserve traditional art forms. For example, Fijians have developed their palm mat and shell jewelry crafts into profitable tourist businesses. They also earn additional income by performing folk dances and fire walking.
① misunderstandings between hosts and tourists
② various ways of creating tourism products
③ negative effects of cultural exchanges
④ disappearance of traditional cultures
⑤ cultural benefits of tourism

정답 ⑤ 관광의 문화적 이점
cultural benefits of tourism

관광은 서로 다른 문화를 가진 사람들이 함께 모여 서로의 차이점과 유사점을 알게 해주며, 한 사회의 문화가 생존할 기회를 제공하는 이점을 가지고 있다는 내용이므로 주제로 적절한 것은 ⑤ '관광의 문화적 이점'이다.

① 호스트와 관광객 간의 오해
misunderstandings between hosts and tourists
② 관광 제품을 창출하는 다양한 방법
various ways of creating tourism products
③ 문화 교류의 부정적인 영향
negative effects of cultural exchanges
④ 전통 문화의 사라짐
disappearance of traditional cultures

DAY 8

고려해야 할 것이 있다.
Here's something to consider:

만일 여러분이 여러분의 여자 형제, 아버지, 혹은 아들에게 사귀라고 추천하지 않을 친구가 있다면, 왜 여러분은 자신을 위해 그런 친구를 두는가?
If you have a friend whose friendship you wouldn't recommend to your sister, or your father, or your son, why would you have such a friend for yourself?

아마도 여러분은 이렇게 말할 것이다. 신의 때문이라고.
You might say: out of loyalty.

identical to ~와 동일한, 똑같은
stupidity 어리석음, 우둔함

글쎄, 신의는 어리석음과 같지 않다.
Well, loyalty is not identical to stupidity.

negotiate 협상하다, 조율하다
fairly 공정하게, 정당하게

신의는 공정하고 정직하게 협상되어야 한다.
Loyalty must be negotiated, fairly and honestly.

reciprocal 상호적인, 서로 주고받는
arrangement 협정, 조정

우정은 상호 합의이다.
Friendship is a reciprocal arrangement.

morally 도덕적으로
obliged to ~할 의무가 있는

여러분은 세상을 더 나쁜 곳으로 만들고 있는 누군가를 도덕적으로 지지할 의무가 없다.
You are not morally obliged to support someone who is making the world a worse place.

완전히 정반대이다. 여러분은 상황이 더 나빠지는 것이 아니라 더 나아지기를 원하는 사람들을 선택해야 한다.
Quite the opposite. You should choose people who want things to be better, not worse.

여러분에게 좋은 사람을 고르는 것은 이기적인 일이 아니라 좋은 일이다.
It's a good thing, not a selfish thing, to choose people who are good for you.

appropriate 적절한, 알맞은
praiseworthy 칭찬할 만한, 바람직한
associate with ~와 어울리다, 교류하다

여러분의 삶이 개선되는 것을 보면 자신의 삶도 개선될 사람들과 사귀는 것은 적절하고 칭찬할 만한 일이다.
It's appropriate and praiseworthy to associate with people whose lives would be improved if they saw your life improve.

....

20. 다음 글에서 필자가 주장하는 바로 가장 적절한 것은?

   Here's something to consider: If you have a friend whose friendship you wouldn't recommend to your sister, or your father, or your son, why would you have such a friend for yourself? You might say: out of loyalty. Well, loyalty is not identical to stupidity. Loyalty must be negotiated, fairly and honestly. Friendship is a reciprocal arrangement. You are not morally obliged to support someone who is making the world a worse place. Quite the opposite. You should choose people who want things to be better, not worse. It's a good thing, not a selfish thing, to choose people who are good for you. It's appropriate and praiseworthy to associate with people whose lives would be improved if they saw your life improve.

① 더 나은 삶과 세상을 지향하는 사람과 사귀어야 한다.
② 부모는 자녀와 교우 관계에 대해 자주 대화해야 한다.
③ 우정을 지키려면 변함없는 신의를 보여줘야 한다.
④ 원만한 인간관계를 위해 이기적인 태도를 버려야 한다.
⑤ 가족의 의사결정은 모든 구성원의 합의로 이루어져야 한다.

정답 ①

이유는 본문에서 필자는 친구 선택의 중요성을 강조하며, 단순한 충성심만으로 관계를 유지해서는 안 된다고 말하고 있다. 필자는 "세상을 더 나쁘게 만드는 사람"을 지지할 도덕적 의무는 없다고 주장하며, 오히려 더 나은 세상과 삶을 지향하는 사람들과 어울려야 한다고 강조하고 있다. 또한, 자신에게 긍정적인 영향을 미치는 사람들과의 관계가 이기적인 것이 아니라 바람직하다고 설명하고 있다.

obsess 집착하다, 몰두하다
fault 잘못, 책임

무언가 잘못되었을 때 사람들이 왜 그런 일이 생겼고, 그것이 누구의 잘못이며, '왜 나인가?'에 집착하는 것은 유감스러운 일이다.
It's unfortunate that when something goes wrong, people obsess about why it happened, whose fault it was, and "why me?"

솔직히, 대부분의 경우 그런 생각이 무슨 소용인가?
Honestly, what good is that thinking in most cases?

여러분의 두뇌가 해결 지향적이 되도록 훈련하라.
Train your brain to be solution-oriented.

지구상에서 가장 간단한 예를 들어 보자.
Let's take the simplest example on the planet.

우유 한 잔이 쏟아지면 무슨 일이 벌어지는가?
What happens when a glass of milk spills?

stain 얼룩지게 하다, 오염시키다
along the lines of ~와 같은 맥락에서, 비슷한 방식으로

그렇다, 여러분은 집착해서, 그것이 어떻게 넘어졌지, 누가 그것을 넘어지게 했지, 그것이 바닥을 얼룩지게 할까 하고 말하거나 '왜 늘 나야? 나는 서둘러야 해서 이런 일은 일어나면 안 되는데.'와 비슷한 무언가를 생각할 수 있다.
Yes, you can obsess and say, how did that fall, who made it fall, will it stain the floor, or think something along the lines of, "Why always me? I'm in a hurry and don't need this."

thought process 사고 과정, 사고 방식

그러나 해결 지향적인 사고 과정을 가진 누군가는 그저 수건을 가져오고, 잔을 집어 들고, 우유 한 잔을 새로 가져올 것이다.
But someone with a solution-oriented thought process would simply get a towel, pick up the glass, and get a new glass of milk.

여러분의 에너지를 현명하게 사용하라. 실수로부터 배우되, 해결책을 가지고 빠르게 넘어가라.
Use your energy wisely; learn from mistakes but then move on fast with solutions.

....

20. 다음 글에서 필자가 주장하는 바로 가장 적절한 것은?
It's unfortunate that when something goes wrong, people obsess about why it happened, whose fault it was, and "why me?" Honestly, what good is that thinking in most cases? Train your brain to be solution-oriented. Let's take the simplest example on the planet. What happens when a glass of milk spills? Yes, you can obsess and say, how did that fall, who made it fall, will it stain the floor, or think something along the lines of, "Why always me? I'm in a hurry and don't need this." But someone with a solution-oriented thought process would simply get a towel, pick up the glass, and get a new glass of milk. Use your energy wisely; learn from mistakes but then move on fast with solutions.

① 문제가 생기면 주위 사람들에게 조언을 구하라.
② 비판하는 사람보다 격려하는 사람을 가까이하라.
③ 실패의 경험을 분석해서 배우려는 자세를 가져라.
④ 문제 자체에 집착하기보다는 문제 해결에 집중하라.
⑤ 예상치 못한 위험에 대비해 항상 경계를 늦추지 마라.

정답 ④

이유는 본문에서 필자는 문제가 발생했을 때 원인이나 잘못을 따지기보다는 해결책에 집중하는 사고방식을 가져야 한다고 주장하고 있다. 예시로 든 우유가 쏟아지는 상황에서도 "왜 이런 일이 생겼지?"라고 고민하기보다는 즉시 수건을 가져와 치우고, 새 우유를 따르면 된다고 설명하며, 문제 해결에 에너지를 집중할 것을 강조하고 있다.

*aloft 높이
flap 날개를 퍼덕이다

새들이 날 때 그것들은 에너지를 절약하기 위해 많은 기술들을 사용하는데, 그중 대부분은 날갯짓을 하지 않고 높이 머무르기 위한 요령이다.
Birds use many techniques to save energy when they are flying, most of which are tricks to stay aloft without flapping.

riding updrafts 상승 기류를 타는 것
gain altitude 고도를 얻다, 높이 오르다
*conspicuous 컨스피큐어스 눈에 띄는, 두드러진

(B) 고도를 확보하기 위해 상승 기류를 타는 것이 가장 뚜렷한 요령 중 하나이다.
(B) Riding updrafts to gain altitude is one of the most conspicuous.

bare ground 맨땅, 노출된 지면
absorb 흡수하다

들판이나 주차장과 같은 텅 빈 지면은 태양으로부터 더 많은 열을 흡수하고, 지면 근처의 공기가 따뜻해지면서 그것이 상승한다.
Bare ground such as fields or parking lots absorbs more heat from the sun, and as air near the ground warms up it rises.

column 기둥, 기류

(C) 이는 상승하는 따뜻한 공기 기둥 즉, '상승 온난 기류'를 형성하며 이것은 수백 혹은 심지어 수천 피트의 높이에 이른다.
(C) This creates a column of rising warm air — a thermal — reaching hundreds or even thousands of feet high.

fly in circles 원을 그리며 날다

날아오르는 새는 이 공기 움직임을 감지할 수 있고 그 기둥에 머무르기 위해 원을 그리며 날 수 있다.
A soaring bird can sense the air movement and fly in circles to stay in the column.

fan 펼치다, 퍼지게 하다

그것은 단순히 그 날개와 꼬리를 펴서 상승하는 공기가 엘리베이터처럼 자신을 들어 올려 주도록 한다.
It simply fans its wings and tail and lets the rising air carry it up like an elevator.

glide 활공하다, 미끄러지듯 날다
*thermal 상승 기류

(A) 그것이 최고점에 도달했을 때 그 새는 날개를 구부려서 자신이 이동하고 싶은 방향으로 활공하며 다음 상승 온난 기류를 탐색한다.
(A) When it reaches the top, the bird bends its wings and glides in the direction it wants to travel, searching for the next thermal.

soaring 솟아오르는, 활공하는
take advantage of ~을 이용하다
species 종(생물)
Broad-winged Hawk 넓적날개말똥가리(맹금류)
specialist 전문가, 특화된 종

모든 날아오르는 새들은 상승 온난 기류를 이용하지만, 넓적날개말똥가리와 같은 몇몇 종들은 전문가여서 적절한 조건에서는 거의 날갯짓을 하지 않고 수백 마일을 이동할 수 있다.
All soaring birds take advantage of thermals, but some species, like the Broad-winged Hawk, are specialists and in the right conditions can travel hundreds of miles with almost no flapping.

....

36. 주어진 글 다음에 이어질 글의 순서로 가장 적절한 것을 고르시오.
Birds use many techniques to save energy when they are flying, most of which are tricks to stay aloft without flapping.
(A) When it reaches the top, the bird bends its wings and glides in the direction it wants to travel, searching for the next thermal. All soaring birds take advantage of thermals, but some species, like the Broad-winged Hawk, are specialists and in the right conditions can travel hundreds of miles with almost no flapping.
(B) Riding updrafts to gain altitude is one of the most conspicuous. Bare ground such as fields or parking lots absorbs more heat from the sun, and as air near the ground warms up it rises.
(C) This creates a column of rising warm air — a thermal — reaching hundreds or even

thousands of feet high. A soaring bird can sense the air movement and fly in circles to stay in the column. It simply fans its wings and tail and lets the rising air carry it up like an elevator. [3점]

* aloft 높이 * thermal 상승 온난 기류 * conspicuous 뚜렷한

① (A) - (C) - (B)   ② (B) - (A) - (C)
③ (B) - (C) - (A)   ④ (C) - (A) - (B)
⑤ (C) - (B) - (A)

정답 ③

주어진 문장은 새들이 비행 중 에너지를 절약하는 다양한 기술을 사용하며, 대부분은 날개를 퍼덕이지 않고 떠 있는 방법과 관련이 있다고 설명하고 있다. 이를 바탕으로 이어질 글의 순서를 분석하면 다음과 같다.

(B) 새들이 상승 기류를 이용하는 방법을 소개
새들이 고도를 얻기 위해 상승 기류를 이용하는 것이 가장 뚜렷한 방법 중 하나라고 설명하며, 지표면의 열이 공기를 데우면서 공기가 상승하는 원리를 설명한다.
(C) 상승 기류가 만들어내는 열기둥(thermal)에 대한 설명
지표면에서 올라간 공기가 열기둥을 형성하며, 새들은 이를 감지하고 원을 그리며 비행하여 열기둥 안에서 떠오를 수 있다.
(A) 열기둥을 활용한 비행 과정과 특정 새의 사례
열기둥의 꼭대기에 도달하면 새는 날개를 접고 원하는 방향으로 활공하며 다음 열기둥을 찾는다. 특히 Broad-winged Hawk 같은 새들은 이 기술을 전문적으로 사용하여 거의 날개를 퍼덕이지 않고도 수백 마일을 이동할 수 있다.

이러한 흐름을 고려할 때 가장 적절한 순서는 (B) → (C) → (A)이며, 정답은 ③이다.

biologist 생물학자
extraordinary 특별한, 놀라운
evolutionary fitness 진화적 적응도

진화 생물학자 Robert Trivers는 자기 (자신의 행동에 의식적인 접근을 하는) 동물이 그 진화적 적합성에 해를 줄 수 있다는 탁월한 사례를 제시한다.
Evolutionary biologist Robert Trivers gives an extraordinary example of a case where an animal (having conscious access to its own actions) may be damaging to its evolutionary fitness.

*hare 산토끼
shake off 따돌리다, 떨쳐내다
pursuer 추격자, 사냥꾼

산토끼가 쫓기고 있을 때, 그것은 추격자를 떨쳐내기 위한 시도로 무작위 방식으로 지그재그로 나아간다.
When a hare is being chased, it zigzags in a random pattern in an attempt to shake off the pursuer.

reliable 신뢰할 수 있는, 확실한
genuinely 진정으로, 실제로
foreknowledge 사전 지식, 예측

산토끼가 다음에 자신이 어디로 뛰어오를 것인지를 미리 알지 못하는 것이 더 좋기 때문에, 그 기술이 정말로 무작위라면 이것은 좀 더 믿을 만한 것이 될 것이다.
This technique will be more reliable if it is genuinely random, as it is better for the hare to have no foreknowledge of where it is going to jump next:

posture 자세, 태도
reveal 드러내다, 보여주다

만약 산토끼가 다음에 자신이 어디로 뛰어오를지 안다면, 그것의 자세가 자신의 추격자에게 단서를 드러낼지도 모른다.
if it knew where it was going to jump next, its posture might reveal clues to its pursuer.

anticipate 예측하다, 예상하다
cue 신호, 단서

fatal 치명적인, 죽음을 초래하는

시간이 지나, 개들이 이러한 신호들을 예상하는 것을 배우게 될 것이고, 이는 산토끼에게 치명적인 결과를 가져올 것이다.
Over time, dogs would learn to anticipate these cues — with fatal consequences for the hare.

self-awareness 자기 인식, 자각
die out 멸종하다, 사라지다
descend from ~의 후손이다, ~에서 유래하다
self-knowledge 자기 이해, 자아 인식

좀 더 자기 인식을 하는 그런 산토끼들이 멸종되는 경향이 있을 것이며, 따라서 대부분의 오늘날의 산토끼들은 아마도 자각을 덜 했던 산토끼들의 후손일 것이다.
Those hares with more self-awareness would tend to die out, so most modern hares are probably descended from those that had less self-knowledge.

conceal 숨기다, 감추다
motive 동기, 이유

마찬가지로, 인간들은 자신의 진짜 동기들을 숨기는 것을 더 잘했던 조상들의 후손일지도 모른다.
In the same way, humans may be descended from ancestors who were better at the concealment of their true motives.

convincing 설득력 있는, 믿을 만한

그것들을 다른 사람들로부터 숨기는 것은 충분치 않으며, 확실히 (행동에) 설득력이 있으려면 여러분 자신으로부터도 그것들을 숨겨야 한다.
It is not enough to conceal them from others — to be really convincing, you also have to conceal them from yourself.

··

32. 다음 빈칸에 들어갈 말로 가장 적절한 것을 고르시오.
  Evolutionary biologist Robert Trivers gives an extraordinary example of a case where an animal (   ) may be damaging to its evolutionary fitness. When a hare is being chased, it zigzags in a random pattern in an attempt to shake off the pursuer. This technique will be more reliable if

it is genuinely random, as it is better for the hare to have no foreknowledge of where it is going to jump next: if it knew where it was going to jump next, its posture might reveal clues to its pursuer. Over time, dogs would learn to anticipate these cues — with fatal consequences for the hare. Those hares with more self-awareness would tend to die out, so most modern hares are probably descended from those that had less self-knowledge. In the same way, humans may be descended from ancestors who were better at the concealment of their true motives. It is not enough to conceal them from others — to be really convincing, you also have to conceal them from yourself.

* hare: 산토끼

① disconnecting the link from its circumstance
② having conscious access to its own actions
③ sharpening its own intuitions and instincts
④ relying on its individual prior experiences
⑤ activating its innate survival mechanism

정답 ②

② 자신의 행동에 의식적으로 접근하다
having conscious access to its own actions

빈칸이 포함된 문장은 "an animal ___ may be damaging to its evolutionary fitness"로, 동물이 특정한 행동을 할 때 그것이 진화적 적응력에 해로울 수 있다는 의미를 전달한다. 이어지는 예시에서 산토끼가 포식자로부터 도망칠 때 무작위로 지그재그로 뛰는 행동을 설명하며, 이러한 움직임이 진정으로 무작위적일수록 생존 확률이 높아진다고 한다.

특히 중요한 점은 토끼가 자신의 움직임을 미리 인식하고 있다면 그 행동이 포식자에게 읽힐 가능성이 커지고, 결국 더 쉽게 잡히게 된다는 의미다. 따라서 "자신의 행동을 의식적으로 인식하는 것"이 오히려 불리하게 작용한다는 점을 강조하고 있다.

① 상황과의 연결을 끊다
disconnecting the link from its circumstance
③ 자신의 직감과 본능을 날카롭게 하다
sharpening its own intuitions and instincts
④ 자신의 개별적인 경험에 의존하다
relying on its individual prior experiences
⑤ 본능적인 생존 메커니즘을 활성화하다
activating its innate survival mechanism

geographic expansion 지리적 확장
cultural innovation 문화적 혁신
experience 경험하다, 겪다

(우리를 새로운 환경에 놓이게 하는) 지리적 확장과 문화적 혁신 모두 인간이 경험하는 선택압을 변화시켰다.
Geographic expansion (which placed us in new environments) and cultural innovation both changed the selective pressures humans experienced.

payoff 보상, 이익
trait 특성, 형질
optimal 최적의

많은 특징들의 이점이 변했고, 그래서 최적의 생존 전략도 변했다.
The payoff of many traits changed, and so did optimal life strategy.

close-in 공격 가까이 접근하는 공격
thrusting spears 찌르는 창

예를 들어, 인간이 10만 년 전에 큰 사냥감을 사냥했을 때, 그들은 가까운 거리에서 창으로 찌르는 공격에 의존했다.
(①) For example, when humans hunted big game 100,000 years ago, they relied on close-in attacks with thrusting spears.

physically demanding 신체적으로 힘든
heavily muscled 근육이 발달한

그러한 공격은 매우 위험하고 신체적으로 힘들어서 그 당시에 사냥꾼들은 근육이 많아야 했고 굵은 뼈를 가져야 했다.
(②) Such attacks were highly dangerous and physically demanding, so in those days, hunters had to be heavily muscled and have thick bones.

if nothing else 최소한, 적어도
on the whole 전체적으로 보면

그러한 신체는 단점을 가지고 있었는데, 다른 것은 몰라도, 그것은 더 많은 식량을 필요로 했지만, 전체적으로 그것은 그 상황에서 최고의 해결책이었다.
(③) That kind of body had its disadvantages — if nothing else, it required more food — but on the whole, it was the best solution in that situation.

atlatl 아틀라틀(창 던지는 도구)
spearthrower 창 던지는 기구
muscle-generated 근육에서 생성된
*biceps 이두근(상완 근육)
robust 튼튼한, 강건한
skeleton 골격, 뼈대

하지만 아틀라틀(투창기)과 활과 같은 새로운 무기는 근육으로 생성되는 에너지를 효과적으로 비축했는데, 이것은 사냥꾼들이 큰 이두박근과 튼튼한 골격 없이도 큰 사냥감을 잡을 수 있다는 것을 의미했다.
(But new weapons like the atlatl (a spearthrower) and the bow effectively stored muscle-generated energy, which meant that hunters could kill big game without big biceps and robust skeletons.)

competitively 경쟁적으로
superior 우월한, 더 나은

그렇게 되자, 더 잘 달리고 그렇게 많은 식량을 필요로 하지 않는 가벼운 체구의 사람들은 경쟁적으로 우위에 있게 되었다.
(④) Once that happened, lightly built people, who were better runners and did not need as much food, became competitively superior.

큰 체구는 비용이 많이 들기만 하고 더 이상 필요하지 않은 과거의 해결책이었다.
(⑤) A heavy build was yesterday's solution: expensive, but no longer necessary.

....

39. 글의 흐름으로 보아, 주어진 문장이 들어가기에 가장 적절한 곳을 고르시오.
  But new weapons like the atlatl (a spearthrower) and the bow effectively stored muscle-generated energy, which meant that hunters could kill big game without big biceps and robust skeletons.

Geographic expansion (which placed us in new environments) and cultural innovation both changed the selective pressures humans experienced. The payoff of many traits changed, and so did optimal life strategy. (①) For example, when humans hunted big game 100,000 years ago, they relied on close-in attacks with thrusting spears. (②) Such attacks were highly dangerous and physically demanding, so in those days, hunters had to be heavily muscled and have thick bones. (③) That kind of body had its disadvantages — if nothing else, it required more food — but on the whole, it was the best solution in that situation. (④) Once that happened, lightly built people, who were better runners and did not need as much food, became competitively superior. (⑤) A heavy build was yesterday's solution: expensive, but no longer necessary.

* biceps: 이두박근

정답 ④

주어진 문장은 "새로운 무기인 아틀라틀(창 던지기 도구)과 활은 근육에서 생성된 에너지를 효과적으로 저장했으며, 이는 사냥꾼들이 큰 근육이나 튼튼한 골격 없이도 대형 동물을 사냥할 수 있게 해 주었다."라는 의미이다.

본문의 흐름을 보면,
①번 앞에서는 지리적 확장과 문화적 혁신이 인간의 선택 압력을 변화시켰다고 설명하고 있다.
②번과 ③번에서는 과거 사냥 방식(근접 공격)이 위험하고 신체적으로 부담이 컸기 때문에, 당시 사냥꾼들은 강한 근육과 튼튼한 뼈를 가질 필요가 있었다는 점을 설명하고 있다.
④번에서는 새로운 무기가 등장하면서 가벼운 체격을 가진 사람들이 더 경쟁적으로 우위를 점하게 되었다고 말하고 있다.

주어진 문장은 새로운 무기의 등장이 결정적 요인이었다는 내용을 전달하므로, 기존의 체격 조건이 필요했던 이유를 설명한 후(③번까지), 그 변화의 원인을 제시하는 ④번 앞에 들어가는 것이 적절하다.

onlooker 구경꾼, 방관자

일단 어떤 사건이 목격되면, 구경하는 사람은 그것이 정말로 비상 상황인지 결정해야 한다.
Once an event is noticed, an onlooker must decide if it is truly an emergency.

label 분류하다, 표시하다

비상 상황은 항상 명확하게 그와 같은 것으로 꼬리표가 붙어 있는 것은 아닌데, 대기실로 쏟아져 들어오는 '연기' 는 화재에 의해 발생할 수도 있고 단순히 증기 파이프의 누출을 나타낼 수도 있다.
Emergencies are not always clearly (a) labeled as such; "smoke" pouring into a waiting room may be caused by fire, or it may merely indicate a leak in a steam pipe.

quarrel 다툼, 언쟁

거리에서의 비명은 공격을 나타내거나 가족 간의 다툼을 나타낼 수도 있다.
Screams in the street may signal an attack or a family quarrel.

lying in a doorway 문간에 누워 있는
*coronary 코로너리 심장병의, 관상동맥의
sleep off 숙취로 자다

출입구에 누워 있는 한 남자는 관상 동맥증을 앓고 있을 수도 있고 그저 술을 깨려고 잠을 자고 있을 수도 있다.
A man lying in a doorway may be having a coronary — or he may simply be sleeping off a drunk.

interpret 해석하다, 이해하다

어떤 한 상황을 해석하려고 하는 사람은 자신이 어떻게 반응해야 하는지 알기 위해 흔히 자기 주변 사람들을 본다.
A person trying to interpret a situation often looks at those around him to see how he should react.

indifferent 무관심한, 냉담한

만약 다른 모든 사람이 침착하고 무관심하다면, 그는 그런 상태를 유지하려는 경향이 있을 것이고,
If everyone else is calm and indifferent, he will tend to remain so;

다른 모든 사람이 강하게 반응하고 있다면, 그는 아마 경계하게 될 것이다.
if everyone else is reacting strongly, he is likely to become alert.

blind conformity 맹목적인 순응

이러한 경향은 단순히 맹목적인 순응이 아닌데,
This tendency is not merely blind conformity;

ordinarily 보통, 일반적으로
derive 얻다, 끌어내다

보통 우리는 우리 주변의 다른 사람들이 어떻게 행동하는지로부터 새로운 상황에 관한 많은 귀중한 정보를 얻는다.
ordinarily we derive much valuable information about new situations from how others around us behave.

길가의 식당을 고를 때 주차장에 다른 차가 없는 곳에서 멈추는 여행객은 드물다.
It's a (b) rare traveler who, in picking a roadside restaurant, chooses to stop at one where no other cars appear in the parking lot.

occasionally 가끔, 때때로

그러나 때때로 다른 사람들의 반응은 정확한(→거짓) 정보를 제공한다.
But occasionally the reactions of others provide (c) accurate (→false) information.

*studied nonchalance 스터디드 넌셸런스 의도적으로 태연한 태도

연구된 치과 병원 대기실 환자의 무관심은 그들의 내면의 불안을 제대로 보여주지 않는다.
The studied nonchalance of patients in a dentist's waiting room is a poor indication of their inner anxiety.

사람들 앞에서 '냉정을 잃는' 것은 창피한 일로 여겨진다.
It is considered embarrassing to "lose your cool" in public.

potentially 잠재적으로
acute situation 심각한 상황
present 참석한, 존재하는
unconcerned 무관심한, 태연한

그렇다면, 잠재적으로 심각한 상황에서, 그곳에 있는 모든 사람은 실제보다 더 무관심한 것처럼 보일 것이다.
In a potentially acute situation, then, everyone present will appear more (d) unconcerned than he is in fact.

crowd 군중, 무리
inaction 무활동, 아무 행동도 하지 않음
passivity 수동성, 소극성

따라서 군중은 수동성을 통해 사건이 비상 상황이 아님을 넌지시 비춤으로써 구성원들이 가만히 있도록 강제할 수 있다.
A crowd can thus force (e) inaction on its members by implying, through its passivity, that an event is not an emergency.

appear a fool 바보처럼 보이다

그런 군중 속에 있는 사람은 누구라도 그 사건이 비상 상황인 것처럼 행동하면 자신이 바보처럼 보일까 봐 두려워한다.
Any individual in such a crowd fears that he may appear a fool if he behaves as though it were.

....

[41~42] 다음 글을 읽고, 물음에 답하시오.
  Once an event is noticed, an onlooker must decide if it is truly an emergency. Emergencies are not always clearly (a) <u>labeled</u> as such; "smoke" pouring into a waiting room may be caused by fire, or it may merely indicate a leak in a steam pipe. Screams in the street may signal an attack or a family quarrel. A man lying in a doorway may be having a coronary — or he may simply be sleeping off a drunk. A person trying to interpret a situation often looks at those around him to see how he should react. If everyone else is calm and indifferent, he will tend to remain so; if everyone else is reacting strongly, he is likely to become alert. This tendency is not merely blind conformity; ordinarily we derive much valuable information about new situations from how others around us behave. It's a (b) <u>rare</u> traveler who, in picking a roadside

restaurant, chooses to stop at one where no other cars appear in the parking lot. But occasionally the reactions of others provide (c) <u>accurate</u> information. The studied nonchalance of patients in a dentist's waiting room is a poor indication of their inner anxiety. It is considered embarrassing to "lose your cool" in public. In a potentially acute situation, then, everyone present will appear more (d) <u>unconcerned</u> than he is in fact. A crowd can thus force (e) <u>inaction</u> on its members by implying, through its passivity, that an event is not an emergency. Any individual in such a crowd fears that he may appear a fool if he behaves as though it were.
* coronary: 관상 동맥증 * nonchalance: 무관심, 냉담

41. 윗글의 제목으로 가장 적절한 것은?
① Do We Judge Independently? The Effect of Crowds
② Winning Strategy: How Not to Be Fooled by Others
③ Do Emergencies Affect the Way of Our Thinking?
④ Stepping Towards Harmony with Your Neighbors
⑤ Ways of Helping Others in Emergent Situations

정답 ①

상황을 판단하는 데 있어서 다른 사람들의 반응은 유용한 준거가 되지만, 때로는 다른 사람들, 즉 군중의 반응이 개인의 독립적인 판단을 방해할 수도 있다는 내용의 글이다. 따라서 글의 제목으로 가장 적절한 것은 ① '우리는 독립적으로 판단을 하는가? 군중의 영향'이다.
② 승리 전략: 다른 사람에 의해 바보 취급을 당하지 않기 위해서는 어떻게 해야 하는가
③ 비상 상황이 우리의 사고방식에 영향을 끼치는가?
④ 이웃과의 조화를 향해 발걸음을 내딛기
⑤ 비상 상황에서 다른 사람을 돕는 방법

42. 밑줄 친 (a)~(e) 중에서 문맥상 낱말의 쓰임이 적절하지 않은 것은?
① (a)　　　② (b)　　　③ (c)　　　④ (d)　　　⑤ (e)

정답 ③

심각한 상황임에도, 군중은 수동성을 이용해 개인이 가만히 있도록 강요할 수도 있다고 언급하는데, 이 경우, 군중이 개인에게 제공하는 정보는 실제 심각성과는 거리가 먼 거짓 정보일 것이다. 따라서 (c)의 accurate(정확한)는 false(거짓의)와 같은 단어로 바꾸어야 한다.

settle down 진정되다, 안정되다
seek 추구하다, 찾다
*famine 기근, 굶주림
*vulnerability 취약성, 약점
enhanced 향상된, 강화된
economic growth 경제 성장
revival 부활, 회복
rural economy 농촌 경제
diversification 다양화, 다변화
economic activity 경제 활동

일단 비상사태의 소요가 진정되고 나면, 주로 강화된 경제 성장이나 지방 경제의 회복, 혹은 경제 활동의 다각화에서 기근 취약성 감소를 모색하는 경향이 있다.
There is a tendency, once the dust of an emergency has settled down, to seek the reduction of famine vulnerability primarily in enhanced economic growth, or the revival of the rural economy, or the diversification of economic activities.

potential 잠재적인
contribution 기여, 공헌
*vulnerable group 취약 계층
deny 부정하다, 부인하다

더 큰 경제적 성공의 잠재적 기여는, 만약 그것이 취약 계층에 영향을 미친다면, 부인할 수 없다.
The potential contribution of greater economic success, if it involves vulnerable groups, cannot be denied.

derive 얻다, 끌어내다
livelihood 생계, 생활 수단
entitlement 권리, 자격
protection mechanism 보호 기제

그와 동시에, 아무리 빠르게 성장하더라도, 인구의 상당수가 그들의 생계를 불확실한 원천으로부터 마련하는 국가는 직접적인 공적 개입을 포함하는 특화된 재정 지원 혜택의 보호 방법 없이는 기근 예방을 기대할 수 없다는 점을 인식하는 것이 중요하다.
At the same time, it is important to recognize that, no matter how fast they grow, countries where a large part of the population derive their livelihood from uncertain sources cannot hope to prevent famines without specialized entitlement protection mechanisms involving direct

public intervention.

agricultural sector 농업 부문
recurrent 반복되는, 재발하는

보츠와나의 경제, 케냐의 농업 부문, 혹은 짐바브웨의 식량 생산의 급속한 성장은 기껏해야 기근의 반복되는 위협을 방지하는 데 있어 그들이 성공한 작은 일부분만을 설명할 뿐이다.
Rapid growth of the economy in Botswana, or of the agricultural sector in Kenya, or of food production in Zimbabwe, explains at best only a small part of their success in preventing recurrent threats of famine.

real achievement 실제 성과, 진정한 업적
direct public intervention 직접적인 공공 개입
time of crisis 위기 시기

이들 국가의 진정한 성과는 위기 상황에서 국민들에게 직접적인 공적 지원을 제공했다는 데 있다.
The real achievements of these countries lie in having provided direct public support to their populations in times of crisis.

somewhat 다소, 어느 정도
diminish 줄이다, 감소시키다
direct approach 직접적인 접근법
affected 영향을 받은, 피해를 입은
play a role 역할을 하다

→ 비록 경제 성장이 한 국가의 기근 위험을 줄이는 데 어느 정도 효과적일 수 있지만, 피해를 입은 사람들을 돕는 것에 대한 직접적인 접근이 이 과정에서 중요한 역할을 한다.
Although economic growth can be somewhat (A) <u>fruitful</u> in diminishing a country's risk of famine, direct approaches to helping the affected people play a(n) (B) <u>critical</u> role in this process.

....

40. 다음 글의 내용을 한 문장으로 요약하고자 한다. 빈칸 (A), (B)에 들어갈 말로 가장 적절한 것은?
　There is a tendency, once the dust of an emergency has settled down, to seek the reduction of famine vulnerability primarily in enhanced economic growth, or the revival of the rural

economy, or the diversification of economic activities. The potential contribution of greater economic success, if it involves vulnerable groups, cannot be denied. At the same time, it is important to recognize that, no matter how fast they grow, countries where a large part of the population derive their livelihood from uncertain sources cannot hope to prevent famines without specialized entitlement protection mechanisms involving direct public intervention. Rapid growth of the economy in Botswana, or of the agricultural sector in Kenya, or of food production in Zimbabwe, explains at best only a small part of their success in preventing recurrent threats of famine. The real achievements of these countries lie in having provided direct public support to their populations in times of crisis.
* famine: 기아 * vulnerability: 취약

→ Although economic growth can be somewhat (A) in diminishing a country's risk of famine, direct approaches to helping the affected people play a(n) (B) role in this process.

      (A)   (B)   (A)   (B)
① productive ...... complicated　　② fruitful　...... critical
③ dominant ...... comprehensive　　④ restrictive ...... appropriate
⑤ desirable　...... cost-effective

답 ②

경제 성장이 기근 취약성 감소에 잠재적 기여를 할 수 있지만, 직접적인 공적 개입이 필수적이라는 내용의 글이다. 따라서 요약문의 빈칸 (A), (B)에 들어갈 말로 가장 적절한 것은 ② '효과적일 – 중요한'이다.

① 생산적일 – 복잡한
③ 우세할 – 포괄적인
④ 제한적일 – 적절한
⑤ 바람직할 – 비용 효율이 높은

fragment 파편, 조각
construction 형성, 구성
debris 잔해, 부스러기
nucleus 핵, 중심
combined with ~와 결합된
radioactive decay 방사성 붕괴

지구는 태양계의 형성 도중 암석과 금속 조각들로부터 만들어졌는데, 이것들은 초기 핵에 의해 휩쓸리고 중력의 힘에 의해 하나의 덩어리로 끌어들여진 파편들이다.
The Earth formed from rocky and metallic fragments during the construction of the solar system — debris that was swept up by an initial nucleus and attracted together into a single body by the force of gravity.

lock inside ~안에 갇혀 있다
individual 개별적인
chemical compound 화합물

(B) 원래 물질들은 우주 공간처럼 차갑고 먼지처럼 건조했는데, 그것들이 포함하는 물과 가스는 무엇이든지 화학 혼합물로서 개별 조각 안에 갇혀 있었다.
(B) The original materials were cold as outer space and dry as dust; whatever water and gases they contained were locked inside individual fragments as chemical compounds.

그 조각들이 모이면서 지구의 중력이 증가했고, 이것은 점점 더 큰 물체들을 끌어당겨 지구에 충돌하게 했다.
As the fragments joined, the Earth's gravity increased, attracting larger and larger objects to impact the Earth.

thorium 토륨

(A) 이러한 증가하는 중력은 우라늄과 토륨과 같은 원소의 끝없는 방사선 붕괴와 결합하여 새로운 지구가 가열되는 것을 유발했다.
(A) This increasing gravity, combined with the timeless radioactive decay of elements like uranium and thorium, caused the new Earth to heat up.

internal 내부의
compound 화합물
break down 분해되다

melt 녹다
release 방출하다, 내보내다

내부 온도와 압력은 많은 혼합물이 분해되거나 녹을 정도로 충분히 높았고, 물과 가스를 방출했다.
The internal temperature and pressure were high enough for many compounds to break down or melt, releasing their water and gases.

(C) 심지어 고체 물질도 그러한 상태에서 움직이고 흐르기 시작할 수 있었다.
(C) Even solid material could begin to move and flow under such conditions.

separation 분리, 구분
organize 정리하다, 구성하다
layered structure 층 구조

밀도에 의한 분리가 시작되었고, 지구는 그것의 현재 지층 구조로 구성되기 시작했다.
Separation by density began, and the Earth started to organize into its present layered structure.

sink to ~로 가라앉다
migrate 이동하다

가장 무거운 금속은 중심부로 가라앉았고, 가장 가벼운 물질은 바깥으로 이동했다.
The heaviest metals sank to the center; the lightest materials migrated outward.

....

36. 주어진 글 다음에 이어질 글의 순서로 가장 적절한 것을 고르시오.
 The Earth formed from rocky and metallic fragments during the construction of the solar system — debris that was swept up by an initial nucleus and attracted together into a single body by the force of gravity.

(A) This increasing gravity, combined with the timeless radioactive decay of elements like uranium and thorium, caused the new Earth to heat up. The internal temperature and pressure were high enough for many compounds to break down or melt, releasing their water and gases.
(B) The original materials were cold as outer space and dry as dust; whatever water and gases they contained were locked inside individual fragments as chemical compounds. As the

fragments joined, the Earth's gravity increased, attracting larger and larger objects to impact the Earth.

(C) Even solid material could begin to move and flow under such conditions. Separation by density began, and the Earth started to organize into its present layered structure. The heaviest metals sank to the center; the lightest materials migrated outward.

① (A) - (C) - (B) ② (B) - (A) - (C)
③ (B) - (C) - (A) ④ (C) - (A) - (B)
⑤ (C) - (B) - (A)

정답 ②

본문에서 지구 형성 과정을 시간 순서대로 설명하고 있기 때문이다. 지구가 형성될 때의 초기 상태에서 시작하여, 내부 가열 과정을 거쳐 현재의 층상 구조로 발전하는 흐름을 따른다.

(B)는 지구 형성 초기의 상황을 설명한다. 원래의 물질들은 차갑고 건조했으며, 조각들이 합쳐지면서 지구의 중력이 증가했고, 더 큰 물체들이 지구로 끌려와 충돌하기 시작했다. 이 부분이 시작점이 된다.

(A)에서는 중력이 증가하면서 방사성 원소(우라늄, 토륨 등)의 붕괴로 지구 내부가 가열되는 과정을 설명한다. 이로 인해 화합물들이 분해되거나 녹으면서 물과 가스가 방출된다.

(C)는 지구 내부의 온도와 압력이 높아지면서 물질들이 움직이기 시작하고, 밀도 차이에 따라 층이 나뉘는 과정을 설명한다. 무거운 금속들은 중심으로 가라앉고, 가벼운 물질들은 바깥으로 이동하며 현재의 지구 구조가 형성된다.

따라서 가장 적절한 순서는 ② (B) - (A) - (C) 이다.

delivery vehicle 배달 차량
suit 적합하게 하다, 맞추다
density 밀도
distribution 분배, 유통
involve 포함하다, 수반하다

도시의 배달 운송 수단은 도시 배치의 밀집 상태에 더 잘 맞도록 개조될 수 있는데, 거기에는 자주 밴과 같은 더 작은 운송 수단을 포함하는데, 자전거도 포함된다.
Urban delivery vehicles can be adapted to better suit the density of urban distribution, which often involves smaller vehicles such as vans, including bicycles.

latter 후자
potential 잠재력, 가능성
preferred 선호되는, 우선적인
particularly 특히
high-density 고밀도의
congested 혼잡한, 붐비는

후자(자전거)는 특히 밀도가 높고 혼잡한 지역에서 선호되는 '최종 단계' 운송 수단이 될 잠재력이 있다.
The latter have the potential to become a preferred 'last-mile' vehicle, particularly in high-density and congested areas.

cargo 화물, 짐

네덜란드와 같이 자전거 사용이 많은 지역에서 배달 자전거가 또한 개인 짐(예를 들어 식료품)을 운반하기 위해 사용된다.
In locations where bicycle use is high, such as the Netherlands, delivery bicycles are also used to carry personal cargo (e.g. groceries).

acquisition 비용 구매, 획득
maintenance 유지보수, 관리
convey 전달하다, 운반하다
developed country 선진국
developing country 개발도상국
becak 베짝 (인도네시아의 삼륜 자전거)

매입과 유지 비용이 낮아서 짐 자전거는 선진국에서 그리고 인도네시아의 becak(바퀴가 세 개 달린 자전거)와 같이 개발도상국에서 똑같이 많은 잠재력을 전달한다.
Due to their low acquisition and maintenance costs, cargo bicycles convey much potential in developed and developing countries alike, such as the becak (a three-wheeled bicycle) in Indonesia.

tricycle 삼륜 자전거
implement 실행하다, 도입하다
parcel 소포, 화물
catering 음식 공급, 출장 요리

전기 보조 배달용 세발자전거를 이용하는 서비스는 프랑스에서 성공적으로 시행되었고 소포나 음식 배달과 같은 다양한 서비스를 위해 유럽 전역에서 점차 도입되고 있다.
Services using electrically assisted delivery tricycles have been successfully implemented in France and are gradually being adopted across Europe for services as varied as parcel and catering deliveries.

encourage 장려하다, 촉진하다
commercial district 상업 지구
dedicated 전용의, 특정 목적의

자전거를 화물 운송 수단으로 사용하는 것은 도심이나 상업 지구처럼 도시의 특정 지역에 자동차 접근을 제한하는 정책이나 자전거 전용 도로의 확장과 결합될 때 특히 장려된다.
Using bicycles as cargo vehicles is particularly encouraged when combined with policies that restrict motor vehicle access to specific areas of a city, such as downtown or commercial districts, or with the extension of dedicated bike lanes.

....

22. 다음 글의 요지로 가장 적절한 것은?

 Urban delivery vehicles can be adapted to better suit the density of urban distribution, which often involves smaller vehicles such as vans, including bicycles. The latter have the potential to become a preferred 'last-mile' vehicle, particularly in high-density and congested areas. In locations where bicycle use is high, such as the Netherlands, delivery bicycles are also used to carry personal cargo (e.g. groceries). Due to their low acquisition and maintenance costs, cargo bicycles convey much potential in developed and developing countries alike, such as the becak (a three-wheeled bicycle) in Indonesia. Services using electrically assisted delivery tricycles have been successfully implemented in France and are gradually being adopted across Europe for services as varied as parcel and catering deliveries. Using bicycles as cargo vehicles is particularly encouraged when combined with policies that restrict motor vehicle access to specific areas of a city, such as downtown or commercial districts, or with the extension of dedicated bike lanes.

① 도시에서 자전거는 효율적인 배송 수단으로 사용될 수 있다.
② 자전거는 출퇴근 시간을 줄이기 위한 대안으로 선호되고 있다.
③ 자전거는 배송 수단으로의 경제적 장단점을 모두 가질 수 있다.
④ 수요자의 요구에 부합하는 다양한 용도의 자전거가 개발되고 있다.
⑤ 세계 각국에서는 전기 자전거 사용을 장려하는 정책을 추진하고 있다.

정답 ①

이유는 본문에서 도시 내 배송을 위해 자전거가 효율적인 수단으로 활용될 수 있음을 강조하고 있기 때문이다. 자전거는 좁은 도로나 혼잡한 지역에서도 원활히 이동할 수 있으며, 비용이 저렴하고 유지비가 적게 든다는 장점을 가지고 있다. 또한, 자전거는 네덜란드, 인도네시아, 프랑스 등 여러 나라에서 개인 물품이나 상업적 물품을 운반하는 데 사용되고 있으며, 전기 사선거나 세발 자전거와 같은 변형된 형태로도 활용되고 있다. 특히, 도심 지역의 차량 진입 제한 정책이나 전용 자전거 도로와 결합될 때 자전거의 효율성이 더욱 높아진다고 언급하고 있다.

DAY 9

motivation 동기부여, 자극
accidental 우연한, 뜻밖의

동기는 우연적일 필요는 없다.
Motivation doesn't have to be accidental.

pick up spirits 기운을 북돋우다

예를 들면, 당신은 라디오에서 기분을 좋게 하는 특정한 노래가 나올 때까지 몇 시간 동안 기다릴 필요는 없다.
For example, you don't have to wait for hours until a certain song that picks up your spirits comes on the radio.

당신은 자신이 듣는 노래를 통제할 수 있다.
You can control what songs you hear.

lift up 기분을 좋게 하다, 고양시키다

만약 항상 당신을 기분 좋게 만드는 특정한 노래가 있다면, 이런 노래들의 모음을 만들고 당신의 차에서 그것을 틀 준비를 해라.
If there are certain songs that always lift you up, make a mix of those songs and have it ready to play in your car.

greatest motivational hits 최고의 동기부여 곡

당신의 모든 음악을 찾아보고 "최고의 동기부여 히트곡" 목록을 스스로 만들어라.
Go through all of your music and create a "greatest motivational hits" playlist for yourself.

또한 영화도 이용해라.
Use the movies, too.

inspired 영감을 받은, 감명을 받은
take on the world 세상과 맞서다, 도전하다

당신은 몇 번이나 감명받고 세상에 맞설 준비가 된 상태로 영화관을 나오는가?
How many times do you leave a movie feeling inspired and ready to take on the world?

그런 일이 일어날 때마다, "적절한 버튼"이라고 이름 붙인 특별한 노트에 그 영화의 이름을 적어놓아라.
Whenever that happens, put the name of the movie in a special notebook that you might label "the right buttons."

6개월에서 1년 후에, 당신은 그 영화를 볼 수 있고 똑같이 감명받은 기분을 느낄 수 있다.
Six months to a year later, you can watch the movie and get the same inspired feeling.

second time around 두 번째로 볼 때

우리에게 감명을 주는 대부분의 영화는 두 번째에 훨씬 더 좋다.
Most movies that inspire us are even better the second time around.

control over ~에 대한 통제력

당신이 깨닫는 것보다 자신의 환경을 더 많이 통제할 수 있다.
You have much more control over your environment than you realize.

consciously 의식적으로, 의도적으로

당신은 더욱더 집중하고 동기부여될 수 있도록 의식적으로 스스로를 프로그래밍하기 시작할 수 있다.
You can begin (programming) yourself consciously to be more and more focused and motivated.

....

31. 다음 빈칸에 들어갈 말로 가장 적절한 것을 고르시오.
 Motivation doesn't have to be accidental. For example, you don't have to wait for hours until a certain song that picks up your spirits comes on the radio. You can control what songs you hear. If there are certain songs that always lift you up, make a mix of those songs and have it ready to play in your car. Go through all of your music and create a "greatest motivational hits" playlist for yourself. Use the movies, too. How many times do you leave a movie feeling inspired and ready to take on the world? Whenever that happens, put the name of the movie in a special notebook that you might label "the right buttons." Six months to a year later, you can watch the movie and get the same inspired feeling. Most movies that inspire us are even better the second time around. You have much more control over your environment than you

realize. You can begin _____ yourself consciously to be more and more focused and motivated.

① isolating   ② denying   ③ programming
④ silencing   ⑤ questioning

정답 ③

빈칸이 포함된 문장은 "You can begin _____ yourself consciously to be more and more focused and motivated."로, "점점 더 집중하고 동기부여가 되도록 스스로를 _____할 수 있다."라는 의미를 전달하고 있다.

앞서 나온 내용은 음악, 영화 등을 이용하여 의도적으로 동기부여를 강화할 수 있다는 점을 설명하고 있다. 특정한 음악을 모아둔 플레이리스트를 만들거나, 자신을 고무시키는 영화를 기록해두고 다시 보는 등의 방법을 제시하며, 동기부여를 의식적으로 조절할 수 있음을 강조하고 있다.

이러한 맥락에서 "스스로를 프로그래밍하다"라는 의미의 "programming"이 가장 적절하다. 자신을 의도적으로 조정하여 원하는 방향으로 유도하는 과정을 나타내기에 문맥에 잘 맞는다.

innately 선천적으로, 본능적으로
programmed 프로그램된, 설계된
behaviour 행동, 습성

어떤 동물이 어떤 종류의 행동을 하도록 선천적으로 타고났다면, 생물학적인 단서가 있을 가능성이 있다.
If an animal is innately programmed for some type of behaviour, then there ① are likely to be biological clues.

streamlined 유선형의, 날렵한
fin 지느러미

물고기가 지느러미와 강력한 꼬리를 갖춘 유선형이고 매끄러운 몸을 가지고 있는 것은 우연이 아니다.
It is no accident that fish have bodies which are streamlined and ② smooth, with fins and a powerful tail.

structurally 구조적으로
adapted 적응된, 맞춰진

그들의 몸은 물속에서 빠르게 움직이는 데 구조적으로 알맞다.
Their bodies are structurally adapted for moving fast through the water.

similarly 마찬가지로, 유사하게

마찬가지로, 여러분이 죽은 새나 모기를 발견한다면, 그 날개를 보고서 비행이 그것의 보편적인 이동 방식이라는 것을 추측할 수 있을 것이다.
Similarly, if you found a dead bird or mosquito, you could guess by looking at ③ its wings that flying was its normal mode of transport.

over-optimistic 지나치게 낙관적인

하지만, 우리는 지나치게 낙관적이어서는 안 된다.
However, we must not be over-optimistic.

생물학적인 단서는 필수적인 것이 아니다.
Biological clues are not essential.

extent 정도, 범위
vary 다르다, 변하다

그것들(생물학적인 단서)이 발견하고 있는(→발견되는) 정도는 동물마다 다르고 행동마다 다르다.
The extent to which they are ④ finding(→found) varies from animal to animal and from activity to activity.

contrary to ~에 반하여, 반대로
physical form 신체적 형태
ghost spider 유령거미
tremendously 엄청나게, 굉장히
weave 짜다, 엮다
web 거미줄
thread 실, 가는 섬유

예를 들어, 새들이 둥지를 짓는 것을 그들의 몸에서 추측하는 것은 불가능하고, 때로 동물들은 유령거미가 엄청나게 긴 다리를 가지고 있지만 매우 짧은 가닥으로 거미집을 짓는 것처럼 그들의 신체적 형태에서 예상될 수 있는 것과는 정반대의 방식으로 행동한다.
For example, it is impossible to guess from their bodies that birds make nests, and, sometimes, animals behave in a way quite contrary to ⑤ what might be expected from their physical form: ghost spiders have tremendously long legs, yet they weave webs out of very short threads.

observer 관찰자
hindrance 방해, 장애물
spin 실을 잣다, 거미줄을 치다
move about 돌아다니다, 움직이다

관찰자인 인간에게는 거미집 둘레를 빙빙 돌며 움직일 때 그것들의 다리는 엄청난 방해물처럼 보인다.
To a human observer, their legs seem a great hindrance as they spin and move about the web.

....

28. 다음 글의 밑줄 친 부분 중, 어법상 틀린 것은?
If an animal is innately programmed for some type of behaviour, then there ① are likely to be biological clues. It is no accident that fish have bodies which are streamlined and ② smooth, with fins and a powerful tail. Their bodies are structurally adapted for moving fast through the

water. Similarly, if you found a dead bird or mosquito, you could guess by looking at ③ <u>its</u> wings that flying was its normal mode of transport. However, we must not be over-optimistic. Biological clues are not essential. The extent to which they are ④ <u>finding</u> varies from animal to animal and from activity to activity. For example, it is impossible to guess from their bodies that birds make nests, and, sometimes, animals behave in a way quite contrary to ⑤ <u>what</u> might be expected from their physical form: ghost spiders have tremendously long legs, yet they weave webs out of very short threads. To a human observer, their legs seem a great hindrance as they spin and move about the web.

정답 ④

주어인 they(biological clues)가 발견하는 동작(find)의 대상이므로, 현재분사 finding을 과거분사 found로 바꾸어 수동태로 표현해야 한다.

① 「There is A」 구문에서 There는 형식상의 주어이고, A가 내용상의 주어이다. 동사의 수는 내용상의 주어의 수에 일치해야 하므로 biological clues에 are로 일치시킨 것은 적절하다.
② are의 주격보어로 형용사 smooth를 사용한 것은 적절하다. streamlined와 smooth는 and로 연결되어 are의 주격보어 역할을 한다.
③ its는 a dead bird or mosquito를 가리킨다.
⑤ what은 선행사를 포함한 관계사로 contrary to의 목적어 역할을 하는 명사절을 유도하고, 관계절 내에서 주어 역할을 한다.

Neanderthal 네안데르탈인
extinct 멸종한, 사라진
debate 논쟁하다, 논의하다
deteriorate 악화되다, 나빠지다

왜 네안데르탈인이 약 4만 년 전에 멸종되게 되어 현생 인류로 대체되었는가가 논의되는데, 가장 선호되는 두 이론은 악화되는 기후 환경과 더불어 새로 도착한 사람들로부터 비롯된 경쟁이다.
Why Neanderthals became extinct about 40,000 years ago to be replaced by modern humans is debated, but the two most favored theories are deteriorating climate conditions together with competition from the new arrivals.

acclimatize 어클라이머타이즈 기후에 적응하게 하다
competition 경쟁
counterintuitive 카운터인투이티브 직관에 반하는, 예상과 다른
lose out 패배하다, 지다
unaccustomed 익숙하지 않은
subtropical 아열대의
via ~을 거쳐, 경유하여

네안데르탈인이 이미 유럽에서 적어도 20만 년 동안 추운 기후 환경에 적응해 왔기 때문에, 추운 기후에 익숙하지 않았을 뿐만 아니라 아열대의 아프리카 기후 지역에서 근동(近東)을 거쳐 온 새로 도착한 사람들에게 그들이 밀려났다는 것은 직관에 반하는 것처럼 보일 수도 있다.
(①) Since the Neanderthals had already become acclimatized to cold conditions for at least 200,000 years in Europe, it may seem counterintuitive that they lost out to the new arrivals, who were not only unaccustomed to cold climate but who came from a subtropical African climate, via the Near East.

technological 기술적인
superiority 우월함, 우세
play a role 역할을 하다

호모 사피엔스의 기술적 우위가 역할을 했던 것으로 보인다.
(②) It appears that the technological superiority of Homo sapiens played a role.

tenfold 열 배로

기존 네안데르탈인의 인구가 줄면서 새로 도착한 사람들의 인구는 10배 증가했다.
(③) The population of the new arrivals increased tenfold as the population of the existing Neanderthals decreased.

speculate 추측하다, 가정하다
involve 포함하다, 수반하다
closely fitting 밀착되는, 꼭 맞는
significant 중요한, 의미 있는

적어도 한 연구자는 피부에 밀착되는 것을 수반하는 보다 발전된 의복을 생산하는 새로 도착한 사람들의 능력이 특별한 의미가 있었다고 추측했다.
(At least one researcher has speculated that the ability of the new arrivals to produce more advanced clothing involving closely fitting skins was significant.)

presumably 아마도, 짐작컨대
sew 바느질하다
hide (동물의) 가죽
peg 말뚝, 고정핀

이것은 가죽을 함께, 아마도 두 겹으로 바느질하고, 그것을 단추나 고정 장치로 고정하는 것을 필요로 했는데, 그것을 착용한 사람이 더 추운 환경에서 사냥할 수 있는 것을 가능하게 했다.
(④) This presumably required sewing hides together, possibly in double layers, and fastening them with buttons or pegs, allowing the wearer to hunt in colder conditions.

in contrast 그에 반해, 대조적으로
wrap-around 감싸는 형태의
sophisticated 정교한, 세련된
tailoring 재단, 재봉

이와는 대조적으로 네안데르탈인은 한 겹으로만 된 옷이나 몸에 둘러서 입는 옷만 가지고 있었을지도 모르는데, 그것은 정교한 맞춤이나 바느질을 수반하지 않았다.
(⑤) In contrast, the Neanderthals may have had only a single layer or wrap-around clothing, which did not involve sophisticated tailoring or sewing.

38. 글의 흐름으로 보아, 주어진 문장이 들어가기에 가장 적절한 곳을 고르시오.

At least one researcher has speculated that the ability of the new arrivals to produce more advanced clothing involving closely fitting skins was significant.

 Why Neanderthals became extinct about 40,000 years ago to be replaced by modern humans is debated, but the two most favored theories are deteriorating climate conditions together with competition from the new arrivals. (①) Since the Neanderthals had already become acclimatized to cold conditions for at least 200,000 years in Europe, it may seem counterintuitive that they lost out to the new arrivals, who were not only unaccustomed to cold climate but who came from a subtropical African climate, via the Near East. (②) It appears that the technological superiority of Homo sapiens played a role. (③) The population of the new arrivals increased tenfold as the population of the existing Neanderthals decreased. (④) This presumably required sewing hides together, possibly in double layers, and fastening them with buttons or pegs, allowing the wearer to hunt in colder conditions. (⑤) In contrast, the Neanderthals may have had only a single layer or wrap-around clothing, which did not involve sophisticated tailoring or sewing.

정답 ④

이유는 주어진 문장이 "새로 온 인류가 밀착된 가죽을 이용해 더 발전된 옷을 만들 수 있었던 능력"에 대한 내용을 담고 있으며, 이는 이들이 더 추운 기후에서 사냥할 수 있게 해주는 기술적 우위를 설명하는 부분이다.
문장 흐름을 보면, ②에서 호모 사피엔스의 기술적 우위가 언급되고, 이어서 주어진 문장이 들어가면 구체적인 예로 발전된 의복 기술이 설명된다. ④번 자리에 주어진 문장을 넣으면, 추운 날씨에도 사냥이 가능했던 이유를 뒷받침하며, 이후 ⑤에서 네안데르탈인의 단순한 옷과의 대비가 자연스럽게 이어진다.
따라서 정답은 ④ 이다.

creativity 창의성, 창조성
commonly 일반적으로, 흔히
define 정의하다
novel 새로운, 독창적인
appropriate 적절한, 알맞은
feasible 피서블 실행 가능한, 실현 가능한

창의성은 참신하고(독창적이고, 새로운) 유용한(적절하고, 실현 가능한) 아이디어를 생산하는 것으로 흔히 정의된다.
Creativity is commonly defined as the production of ideas that are both novel (original, new) and useful (appropriate, feasible).

irrelevant 무관한, 관련 없는
unremarkable 평범한, 특별할 것 없는

독창적이지만 유용하지 않은 아이디어는 무의미하고, 유용하지만 독창적이지 않은 아이디어는 특별한 것이 없다.
Ideas that are original but not useful are irrelevant, and ideas that are useful but not original are unremarkable.

definition 정의, 의미

이러한 정의가 연구에서 널리 사용되지만, 창의성의 중요한 측면이 흔히 간과되는데,
While this definition is widely used in research, an important aspect of creativity is often ignored:

창의적인 아이디어를 생성하는 것이 최종 목표인 경우는 거의 없다는 것이다.
Generating creative ideas rarely is the final goal.

오히려, 문제를 성공적으로 해결하거나 혁신하기 위해서는, 실제로 작동하고 이전 접근 방식보다 더 잘 작동하는 하나 또는 몇 개의 좋은 아이디어가 필요하다.
Rather, to successfully solve problems or innovate requires one or a few good ideas that really work, and work better than previous approaches.

promising 유망한, 가능성이 있는
develop further 더 발전시키다, 심화하다

abandon 버리다, 포기하다

이를 위해 사람들은 자기 자신 또는 서로의 상상력 산물을 평가하고, 더 발전시킬 수 있을 정도로 유망해 보이는 아이디어를 선택하며, 성공 가능성이 작은 것들은 포기해야 한다.
This requires that people evaluate the products of their own or each other's imagination, and choose those ideas that seem promising enough to develop further, and abandon those that are unlikely to be successful.

따라서 창의적인 것은 (아이디어 생성에서 멈추지 않는다.)
Thus, being creative (does not stop with idea generation.)

subsequently 그 이후에, 결과적으로
die a silent death 조용히 사라지다, 주목받지 못하고 없어지다

사실, 창의적인 아이디어를 생성하는 능력은 이러한 아이디어가 이후 조용히 죽어 없어진다면 본질적으로 쓸모가 없다.
In fact, the ability to generate creative ideas is essentially useless if these ideas subsequently die a silent death.

··

32. 다음 빈칸에 들어갈 말로 가장 적절한 것을 고르시오.
 Creativity is commonly defined as the production of ideas that are both novel (original, new) and useful (appropriate, feasible). Ideas that are original but not useful are irrelevant, and ideas that are useful but not original are unremarkable. While this definition is widely used in research, an important aspect of creativity is often ignored: Generating creative ideas rarely is the final goal. Rather, to successfully solve problems or innovate requires one or a few good ideas that really work, and work better than previous approaches. This requires that people evaluate the products of their own or each other's imagination, and choose those ideas that seem promising enough to develop further, and abandon those that are unlikely to be successful. Thus, being creative ____. In fact, the ability to generate creative ideas is essentially useless if these ideas subsequently die a silent death.

① does not stop with idea generation
② rarely originates from practical ideas
③ is often regarded as a shortcut to innovation

④ frequently gives way to unanticipated success
⑤ brings out tension between novelty and relevancy

정답 ①

아이디어 생성에 그치지 않는다
does not stop with idea generation

창의적인 것은 창의적인 아이디어 생성으로 끝나는 것이 아니라, 아이디어를 생성하여 평가하고 선택하는 과정이
이어져야 한다는 내용의 글이다.

② 실용적인 아이디어에서 거의 기원하지 않는다
rarely originates from practical ideas
③ 종종 혁신을 위한 지름길로 여겨진다
is often regarded as a shortcut to innovation
④ 예상치 못한 성공으로 이어지는 경우가 많다
frequently gives way to unanticipated success
⑤ 새로움과 관련성 사이의 긴장을 불러일으킨다
brings out tension between novelty and relevancy

notably 특히, 눈에 띄게
special status 특별한 지위
*leeway 여유, 자유
granted 부여된, 허락된

특히, 많은 종의 어린 동물들은 집단에서 나이가 더 많은 구성원들로부터 부여받는 자유 시기라는 특별한 지위를 갖는다.
Notably, young animals of many species have a special status, a leeway period granted by older members of the group.

hierarchy 하이어알키 계층, 서열
behaviorist 행동주의자
puppy license 강아지 면허
family dynamics 가족 역학, 가족 내 관계

그 계층으로부터의 잠깐의 휴식 기간은 그것을 개에서 본 행동학자들에 의해 '강아지 면허'라고 불리는데, 그것은 다양한 종에서 가족 역학 관계의 특징이다.
This break from the hierarchy is called "puppy license" by the behaviorists who see it in dogs, but it's a feature of family dynamics in a range of species.

overlook 간과하다, 눈감아 주다
inappropriate 부적절한
display of dominance 지배적 행동 표현
offender 위반자, 잘못한 개체

나이가 더 많은 동물은 나쁜 짓을 하는 어린 동물이 어려서 더 잘 알지 못하는 만큼, 적절치 않은 우월의 과시를 눈감아 주거나, 부드럽게 교정해 줄 것이다.
Older animals will ① <u>overlook</u>, or gently correct, an inappropriate display of dominance as long as the offender is young enough not to know better.

'강아지 면허'는 놀이도 포함하는데,
Puppy license also ② <u>covers</u> play:

playfulness 장난기
encourage 격려하다, 장려하다

wrestle 레슬링하다, 몸싸움하다
bark 짖다

나이가 더 많은 개들은 강아지들의 장난기를 즐기는 듯 보이고, 더 부드럽게 몸싸움을 벌이며, 더 부드럽게 짖고, 때로는 강아지들이 이기게 함으로써 어린 개들에게 용기를 북돋워 줄 수도 있다.
older dogs seem to enjoy puppy playfulness, and may encourage young dogs by wrestling more gently, barking more softly, and sometimes letting the puppies win.

adolescence 청소년기, 사춘기

그러나 그 어린 개가 사춘기의 특정 시점에 이르자마자, 그것의 '강아지 면허'는 연장된다(→ 만료된다).
As soon as that young dog hits a certain point in adolescence, however, its puppy license ③ extends (→expires).

lightheartedly 즐겁게, 가볍게
*tolerate 용인하다, 참다
pushback 저항, 반발

불과 며칠 전만 해도 가볍게 용인되었던 행동들이 이제는 성체의 반발을 겪는다.
Behaviors that were lightheartedly tolerated just a few days before are now met with adult pushback.

개가 여전히 어리고 경험이 부족할 수도 있지만, 그것은 도전받고 성체처럼 대해진다.
Although the dog is still young and may lack experience, it is ④ challenged and treated like an adult.

*juvenile 청소년, 미성숙한 개체
mature 성장하다, 성숙해지다
wildhood 야생기 (어린 동물이 독립하는 시기)
valid 유효한, 인정받는
tolerant 관대한, 참을성 있는
irritated 짜증난, 화난
intolerant 참을 수 없는, 불관용적인

인간계와 개의 세계에서, 청소년들이 와일드후드(진화의 세월 동안 모든 종이 경험하는 유년기와 성인기 사이의 시기를 이르는 말)로 성장하고 그들의 강아지 면허가 더 이상 유효하지 않을 때, 관대한 세계는 짜증스럽고 너그럽지 못하게 된다.
In the human world and in the dog world, as juveniles mature into wildhood and their puppy

licenses are no longer ⑤ <u>valid</u>, a tolerant world becomes irritated and intolerant.

....

30. 다음 글의 밑줄 친 부분 중, 문맥상 낱말의 쓰임이 적절하지 않은 것은?

Notably, young animals of many species have a special status, a leeway period granted by older members of the group. This break from the hierarchy is called "puppy license" by the behaviorists who see it in dogs, but it's a feature of family dynamics in a range of species. Older animals will ① <u>overlook</u>, or gently correct, an inappropriate display of dominance as long as the offender is young enough not to know better. Puppy license also ② <u>covers</u> play: older dogs seem to enjoy puppy playfulness, and may encourage young dogs by wrestling more gently, barking more softly, and sometimes letting the puppies win. As soon as that young dog hits a certain point in adolescence, however, its puppy license ③ <u>extends</u>. Behaviors that were lightheartedly tolerated just a few days before are now met with adult pushback. Although the dog is still young and may lack experience, it is ④ <u>challenged</u> and treated like an adult. In the human world and in the dog world, as juveniles mature into wildhood and their puppy licenses are no longer ⑤ <u>valid</u>, a tolerant world becomes irritated and intolerant.
* leeway 자유 * tolerate 용인하다 * juvenile 청소년

정답 ③

이유는 문맥상 "puppy license"가 더 이상 유효하지 않게 되는 시점을 설명하고 있기 때문이다. "extend"는 "연장하다"라는 뜻으로, 문맥에 맞지 않는다. 여기서는 "puppy license"가 끝나는 것을 표현해야 하므로 "expires" 또는 "ends" 같은 표현이 적절하다.

agricultural production 농업 생산
desired 원하는, 바람직한
practically 사실상, 거의 모든

인구 증가가 둔화됨에 따라, 더 많은 농업 생산에 대한 수요를 증가시키는 가장 강력한 힘은 '높아지는 소득'일 것인데, 그것은 거의 모든 정부와 개인이 원하는 바이다.
With population growth slowing, the strongest force increasing demand for more agricultural production will be rising incomes, which are desired by practically all governments and individuals.

proportion 비율, 부분
consume 소비하다, 섭취하다
richer food 더 기름지고 영양가 높은 음식
contribute 기여하다, 초래하다
*debilitation 데빌리테이션 쇠약, 약화

비록 더 부유한 사람들이 자신들의 소득의 더 낮은 비율을 음식에 소비하지만, 통틀어 그들은 더 많은 음식 그리고 더 기름진 음식을 섭취하는데, 그것은 다양한 종류의 질병과 건강 악화의 원인이 된다.
Although richer people spend smaller proportions of their income on food, in total they consume more food — and richer food, which contributes to various kinds of disease and debilitation.

relatively 상대적으로
feed grain 사료용 곡물
food grain 식량용 곡물
animal origin 동물성 식품

보통 더 높은 소득에 수반하는 식단의 변화는 식용 곡물보다는 사료용 곡물의 생산에서 상대적으로 더 큰 증가를 요구할 것인데, 그 이유는 동물성 식품이 부분적으로 사람들의 식단에서 식물에 기반한 식품을 대체하기 때문이다.
The changes in diet that usually accompany higher incomes will require relatively greater increases in the production of feed grains, rather than food grains, as foods of animal origin partly (displace plant-based foods in people's diets.)

equivalent value 동등한 가치

동물을 통해 영양가를 생산하려면 식물에서 직접 그와 동등한 영양가를 얻는 것보다 2배에서 6배 더 많은 곡물이 필요하다.
It takes two to six times more grain to produce food value through animals than to get the equivalent value directly from plants.

credible 신뢰할 만한, 믿을 수 있는
decade 10년
at present 현재
accessible 접근 가능한, 이용할 수 있는
food-insecure 식량 불안정한, 영양 부족 상태인

따라서 향후 30년에서 50년 이내에 경제적 그리고 사회적 요구를 충족시키기 위해서는 세계가 현재보다 2배가 넘는 곡물과 농산물을, 그러면서도 식량이 부족한 사람들도 이것들을 얻을 수 있는 방식으로 생산해야 한다고 추정하는 것은 꽤 설득력이 있다.
It is thus quite credible to estimate that in order to meet economic and social needs within the next three to five decades, the world should be producing more than twice as much grain and agricultural products as at present, but in ways that these are accessible to the food-insecure.

....

32. 다음 빈칸에 들어갈 말로 가장 적절한 것을 고르시오.
With population growth slowing, the strongest force increasing demand for more agricultural production will be rising incomes, which are desired by practically all governments and individuals. Although richer people spend smaller proportions of their income on food, in total they consume more food — and richer food, which contributes to various kinds of disease and debilitation. The changes in diet that usually accompany higher incomes will require relatively greater increases in the production of feed grains, rather than food grains, as foods of animal origin partly ____. It takes two to six times more grain to produce food value through animals than to get the equivalent value directly from plants. It is thus quite credible to estimate that in order to meet economic and social needs within the next three to five decades, the world should be producing more than twice as much grain and agricultural products as at present, but in ways that these are accessible to the food-insecure.
* debilitation: 건강 악화

① displace plant-based foods in people's diets
② demand eco-friendly processing systems
③ cause several nutritional imbalances

④ indicate the consumers' higher social status
⑤ play an important role in population growth

정답 ①

사람들의 식단에서 식물 기반 음식을 대체하다
displace plant-based foods in people's diets

사람들이 더 부유해질수록 더 기름진 음식을 섭취하고, 동물을 통해 영양가를 생산하 는 것은 식물을 통해 그와 동등한 영양가를 생산하는 것보다 더 많은 곡물을 필요로 한다는 내용으로 보아, 빈칸에 들어갈 말로 가장 적절한 것은 ① 이다.

② 친환경적인 가공 시스템을 요구하다
demand eco-friendly processing systems
③ 여러 영양 불균형을 초래하다
cause several nutritional imbalances
④ 소비자의 높은 사회적 지위를 나타내다
indicate the consumers' higher social status
⑤ 인구 증가에 중요한 역할을 하다
play an important role in population growth

yield 수확량, 생산량
*cultivar 재배 식물, 품종
management method 관리 방법
pest 해충, 유해 생물
aspect 측면, 요소
social environment 사회적 환경

단지 현재의 수준으로 수확량을 유지하는 것만도 해충과 질병이 계속 진화하고 있고 화학적, 물리적, 사회적 환경의 양상이 수십 년에 걸쳐 변할 수 있으므로, 보통 새로운 품종과 관리 기법이 필요하다.
Simply maintaining yields at current levels often requires new cultivars and management methods, since pests and diseases continue to evolve, and aspects of the chemical, physical, and social environment can change over several decades.

*pesticide 농약, 살충제

1960년내에 많은 사람은 살충세가 사람들에게 내체로 유익한 것으로 여겼나.
(①) In the 1960s, many people considered pesticides to be mainly beneficial to mankind.

broadly 효과가 넓은, 광범위한
persistent 지속적인, 오래가는
control 통제하다, 억제하다
crop plant 작물 식물

새롭고 널리 효과를 거두고 지속하는 살충제를 개발하는 것은 흔히 농작물 해충을 통제하는 최고의 방법으로 여겨졌다.
(②) Developing new, broadly effective, and persistent pesticides often was considered to be the best way to control pests on crop plants.

apparent 분명한, 명확한
negate 무효화하다, 상쇄하다
non-target organism 비표적 생물

그때 이래로, 널리 효과를 거두는 살충제가 유익한 곤충에 해로운 영향을 미칠 수 있어서 그것이 해충 통제 효과를 무효화할 수 있으며, 그 지속하는 살충제는 새와 사람 같은, 생태계의 목표 외 생물에게 해를 줄 수 있다는 것이 분명해졌다.
(③) Since that time, it has become apparent that broadly effective pesticides can have

harmful effects on beneficial insects, which can negate their effects in controlling pests, and that persistent pesticides can damage non-target organisms in the ecosystem, such as birds and people.

또한, 기업들이 새로운 살충제를, 주요한 이로운 효과는 있지만 부정적인 효과는 거의 없을 수 있는 것들조차, 개발하는 것이 어려워졌다.
(Also, it has become difficult for companies to develop new pesticides, even those that can have major beneficial effects and few negative effects.)

procedure 절차, 과정
government approval 정부 승인

매우 높은 비용이 새로운 살충제에 대한 정부의 승인을 얻는 데 필요한 모든 절차를 따르는 것에 수반된다.
(④) Very high costs are involved in following all of the procedures needed to gain government approval for new pesticides.

consequently 결과적으로, 따라서
consideration 고려, 숙고
incorporate 포함하다, 통합하다
resistance 저항성, 내성
*breeding 육종, 번식
biological control method 생물학적 방제법

결과적으로, 다른 생물학적 통제 기법을 개량하여 사용함으로써 품종에 더 강한 해충 저항력을 포함하는 것 같은, 해충을 관리하는 다른 방법들이 더 많이 고려되고 있다.
(⑤) Consequently, more consideration is being given to other ways to manage pests, such as incorporating greater resistance to pests into cultivars by breeding and using other biological control methods.

....

38. 글의 흐름으로 보아, 주어진 문장이 들어가기에 가장 적절한 곳을 고르시오.
Also, it has become difficult for companies to develop new pesticides, even those that can have major beneficial effects and few negative effects.

 Simply maintaining yields at current levels often requires new cultivars and management

methods, since pests and diseases continue to evolve, and aspects of the chemical, physical, and social environment can change over several decades. (①) In the 1960s, many people considered pesticides to be mainly beneficial to mankind. (②) Developing new, broadly effective, and persistent pesticides often was considered to be the best way to control pests on crop plants. (③) Since that time, it has become apparent that broadly effective pesticides can have harmful effects on beneficial insects, which can negate their effects in controlling pests, and that persistent pesticides can damage non-target organisms in the ecosystem, such as birds and people. (④) Very high costs are involved in following all of the procedures needed to gain government approval for new pesticides. (⑤) Consequently, more consideration is being given to other ways to manage pests, such as incorporating greater resistance to pests into cultivars by breeding and using other biological control methods.
* pesticide 살충제 * cultivar 품종 * breed 개량하다

정답 ④

주어진 문장은 기업들이 새로운 살충제를 개발하는 것 또한 어려워졌다는 내용이다. 따라서 이 문장 바로 앞에는 지속하는 살충제가 유익한 곤충 및 다른 생물에게도 해를 줄 수 있다는 점이 분명해졌다는 내용, 즉 살충제 사용의 문제점에 관한 내용의 문장이 있어야 하고, 바로 뒤에는 새로운 살충제 개발이 어려운 이유를 설명하는 내용의 문장이 이어져야 한다. 따라서 주어진 문장이 들어가기에 가장 적절한 곳은 ④이다.

savanna 사바나 (열대 초원)
pose 제기하다, 야기하다
ecologist 생태학자

사바나는 생태학자에게 약간의 문제를 제기한다.
Savannas pose a bit of a problem for ecologists.

*axiom 엑시옴 자명한 이치, 공리
ecology 생태학
complete competitor 완전한 경쟁자
coexist 공존하다

'완전한 경쟁자는 공존할 수 없다'는 생태학의 원리가 있다.
There is an axiom in ecology that 'complete competitors cannot coexist':

organism 생물, 유기체
dominate 지배하다, 우세하다

다시 말해, 두 개의 유기체 개체군이 정확히 동일한 자원을 사용하는 곳에서는 한 개체군이 다른 개체군보다 약간 더 효율적으로 그렇게 해서 따라서 장기적으로는 우세하게 될 것으로 기대될 것이다.
in other words, where two populations of organisms use exactly the same resources, one would be expected to do so slightly more efficiently than the other and therefore come to dominate in the long term.

지구상의 온화한 지역에서 (숲에서는) 나무가 우세하거나 혹은 (초원에서는) 풀이 우세하게 된다.
In temperate parts of the world, either trees dominate (in forests) or grasses dominate (in grasslands).

하지만 사바나에서는 풀과 나무가 공존한다.
Yet, in savannas grasses and trees coexist.

propose 제안하다, 주장하다

전형적인 설명에 의하면 나무는 뿌리가 깊고, 반면에 풀은 뿌리가 얕다.

The classic explanation proposes that trees have deep roots while grasses have shallow roots.

competitor 경쟁자

따라서 그 두 가지 식물 형태는 공존할 수 있는데 그 이유는 그것들이 사실은 경쟁자가 아니기 때문이다.
The two plant types are therefore able to coexist because they are not in fact competitors:

penetrate 침투하다, 스며들다

나무는 더 습한 기후에서 그리고 모래가 더 많은 토양에서 숫자가 더 많아지는데 그 이유는 더 많은 물이 깊은 뿌리까지 침투할 수 있기 때문이다.
the trees increase in wetter climates and on sandier soils because more water is able to penetrate to the deep roots.

indeed 확실히, 정말로
top half-metre 지표에서 50cm 깊이
just where 바로 그곳에서

나무는 사실 상당한 깊이까지 침투하는 약간의 작은 뿌리들을 정말 가지고 있긴 하지만, 뿌리의 대부분은 표면으로부터 0.5미터 깊이의 토양에 있는데, 바로 거기에 풀뿌리들도 있다.
Trees do indeed have a few small roots which penetrate to great depth, but most of their roots are in the top half-metre of the soil, just where the grass roots are.

....

23. 다음 글의 제목으로 가장 적절한 것은?
Savannas pose a bit of a problem for ecologists. There is an axiom in ecology that 'complete competitors cannot coexist': in other words, where two populations of organisms use exactly the same resources, one would be expected to do so slightly more efficiently than the other and therefore come to dominate in the long term. In temperate parts of the world, either trees dominate (in forests) or grasses dominate (in grasslands). Yet, in savannas, grasses and trees coexist. The classic explanation proposes that trees have deep roots while grasses have shallow roots. The two plant types are therefore able to coexist because they are not in fact competitors: the trees increase in wetter climates and on sandier soils because more water is able to penetrate to the deep roots. Trees do indeed have a few small roots which penetrate to great depth, but most of their roots are in the top half-metre of the soil, just where the

grass roots are.
* axiom 원리, 공리
① A War at Hand Between Plants in Savannas
② A Rivalry for Wetter Soils among Savanna Trees
③ Are Savannas a Hidden Treasure of Bio-Diversity?
④ Cyclic Dominance of Trees over Grasses in Savannas
⑤ Strange Companions: Savanna Plants Confuse Ecologists

정답 ⑤

이상한 동료들: 사바나 식물들이 생태학자들을 혼란스럽게 하다
Strange Companions: Savanna Plants Confuse Ecologists

'완전한 경쟁자는 공존할 수 없다'는 생태학의 원리에 대해 사바나에 공존하는 나무와 풀의 사례를 들어 사바나가 생태학자에게 약간의 문제를 제기한다는 내용을 이야기하 고 있는 글이므로 글의 제목으로는 ⑤ '이상한 동반자: 사바나의 식물들은 생태학자를 혼란스럽게 만든다'가 가장 적절하다.

① 사바나 식물들 간의 전쟁
A War at Hand Between Plants in Savannas
② 사바나 나무들 간의 더 습한 토양을 위한 경쟁
A Rivalry for Wetter Soils among Savanna Trees
③ 사바나는 숨겨진 생물 다양성의 보물인가?
Are Savannas a Hidden Treasure of Bio-Diversity?
④ 사바나에서 나무가 풀보다 주기적으로 우세를 보이다
Cyclic Dominance of Trees over Grasses in Savannas

assess 평가하다, 판단하다
potential 잠재력, 가능성
*cardinal 중대한
immediately 즉시, 곧바로

우리가 잠재력을 평가할 때, 우리는 출발점, 즉 즉각적으로 눈에 보이는 능력에 집중하는 아주 중요한 실수를 한다.
When we assess potential, we make the cardinal error of focusing on starting points — the abilities that are immediately visible.

obsessed with ~에 집착하는
innate talent 타고난 재능
assume 가정하다, 추정하다
stand out 눈에 띄다, 두드러지다

내재된 능력에 집착하는 세상에서, 우리는 가장 기대되는 사람들은 즉시 눈에 띄는 사람들이라고 가정한다.
In a world obsessed with innate talent, we assume the people with the most promise ① are the ones who stand out right away.

vary 다르다, 차이가 있다
dramatically 극적으로, 현저하게
initial 처음의, 초기의
aptitude 적성, 재능

그러나 높은 성취를 하는 사람들은 초기 자질에 있어서 크게 다르다.
But high achievers vary dramatically in their initial aptitudes.

judge 평가하다, 판단하다

우리가 사람들이 첫날에 할 수 있는 것으로만 그들을 판단한다면 그들의 잠재력은 숨겨진 채로 남는다.
If we judge people only by what they can do on day one, their potential remains hidden.

land 도달하다, 도착하다

당신은 사람들이 어디에서 시작하는가로부터는 어디에 도착할지 알 수 없다.

You can't tell ② <u>where</u> people will land from where they begin.

학습할 수 있는 적절한 기회와 동기가 있다면, 누구라도 더 큰 것을 성취할 기술을 쌓을 수 있다.
With the right opportunity and motivation ③ <u>to learn</u>, anyone can build the skills to achieve greater things.

잠재력은 당신이 어디에서 출발하는지에 대한 문제가 아니라, 얼마나 멀리 나아가는지에 대한 문제이다.
Potential is not a matter of where you start, but of how far you travel.

focus less on ~에 덜 집중하다
distance traveled 이동 거리

우리는 출발점에 덜 집중하고 나아간 거리에 더 많이 집중해야 한다.
We need to focus less on starting points and more on distance ④ traveled.

Mozart 모차르트
make a big splash 크게 성공하다, 큰 반향을 일으키다
Bach 바흐 (점진적으로 성장한 음악가)
ascend slowly 서서히 발전하다
bloom late 늦게 꽃을 피우다, 늦게 성공하다
homegrown 자체 개발된, 스스로 키운

초기에 큰 성공을 거두는 각각의 Mozart에 대하여, 천천히 올라가고 늦게 꽃을 피우는 다수의 Bach가 있다.
For every Mozart who makes a big splash early, there are multiple Bachs who ascend slowly and ⑤ <u>blooming</u> (→bloom) late.

그들은 보이지 않는 초능력을 갖고 태어나지 않는다.
They're not born with invisible superpowers;

그들의 재능 대부분은 집에서 길러지거나 만들어진 것이다.
most of their gifts are homegrown or homemade.

29. 다음 글의 밑줄 친 부분 중, 어법상 틀린 것은?

When we assess potential, we make the cardinal error of focusing on starting points — the abilities that are immediately visible. In a world obsessed with innate talent, we assume the people with the most promise ① are the ones who stand out right away. But high achievers vary dramatically in their initial aptitudes. If we judge people only by what they can do on day one, their potential remains hidden. You can't tell ② where people will land from where they begin. With the right opportunity and motivation ③ to learn, anyone can build the skills to achieve greater things. Potential is not a matter of where you start, but of how far you travel. We need to focus less on starting points and more on distance ④ traveled. For every Mozart who makes a big splash early, there are multiple Bachs who ascend slowly and ⑤ blooming late. They're not born with invisible superpowers; most of their gifts are homegrown or homemade.

* cardinal 아주 중요한

정답 ⑤ blooming → bloom

문장에서 "there are multiple Bachs who ascend slowly and blooming late."라고 되어 있는데, "ascend"는 동사 원형이므로, 병렬 구조를 유지하려면 "blooming late"가 아니라 "bloom late"로 수정해야 한다.

① are the ones who stand out right away
"are"는 주어 "the people with the most promise"를 받는 동사로 적절하다. 관계대명사 "who" 이하의 "stand out right away"는 "두드러지다, 눈에 띄다"라는 의미로 문맥에 맞게 쓰였다.

② where people will land from where they begin
"where people will land"는 "사람들이 어디에 도달할지"라는 의미로, "from where they begin(그들이 시작하는 곳으로부터)"와 함께 문맥상 자연스럽다.

③ With the right opportunity and motivation to learn
"With + 명사" 구문은 "적절한 기회와 학습에 대한 동기부여가 있다면"이라는 뜻으로 적절하다. "to learn"은 motivation을 수식하는 적절한 용법이다.

④ more on distance traveled
"distance traveled"에서 "traveled"는 과거분사로서 "이동한 거리"라는 의미를 가지며, 명사 "distance"를 수식하는 형용사적 용법으로 적절하다.

*shrinkflation 슈링크플레이션 제품 크기를 줄여 사실상 가격을 인상하는 현상
basket of products 제품 묶음
inflation 인플레이션, 물가 상승

한 바구니의 제품은 부피나 무게가 아니라 가격에 의해 인플레이션이 측정된다.
A basket of products is measured for inflation by price, not by volume or weight.

shrink 줄어들다, 축소되다
technically 기술적으로, 엄밀히 말하면
occur 발생하다, 일어나다

만일 제품의 크기가 줄어들지만 가격은 그대로 유지된다면, 기술적으로 어떤 가격 상승도 일어나지 않는다.
If the products shrink in size but the price stays the same, technically no price (a) <u>increase</u> has occurred.

그러나 사람들은 바보가 아니고, 그들은 그것이 무엇을 의미하는지 알고 있다.
But people aren't stupid, they know what that means.

여러분은 이것을 상자에 든 시리얼의 감소된 양부터 더 작은 크기의 초콜릿 바에 이르기까지 모든 것에서 볼 수 있다.
You can see this in everything from the reduced amount of cereal in a box to smaller-sized chocolate bars.

*aperture 구멍, 틈, 입구
various sorts 다양한 종류

여러분은 이것을 치약 튜브와 다양한 종류의 가루제품의 그 어느 때보다 더 큰 입구의 형태에서 볼 수 있다.
You can see it in the form of ever-larger apertures in toothpaste tubes and powders of various sorts.

use up 다 쓰다, 소진하다

이러한 변화의 목적은 소비자가 제품을 더 빨리 다 써버리고 무게당 더 많은 돈을 지불하도록 만드는 것이다.
The purpose of these changes is to make the consumer use up the product (b) <u>faster</u> and to pay more per weight.

tube centre 두루마리 중앙 부분

가격은 그대로인 반면에, 화장지와 종이 타월 롤은 그 어느 때보다 더 큰 튜브 중심과 그 어느 때보다 더 적은 면 수를 가지고 있다.
Toilet paper and paper towel rolls have ever-larger tube centres and ever-fewer sheets, while the price remains the same.

봉지에는 더 적은 수의 감자칩이 있고 상자에는 더 적은 수의 쿠키가 있다.
There are (c) <u>fewer</u> potato crisps in the bag and cookies in the box.

*dimple 움푹 들어간 부분
displace 이동시키다, 대체하다

향수와 같은 액체 병의 바닥에는 제품을 대체하고 내부에 있는 것보다 더 많이 있다는 착각을 방지하는(→ 만드는) 그 어느 때보다 더 큰 움푹 들어간 곳이 있다.
Bottles of liquids such as perfumes have ever-larger dimples on the bottom that displace the product and (d) <u>prevent</u> (→ cause) the illusion of more inside than there is.

restricted 제한된, 국한된

shrinkflation은 소매 제품에만 국한되지 않는다.
Shrinkflation is not restricted to retail products.

아파트도 줄어들고 있다.
Apartments are shrinking, too.

square foot 제곱피트 (면적 단위)

초소형 아파트는 우리가 전에 살았던 그 어떤 것보다 작지만 평방 피트당 비용이 더 든다.
Micro apartments are smaller than anything we lived in before but cost more per square foot.

shrinkflation은 회사들이 더 높은 비용에 직면하고 있다는 것을 알려주는 신호이다.
Shrinkflation is a signal that tells us that companies are facing higher costs.

그것은 가격 압박이 심해지기 시작했다는 신호이다.
It is a signal that price pressures are starting to (e) <u>build</u>.

[41~42] 다음 글을 읽고, 물음에 답하시오.

We have seen a clear rise in something called 'shrinkflation'. A basket of products is measured for inflation by price, not by volume or weight. If the products shrink in size but the price stays the same, technically no price (a) <u>increase</u> has occurred. But people aren't stupid, they know what that means. You can see this in everything from the reduced amount of cereal in a box to smaller-sized chocolate bars. You can see it in the form of ever-larger apertures in toothpaste tubes and powders of various sorts. The purpose of these changes is to make the consumer use up the product (b) <u>faster</u> and to pay more per weight. Toilet paper and paper towel rolls have ever-larger tube centres and ever-fewer sheets, while the price remains the same. There are (c) <u>fewer</u> potato crisps in the bag and cookies in the box. Bottles of liquids such as perfumes have ever-larger dimples on the bottom that displace the product and (d) <u>prevent</u> the illusion of more inside than there is. Shrinkflation is not restricted to retail products. Apartments are shrinking, too. Micro apartments are smaller than anything we lived in before but cost more per square foot. Shrinkflation is a signal that tells us that companies are facing higher costs. It is a signal that price pressures are starting to (e) <u>build</u>.
* aperture: 입구 ** dimple: 움푹 들어간 곳

41. 윗글의 제목으로 가장 적절한 것은?
① Small Sizes Win Consumers Over in the Era of Shrinkflation
② Hidden Inflation: Paying the Same for Shrunken Goods
③ Business Marketing Strategy: Stand Out, Don't Shrink
④ Innovative Changes in Smaller-Sized Daily Products
⑤ Buy One, Get One Free: How Companies Attract You

정답 ②

숨겨진 인플레이션: 축소된 상품에 같은 가격을 지불하다
Hidden Inflation: Paying the Same for Shrunken Goods

글의 핵심 내용은 제품의 크기는 줄어들지만 가격은 동일하게 유지되어 소비자가 실질적으로 더 많은 비용을 지불하게 되는 'shrinkflation' 현상에 대한 것이다. 특히 "technically no price increase has occurred"라는 부분에서 가격은 그대로지만 실제로는 소비자가 손해를 보고 있음을 강조하고 있다.

① 수축 인플레이션 시대에 작은 크기가 소비자를 끌어들이다
Small Sizes Win Consumers Over in the Era of Shrinkflation
③ 비즈니스 마케팅 전략: 축소하지 말고 돋보이게 하라
Business Marketing Strategy: Stand Out, Don't Shrink

④ 더 작은 크기의 일상 제품에서 혁신적인 변화
Innovative Changes in Smaller-Sized Daily Products
⑤ 하나를 사면 하나를 무료로: 기업들이 당신을 끌어들이는 방법
Buy One, Get One Free: How Companies Attract You

42. 밑줄 친 (a)~(e) 중에서 문맥상 낱말의 쓰임이 적절하지 않은 것은?
① (a)   ② (b)   ③ (c)   ④ (d)   ⑤ (e)

정답 ④

(d) prevent → "움푹 들어간 바닥이 제품의 양을 착각하게 만든다"는 의미를 전달해야 하는데, prevent는 착각을 막는다는 의미가 되어 문맥상 부적절하다. 올바른 표현은 create 또는 cause가 되어야 한다.